How I wrote the story

Second edition

How I wrote the story
Second edition
Edited by Christopher Scanlan

Poynter Institute for Media Studies
Library

JUN 26 '87

ISBN: 0-937550-09-4

Published by the Providence Journal Co.
© 1986, Providence, Rhode Island

Address inquiries about this book to:
Providence Journal Book Club
75 Fountain St.
Providence, R.I. 02902
Telephone: 401-277-7594

Table of contents

Acknowledgments		vii
Foreword	Charles McCorkle Hauser	ix
Introduction	Christopher Scanlan	xi

PART I: THE PROCESS OF NEWS WRITING

Chapter 1	The process approach	Donald M. Murray and Christopher Scanlan	3
Chapter 2	Problems and solutions	Donald M. Murray	9
Chapter 3	Help or hindrance?	*Journal-Bulletin* writers and editors	15
Chapter 4	Talk talk: Notes on the art of interviewing	Berkley Hudson	19
Chapter 5	The Write Stuff: Sharing the lessons of good writing	Christopher Scanlan	27

PART II: THE PROCESS OF EDITING

Chapter 6	Consultive editing	Donald M. Murray and *Journal-Bulletin* editors	33
Chapter 7	Editing people, not copy	An interview with Joel Rawson	41

PART III: HOW I WROTE THE STORY

Chapter 8	How I wrote the story: Accounts of the news-writing process		49
	Maine budworm war: What poisons pests may poison people	Carol McCabe	50
	Breakfast with the President	Charles McCorkle Hauser	61
	Having a baby: 'In sorrow thou shalt bring forth children'	Christopher Scanlan	63
	Burning wire	Barbara Carton	71
	Working in jewelry: Behind the glitter	Bruce D. Butterfield	80
	The class of '56: It was a very good year	Doug Cumming	92
	Incident in Ward 4	Bruce DeSilva	95
	VonBulow sentenced to 30 years	Gayle Gertler	102
	Our stolen cars	Ira Chinoy and Ward Pimley	106
	A death in the family	Jeanne Edwards	112
	As an orator, Pastore is a Rolls amid the Cadillacs	M. Charles Bakst	115
	Senate returns to Square One	Thomas E. Walsh	120
	Darigan has learned to relax	Bob Wyss	123
	The interns: First crisis comes quickly as lives replace textbooks	Irene Wielawski	126
	Crissie's last chance: She gambled trip to edge of death	Marialisa Calta	132
	How I edited the story	Michael R. Young	138
	Rosa Parks visits and recalls her ride into history	Brian C. Jones	141
	Nicaraguan Indians fight Sandinista 'liberators'	Randall Richard	145
	The Appalachian Trail: Lessons in humility	Berkley Hudson	152
	Building new lives: 'Fragile' people find new security	G. Wayne Miller	161
	A simple story of loss that speaks to all people	Mark Patinkin	166
	One soldier's story: A cocky adventure that turned out wrong	Joel Rawson	171
	Summer dreams, vacation fantasies and the annual purge	S. Robert Chiappinelli	177
	The natural	Bill Parrillo	181
Chapter 9	Bookbag: A reading list for writers and editors		187

Acknowledgments

Like the volume that precedes it, the second edition of "How I Wrote the Story" owes its existence to the generous contributions of scores of *Journal-Bulletin* writers and editors, past and present. Both editions would have been impossible without the support and assistance of Executive Editor Charles McCorkle Hauser; Deputy Executive Editor James V. Wyman; Managing Editor, Graphics, David B. Gray; Metropolitan Managing Editor Joel P. Rawson (now executive editor of the Lexington, Ky., *Herald-Leader*); staff writer Berkley Hudson; Joyce Olson, Ann McGarry, Phyllis Trementozzi and Maria Balasco, newsroom secretaries whose considerable skills have helped keep alive the weekly writing contest that is the heart of these books; and Joseph O. Mehr, Susan Fedorzyn-Edgar and the entire *Journal-Bulletin* library staff, collaborators in the writing process who all too often remain unsung heroes.

Since his arrival at the *Journal-Bulletin,* in 1981, Donald M. Murray has been a constant source of guidance. As our writing coach, he has inspired this book by teaching us that the best way to learn how to write well is to share the lessons of good writing with one another.

— C.S.

Foreword

By Charles McCorkle Hauser, executive editor
The Providence Journal-Bulletin

What do we mean when we say the Providence *Journal-Bulletin* has become a "writer's newspaper"? Do our editors pretty much step aside and let the reporters do their own thing?

No. We operate on the principle that good editing is an integral component of good writing. The editor and writer work as a team. If possible, their collaboration begins with the embryo of the story idea and continues until the final rewrite is released to the copy desk.

Our goal is to make our newspaper stories do more than inform; we want them to be a pleasure to read. The essentials of journalism — accuracy, fairness, completeness — are still the first requirements. But we believe grace of language is the extra element that attracts and holds readers.

How did we reach this point?

We started, more than a dozen years ago, by changing our hiring practices. We dropped a longstanding policy of recruiting reporters right out of college or graduate journalism school and began requiring several years of experience. In screening candidates, we asked for lots of clippings, and we put quality of writing at the top of our checklist.

We created in-house training programs to develop the writing skills of the staff. We invited visitors in to conduct seminars. We held weekly brown-bag lunches in our conference room for bull sessions on writing. We acquired the services of a former Pulitzer Prize-winning newspaperman, Professor Donald M. Murray of the University of New Hampshire, as our part-time writing coach. We created a weekly writing-awards program — with cash prizes and judging by a rotating panel of previous winners.

And over the years we more and more came to appreciate the importance of what Don Murray identified as "consultive editing." We started spending more time on editor training. In this second edition of "How I Wrote the Story," we have added new material on the editor's role.

One final word: There is a key element that is perhaps the most important of all in creating a climate of good writing in our newsroom — it is the willingness of our staff members to help one another and to seek help from one another. The jealousies and insecurities that can be found in some newsrooms around the country seem to be absent here; our writers are willing to be vulnerable and to admit they can learn from their colleagues.

We're still learning, all of us, and these books are part of the process.

Charles Hauser

Introduction

> **"** *Do not be afraid to acknowledge that you have learned from other writers. Do not spend your time trying to kill off other writers and reporters. The more talented you are, the more you can learn from other writers, and the freer you are to admit that you have learned.* **"**
>
> — Lillian Ross

By Christopher Scanlan

That bit of wisdom — offered by Lillian Ross in the introduction to "Reporting," her collection of classic nonfiction from *The New Yorker* — is the guiding light of this book.

The roots of "How I Wrote the Story" can be traced, however, to a series of writing workshops at the Providence *Journal-Bulletin* that began in 1981 after Donald M. Murray, author, Pulitzer Prize winner and professor of English at the University of New Hampshire, had been hired as the paper's part-time writing coach.

Baseball players have batting coaches. Opera singers have voice coaches. But what in the world is a writing coach — and why should the *Journal-Bulletin,* which has won its share of writing awards, need one?

Hiring a consultant to work with writers and editors between deadlines is a relatively new idea. But it's one that is becoming more popular as newspapers around the country strive to improve the quality of their writing. Don Murray, as one example, has worked as a writing coach at the Boston *Globe* and the Raleigh *Times* and *News and Observer,* and has provided consultation for other papers from Alaska to Florida.

Loren Ghiglione, editor and publisher of the *News* in Southbridge, Mass., described the writing movement in "Improving Newswriting," a 1982 collection of essays from the *Bulletin of the American Society of Newspaper Editors.*

"In the mid-1970s," Ghiglione observed, "editors began to worry about writing. Aware that newspaper circulation was lagging behind population growth, they started to fret over how newspapers could compete with the visual fireworks of television. One possibility: four-color writing to create striking word pictures in readers' minds. . . .

"So newspapers hired writing coaches to work with reporters. Editors attended writing seminars. Papers appointed assistant managing editors whose primary responsibility was to overcome the second half of Oscar Wilde's line about the difference between literature and journalism: 'Literature is not read and journalism is unreadable.' "

The *Journal-Bulletin* has been at the forefront of the writing movement almost from its beginning. In 1975, Metropolitan Managing Editor Joel Rawson began conducting a series of writing workshops.

Since the late 1970s, *Journal* News Editor Len Levin has waged a crusade for good writing, first in his "Excellence Memo" and now in "Errata," a regular feature in the newspaper's computer bulletin board that points out stylistic lapses in *Journal-Bulletin* stories. In 1979, *Journal* Section Editor Dave Korb and then *Bulletin* Assistant City Editor Jim Rosenthal started a program for state-staff reporters, who met weekly to critique one another's work.

And in 1980, writers and editors who thought the newspaper's already good writing could be even better suggested that the *Journal-Bulletin* hire Don Murray.

Despite a distinguished career writing and

teaching, Murray describes himself as "a writer who's still learning to write." As a writing coach, he says, "my job is to stimulate an interest in writing and to provide a means for professionals to share the techniques they use when writing goes well."

Murray's chief contribution to good writing at the *Journal-Bulletin* has been to introduce the staff to the process approach to news writing. This is based, he explains, "on the assumption that using language to collect information, understand it and communicate it is a logical process that can be described and, therefore, understood and learned."

Murray's process approach is the core of "How I Wrote the Story." That core combined with the contributions of more than 100 *Journal-Bulletin* writers and editors who have shared their knowledge of news writing have resulted in this book.

When this book was first conceived, in 1981, several writers had written "How I Wrote the Story" accounts for writing workshops then under way.

Exploring the process of news writing then became a weekly routine at the *Journal-Bulletin* when, in April, 1982, the paper began a weekly writing contest open to all departments and carrying a prize of $25 (it is now $50).

The best story of the week is chosen by five writers — previous winners who do the judging for the five weeks following their winning. The prize carries one stipulation: To receive the money, the winner must write an account of the writing of his or her winning story, which is then posted in all departments and bureaus.

"How I Wrote the Story" contains writing descriptions culled from both the workshops and the weekly contest. Several of the stories described were written on deadline for the next day's paper; in other cases, the writer had several days or even weeks to report and write, while one story was an installment of a series produced over 18 months.

In sum, the time these stories took to be produced was not the criterion for their selection as winners. The stories printed here were chosen simply as examples of good writing. The accounts of these stories are effective explorations of the decisions behind good writing.

The stories cover the gamut of news writing today: reporting on politics and government, sports, criminal justice, medicine, the environment; investigative reporting; feature writing; foreign correspondence; column writing; writing on deadline and writing the developed story and series. The stories include several major prize winners.

Bruce Butterfield's series "Working in Jewelry" was a finalist for the 1982 Pulitzer Prize for public service and won the 1981 Public Service Award of the Associated Press Managing Editors Association, the New England Associated Press News Executives Association (NEAPNEA) Sevellon Brown Award for outstanding public service, second prize in the William S. Miller Awards for Enterprise Reporting and an honorable mention in the Heywood Broun Award competition.

Carol McCabe's "Maine Budworm War" was part of the 1980 winning entry in the American Society of Newspaper Editors (ASNE) competition for deadline and non-deadline writing, and was also judged by the NEAPNEA to be the best-written series that year in a paper of over-60,000 circulation. Christopher Scanlan's "Having a Baby" was the 1981 winner of the NEAPNEA's prize for the best-written feature. "Burning Wire," by Barbara Carton, was a finalist in the 1981 magazine-article competition sponsored by the New England Women's Press Association.

"The Interns," a six-part series by Irene Wielawski, won the 1983 J.C. Penney - University of Missouri's Paul Myhre Award for best series. Mark Patinkin's "African Journey" was named a finalist in the ASNE's deadline-writing competition in 1984. G. Wayne Miller's 1984 series "Building New Lives" won several public-service awards from mental-health organizations and took second place in the series category of the NEAPNEA's annual competition. Joel Rawson's "One Soldier's Story" won third prize in the NEAPNEA's 1985 feature-writing competition.

In addition to the reprinted stories and accounts of "How I Wrote the Story," this book offers as an aid to writers and editors a reading list, updated for this edition. It appears in Chapter 9, "Bookbag."

In Shakespeare's time, actors carried bags containing the tools of their art — jars of paint, props, scraps of costume — so they could quickly change into a new character. We hope this book can be such a resource: something to dip into when a quick change in writing or editing seems called for if the performance is to be a success.

Journalists are by nature restless wanderers, moving from story to story and job to job. But there are always special places for these people, where the lessons that they never forget were learned. For me and other writers and editors whose work appears here, the Providence *Journal-Bulletin* will always be such a place. Even when we move on — as I did shortly after completing this second edition — our ties remain strong to this writing community and the standards of excellence its work represents. Today, working in a newsroom 1,500 miles from Providence, I am still just a phone call away from Berkley Hudson, who is as willing to listen to a lead as he was when we sat 10 feet apart. Berkley continues the work I did as the staff liaison to our writing coach, Don Murray. He deserves special recognition for his dedication to publication of this second edition of "How I Wrote the Story" and for his continuing efforts as coordinator of the paper's writing program.

Part I: The Process of News Writing

Chapter 1
The process approach

> *" I don't know how to deal with this subject helpfully to others, but much of what I do is based on luck and intuition. I have unaccountably good luck on stories. The only useful observation I have to pass along is that luck gives me confidence, and confidence often gives me the story. I know it's going to be there, because it always is, so I don't shrink up. "*
>
> — Carol McCabe, *Journal-Bulletin* staff writer

**By Donald M. Murray and
Christopher Scanlan**

Carol McCabe is modest. There's a lot more to writing good stories than luck and intuition. Writing that seems like magic is usually the reward for hard work.

Still, her attitude is a common one among newspaper writers who produce stories on deadline for a living. They're much too busy doing it to think too much about how they go about it.

Athletes study films of themselves to isolate what works and what doesn't. Why can't news writers do the same?

"How I Wrote the Story" is an attempt to do that, by publishing a collection of accounts by Providence *Journal-Bulletin* writers who agreed to describe the process of writing a story and share it with their colleagues.

The process, as these accounts show, changes with the individual writer, the writing task, the writer's experience and the writer's conditions of work.

For news writers, the process may seem to vary with the assignment. A two-graf short on a car accident, two takes on a city-council meeting and two columns detailing the life of a pregnant teenager seem to require totally different approaches.

But in fact, reporting and writing every news story — whether spot, or "hard," news; "soft," or feature, stories — require the same process: collecting, focusing, ordering, developing and clarifying information in understandable prose. The successful writer — whether journalist, novelist, historian, advertising copywriter or scientist — has the same goal: to convey information, ideas and experience across the barriers of time and distance.

Writing is usually discussed from the point of view of the finished product. This is backward — like trying to imagine a pig from a sausage. Instead, the process approach attempts to understand writing from before the story idea through to the published story.

By articulating the process that has produced effective writing, the writer learns to write better. Even though writers may believe their stories are produced by luck or instinct, accounts of the writing process can isolate the rational decisions that produce good writing. Like the baseball player watching himself on film hit a home run, the writer (and the editor) studying an account of the creation of an effective story can learn the conditions that produced that story.

The athlete has an advantage over the writer, of course. A home run can be captured in a few seconds of film. To do the same thing with a great story would take hours of footage, perhaps even days.

Still, the concept can be borrowed, as the accounts in this collection illustrate.

Listen to Carol McCabe discussing how she put together one of the five stories about man's manipulation of nature that won her awards in 1980 from the American Society of Newspaper

Editors and the New England Associated Press News Executives Association.

Watch Bruce DeSilva at work tracing the final hours of Albert Farrands, an elderly patient who died accidentally at the state hospital for the chronically ill.

Go along with Berkley Hudson as he follows the Appalachian Trail from Georgia to Maine. Spend Christmas Eve with Mark Patinkin in a village deep in the famine region of Africa, and accompany Randall Richard to the Miskito Coast in northern Nicaragua. Each of these writers takes away from his or her voyage new lessons about human nature, as well as about reporting and writing.

Follow Gayle Gertler through the two hours she has to write a deadline account of the sentencing of socialite Claus vonBulow. Take a longer journey with Bruce Butterfield, who spent 18 months documenting conditions in Rhode Island's jewelry industry, and Irene Wielawski, who chronicled the year-long rigors of medical internship.

Their accounts, like the others included in "How I Wrote the Story," show the newspaper writer at work: getting an idea or an assignment for a story, reporting the story, trying to decide on a theme and an approach, organizing the material, beginning to write, doing more reporting to fill the holes, writing, rewriting and, finally, seeing his or her work appear in print.

These writers may go about their jobs differently, but the essential qualities of good reporting and writing remain the same: perseverance, curiosity, caring and, above all, determination to find the truth and convey it in the most effective way in the time available.

If writers look at what they do when they write well, they will see significant patterns.

First, there is the ASSIGNMENT, sometimes made by an editor, often conceived by the reporter. It can be vague or highly defined. Whatever the case, the reporting often reshapes the original idea.

Carol McCabe's prizewinner about the budworm-spraying program in Maine began when then-Sunday Editor Joel Rawson gave her "a two- or three-graf wire story clipped from the *Journal*" about an effort by local residents to stop the spraying.

Doug Cumming and Gayle Gertler began with assignments to cover specific events: a high school reunion and the sentencing of a man convicted of attempting to murder his wife.

Writers interested in the personal essay should keep in mind the principle that "City Life" columnist Bob Chiappinelli applied to his idea for a "post-vacation-blues story":

"One thing I have discovered in writing a column is that the more uncomfortable I feel while writing a story, the more people respond to it.

"You might call it the squirm effect.

"I squirmed last year when I wrote about turning 44, and I squirmed again when I wrote about my post-vacation blues. Both columns got a lot of response, even though I wondered all through them why anybody would care. But apparently misery does love company.... What it comes down to, I think, is that it is OK for reporters — the Fourth Estate, the champions of the First Amendment — to let on that we are human beings, not just smart tape recorders who can craft a lead and build a pyramid upside down."

Beat reporters often come up with their own assignments. When Chief Political Writer M. Charles Bakst heard that former U.S. Sen. John O. Pastore, a celebrated speaker, would deliver the keynote speech at a political dinner, he remembered watching a memorable Pastore speech on television 18 years before:

"I had heard the 1964 speech on television, but remembered virtually nothing of it except for the cry 'Shame, shame on all your houses.'

"So what I wanted to do was go to hear Pastore and a real stemwinder of a speech, and see what it is he does (or did), and play it off against the 1964 performance."

Armed with an idea, the writer begins to report: to COLLECT the information that makes good writing possible.

For many reporters, their first stop is the newspaper library to check previous stories on the subject. Under Joseph O. Mehr, the *Journal-Bulletin* library has entered the computer age of reference material, with all clippings since 1982 now available via computer terminals in the newsroom. Susan Fedorzyn-Edgar, formerly the library's data-base expert, routinely provided writers with instant access to reams of material on their subject from a wide variety of sources.

But the library is just the beginning.

"My greatest lesson as a journalist," former St. Petersburg *Times* writing coach Roy Peter Clark concluded, after a reporting stint at that paper, "... is the importance of reporting. Without it, there is no good writing. You may have a facility with language. But if you don't have the interesting facts, the details, the quotations, the description, the anecdotes, your writing will have all the substance of a Fanny Farmer nougat."

Blocked by Electric Boat's refusal to allow a reporter inside its submarine-building operation, Barbara Carton had to reconstruct a day in a welder's life through extensive interviews with her subject. But she went one step further: Eager to convey the mood, she persuaded a contractor friend to let her try on his leathers and hood. "He struck an arc, ran a weld bead or two and generally made the whole experience come alive." It gave her the confidence, she says, to write about an art she had known nothing about before writing "Burning Wire."

For Doug Cumming, the challenge of writing a high-school-reunion feature was "to tap the inner meaning, music and pathos of the thing." That meant not only attending the event, where he used a tape recorder and "eavesdropped all over the place," but also reading short stories and poring over yearbooks and even microfilm of 25-year-old *Journals* — the last "an experience no reporter should miss; if not for a story, then simply for the way the Zeitgeist lingers, in old news and ads."

As is illustrated here, good writing demands more information than writers can possibly use in a story. This abundance of material is necessary for them to understand what to write about and what to leave out.

To document the training of three young doctors, Irene Wielawski told her subjects before the project began that she "would attempt to verify much of what they told me through third-party interviews, so they had to be scrupulously accurate. I didn't want them to exaggerate; I knew much of the story would depend on their veracity. If they knew at the outset that I'd be checking on their versions, I figured it might encourage their accuracy the first time around — and I wanted what they themselves experienced, not hearsay. In the verification period of the research, I interviewed many people who never appeared in the series."

"You really don't know what you're going to need until after you get into the writing," observed Executive Editor Chuck Hauser in an account of his coverage of an editors' briefing by President Reagan. "The material you ignored as irrelevant to your mission may turn out to be essential to the piece you wind up writing."

The information that has been collected now begins to define the story, giving it a FOCUS it may not have had — clarifying the story's original idea. Reaching the FOCUS is a crucial step in the writing process. The writer knows that an effective piece of writing has to say one dominant thing, and that everything in the piece should advance that meaning. That meaning will also dictate the form and structure of the story, and the appropriate voice.

"The most important question as you approach a piece is 'What's this story about?'" says Carol McCabe. "I've skipped it, and so have you. And the result can be a story that's too long or too vague, or races off in several directions at once, softening its impact with irrelevant information."

When Bob Wyss, who was covering Providence City Hall, was assigned to write a profile of mayoral candidate Frank Darigan, he knew the major task "was to make it fresh. That was a challenge because I have been covering the man for five years and he has been in the public eye, off and on, for the last twelve years. But as I thought about it I realized that the key was to concentrate on what has happened to him in the last four years, since his crushing defeat to Cianci."

Often, the focus of a story changes as the reporting proceeds. Writers accept change as a condition of their work.

Bruce DeSilva's story on the elderly patient who died "immediately took a turn" after DeSilva read the medical records and learned that the man not only had been burned seriously, but also had been given "nothing but Vaseline and Tylenol for at least the first five hours. And at the end of those five hours, Farrands was near death."

DeSilva saw he had a different story now. "Not only the accident itself but also the treatment Farrands received afterwards had to be researched."

The writer now begins to ORDER the material — in the mind or on the note pad or VDT screen. Each point grows from the preceding point and leads to the next. This is an "answer and question" technique: Each part of the story answers a question and asks a new question. The reader is simultaneously satisfied and enticed.

At this stage, many writers find the outline a great help.

When Metropolitan Managing Editor Joel Rawson set out to write about his experiences as a pilot in Vietnam, on the 10th anniversary of the fall of Saigon, "This outline resulted," he recalled:

Bennington, Memorial Day, 1980
Helicopters
Orono, 1966. We were so sure
DaNang, summer 1968. What's worth dying for war and politics, war is not diplomacy by another name, they fight to kill, the barroom The Aytollah and limits of power Nixon on the beach and the changing nature of war
Saigon, Thanksgiving, 1968. War by machine and data analysis, garbage in - garbage out, Westmoreland's body count
1975, the newsroom and the wirephoto images of the beach and DaNang, defeat changes the way you think, no longer so sure
Bennington, Memorial Day, 1980

"All of the points did not survive the writing," Rawson recalls, "but the above outline served as the rough guide and a reminder of the points I wanted to touch."

Other writers look for a specific detail and listen for a quote, a statistic — something to "shine a flashlight into the story," as author John McPhee says. Some writers find their organization by writing a lead and an ending, and then listing three to five points they know they must cover.

Gayle Gertler led her story about the vonBulow sentencing with a traditional inverted pyramid, which delivered the news — 30-year jail term, release on bail pending appeal, reaction of vonBulow and courtroom spectators — but then quickly shifted to a chronological narrative that led the reader from the beginning to the end of the event. Roy Peter Clark calls this form the "hourglass," and believes it serves the reader more effectively than the pyrmaid, which begins with the most important information and ends with the least important. The inverted pyramid is just one possible form of journalistic prose; depending on their material, writers look for various ways to write their stories.

"A news story, by my definition, has plot; that is, the organization of incidents into a narrative," says Carol McCabe. "A good plot, according to Aristotle, ought to have a beginning, a middle and an end, and be constructed so that no incident can be displaced or omitted without destroying the unity of the whole. Aristotle never had to cover the closing of a rubber plant."

Barbara Carton had a natural order to her story: a day in the life of a submarine welder. For his description of the high school reunion, Doug Cumming chose a pattern common to fiction but unusual in a newspaper: "I started big and abstract, and then focused on a scene." Working with editor Joel Rawson, Irene Wielawski decided to tell the story of her three interns in episodic, narrative style.

Some writers discover the order of their story by writing a "discovery draft," which teaches them what they know and what they need to know. Bruce Butterfield reports that in retrospect it was "hard to separate the writing from the organization" of the installment he describes of his prizewinning series on Rhode Island's jewelry industry. The decision to write a story that took the reader on "a journey of sorts" into a mill complex "came about in part by trial and error. The lead stayed the same, but a lot of decisions on what would be used and what would not came about by trial and error in the writing," he says.

The writer is now ready to write: to DEVELOP the material collected, focused and ordered into publishable shape.

The writer knows it is more effective to show than to tell, and that shorter is better. The piece of writing should give the reader the information he or she needs in as short a space as possible. A good piece of writing may be judged by the good material that is left out: Shortness is achieved by selection, not compression.

Many writers begin by writing a lead, or several leads. Others plow through a full draft. Overwhelmed by the amount of their material, some writers have learned to write their first draft without their notes, knowing that they will remember the most important points, and that they can always return to the notebook to make sure they haven't left anything out. Once into the writing, the writer may see holes that need filling. That means more more reporting, rethinking the focus, reshaping the lead.

"When I began writing," Doug Cumming says of his high-school-reunion piece, "I set the scene with the red banner at the end of the room. I knew my ending would be with Joan Crocker Pfeiffer's speech, because it seemed to give meaning to the event, and also to express her character.

"But beginning with the red banner wasn't satisfying. So I added an introductory sentence about reunions — something about the bittersweet feeling, I think. I expanded on this. I wrote slowly, polishing as I went, as if writing poetry."

Process approach

The decision facing Bruce DeSilva when he sat down to write about the elderly patient was whether to write a detailed account of Farrands's last days, or an accusatory piece, charging that the patient had received inadequate treatment.

DeSilva had "more than enough" to write the latter, he says, but decided against it. This "was the case of a single mistake by a single, probably overworked physician. Turning the full wrath of the Providence *Journal* on him seemed ridiculously out of proportion — like nuking a shoplifter." But there was another consideration. There was "too much more in the Farrands story that intrigued me: the characters, the ironies, the sights and sounds of the hospital, and most of all, the dramatic moments."

"Good news writing is not the use of words," Carol McCabe maintains. "It's the use of people.

"During the time I'd spent in Maine, I had been collecting people, as well as information, and the people would be infinitely more important to the story. They, and not facts about papermaking or chemical properties, would bring readers into the story.

"If I could make readers care enough about those people to want to know what happened to them, the story would be read. I don't have any tricks for accomplishing this; I just believe that if the writer cares about the people, the reader will, too," she says.

Writers know that the way they end their story is as important as their lead. "We often neglect endings of stories, but in some ways I think they're more important than leads; it's the final point readers take away," Mark Patinkin observes in his account of the writing of a Christmas Eve story from Timbuktu, Mali, the last in his moving series from Africa's famine region.

Deadline approaches. The writer now begins to CLARIFY the story, revising by cutting a line or a graf to quicken the pace, adding a fact, or deleting a section to strengthen the focus. The writer may read the story aloud and cut or change what sounds off-key before hitting the Send button on the terminal. Frequently, other writers and editors are asked for their reaction; every reader is an editor.

When Jeanne Edwards wrote about a teenager fatally shot in a gas-station holdup, "Initially, the description of Mrs. Caldwell ordering the respirator shut off was nearer the top of the story," she said. (Then-Sunday Editor) Mark Silverman suggested it would be more effective at the end. And it was."

In this stage of the process, the writer knows that the decisions to add, cut or reorder are within the text — not in a rule book.

Bob Chiappinelli, who has to tailor his column to a specific length, often spends "two hours paring it.

"I follow the Joel Rawson technique for that, first going through and finding grafs where one or two words tag over onto a new line. A little weeding in a few of those gardens sometimes is all you need.

"Other times, though, I have to chop larger weeds. That usually becomes an individual choice, depending on what I think I can spare from the story, which quotes are similar, etc."

The time it takes to move through the process depends on the deadline. Gayle Gertler finished her vonBulow piece in two hours; other writers worked on their pieces for days, even weeks and months.

Whatever the time spent, the process is recursive. The writer usually has to work back and forth, circling back through the process during the act of writing — repeating the cycle of collect-focus-order-develop-clarify as many times as necessary to discover meaning and to make it clear.

Chapter 2

Problems and solutions

Each step in the writing process has its own problems — and possible solutions. None of the solutions listed here is chiseled in stone, but writers have found them a handy guide for when they're searching for a lead, when their copy is muddy, when they're stuck on the reporting or writing of a story. The techniques also help editors get the best work from their writers.

By Donald M. Murray

PROBLEM: How do I get ideas for stories?

SOLUTIONS:

- Brainstorming. Brainstorming can be a solitary exercise or can be done with other reporters and editors. The key to brainstorming is to suspend critical judgment and write down — as quickly as possible — all the ideas and related thoughts that surface on a particular topic. Don't stop to evaluate items, and don't discard or bypass anything. Write in your personal shorthand, without filling in the details.

  Once the flow of ideas has petered out, then — and only then — do you review and evaluate, discard and organize, clarify and expand. Look for the information that surprises you, or that connects with other information in an interesting unexpected way.

- Mapping. Whereas brainstorming follows a linear progression of thought, mapping calls for the topic to be placed in the middle of a page in a circle, with related ideas leading out from it in many directions.

  Researchers interested in left-brain - right-brain activities feel that this approach more accurately reflects the way the mind works: not in a straight line but more like a pinball machine, bouncing ideas off one another helter-skelter.

- Daybook. Keep a daybook, or journal, that brings together observations, ideas, recollections, possibilities, revealing details and possible lines of writing. Carry it with you and write in it on the spot as ideas occur. In addition, you might set aside a particular time each day to expand on your thoughts.

  Sources of ideas: friends, neighbors, spouses, children, television, movies, magazines, books. Try eavesdropping, observing, wondering. Ideas are everywhere.

PROBLEM: How do I report the story better so I can COLLECT the information needed for good writing?

SOLUTIONS:

- Seek specific, accurate information. We do not write with words; we write with information: who, what, where, when, how and why.

- Collect much more information than you can use, so you can select from this inventory when you write.

- Revel in information you do not yet understand, because writing is a process of discovering meaning.

- Make quick notes on how people move, dress, speak; how the place feels; how people react to one another.

- Use all your senses. See, but also hear, smell, touch, taste.

- Role-play. Practice empathic reporting, in which you become, for a moment, the people in the story.

- Adjust distance. Move in close on an unfamiliar subject; back off on a familiar subject.

- Interview yourself: What makes me mad, what worries me, what makes me happy, what do I want?

- Learn to use scholarly and statistical research so that you can mine for what your reader needs to know.

- Keep and update a checklist of what you know and need to know.

- Write and revise the three to five obvious questions that must be answered in the story.

- Remember Hemingway's advice: "The most essential gift for a good writer is a built-in shockproof shit detector."

PROBLEM: The reporting's done, but what do all these notes mean? How do I find the FOCUS of the story?

SOLUTIONS:

- Answer the question "What's this story about?"

- State the *single dominant* meaning of the story, in one sentence or less. It may be changed by the experience of reporting and writing.
  - The statement should not be a label, such as "War." It should be a title that limits the subject, helps the writer focus on it and may even establish the voice with which the piece will be written.
  - The statement should have what Virginia Woolf called "the power of combination." It should contain the tensions within the story: "They had to destroy the village to save it."
  - It may help to list the elements of the story that relate to the statement. Everything in the story must advance that single meaning.

- Rehearse this statement of focus, in your head and on paper, while working on the story.

- Tell an editor or colleague about the story, to hear what you say about it.

- Draft the end of the story, to give yourself a sense of destination.

- Draft the lead of the story, to reveal the direction and the voice of the story.

- Free-write — as fast as possible — a discovery draft or discovery grafs, to reveal the meaning and the voice of the story. They can be any part of the story as long as they reveal tone, mood, voice. Am I sad, joyous, incredulous, detached, warm, cold? Do I smell earth or engine oil or chalk dust?

- Listen to what your voice is telling you about the meaning of the story. The intensity, rhythm and tone of voice often reveal the meaning of the story.

- Put down what the reader needs to know about the story. How will this story serve the reader?

- Form is meaning. Try on different approaches to the story, such as narrative, profile, inverted pyramid, interview, problem-and-solution.

- Rehearse the story, in your head and on paper, to hear what the story means.

- Look at the story from different points of view.

Problems and solutions

- Focus in writing may be achieved the way focus in photography is achieved: by adjusting the distance. Zoom in close, stand way back; move back and forth until the story comes into focus.

- A revealing detail may give the story focus: Look for the significant detail that reveals the central meaning of the story. That detail may be a fact, a quote, an action, a scene, a name, a face, a place, an act committed, an act not committed. Look for the image that reveals — the specific that controls the vision of the piece.

- Look for the anecdote (the little story or parable that combines character, dialogue, action and place) that reveals the significance of the story — that shows rather than tells the reader.

- You work for a newspaper. What's new?

PROBLEM: How do I ORDER the story?

SOLUTIONS:

- Ask the questions the reader will ask, and put them in the order they will be asked.

- Decide on the information your reader needs to know, and the order in which the reader needs to know it.

- Give information in the lead that makes the reader ask a question. Answer it with information that sparks a new question. Continue until all the questions are answered.

- Draft many possible leads — a dozen, two dozen, three dozen — as quickly as possible.

- Pick a starting point as near the end as you can.

- Seek a natural order for the story: narrative, chronology, inverted pyramid, problem-and-solution, follow-up, a visit with ..., a walk through ..., etc.

- Draft a lead and indicate three to five main points and an ending. Consult an editor.

- Draft many endings as quickly as possible. Once you know where you're going, you may see how to get there.

- Diagram the pattern of the story.

- Write an outline.

- Write out the thread that holds the story together.

- Clip together the notes on each part of the subject. Move the piles around until you discover a working order.

- Play with the key revealing specifics to see what pattern they form.

- List all the items in the story down the left side of the page, and then move each important item into one of three columns, labeled "beginning," "middle" and "end." (Draw arrows or number the items.)

PROBLEM: How do I write — and keep writing — to DEVELOP the story into publishable shape?

SOLUTIONS:

- Write early, to discover what you know and what you need to know.

- Write fast — without notes. The subconscious is a good editor. What is remembered probably should be, what is forgotten probably should be. And you can go back to your notes when the draft is done.

- Select the important points and take the

time to develop them adequately. Brevity is achieved by selection, not compression.

• Write with your ear. Listen to what you are saying, and how you are saying it. (If stuck, dictate into a tape recorder.)

• When possible, reveal the story to the reader: Show, don't tell. Use scene and anecdote. Let the reader experience the story to discover its meaning.

• Let action or the natural order of the story carry the exposition and description.

• If there is a serious problem in organization that hasn't been solved during the Order stage of the process, type your paragraphs with six spaces between them. Make a printout, cut the paragraphs apart, and play "solitaire" with them until you find their natural sequence.

• If blocked, follow poet William Stafford's advice: Lower your standards. Or heed William Faulkner: "Get it down. Take chances. It may be bad, but that's the only way you can do anything really good." Writer's block often comes when the writer has set impossible standards.

• Provide the reader with the evidence an intelligent but uninformed person will need in order to believe the story.

• Type "TK" (to come) or an underlined blank space in the text for details that you have forgotten but can be inserted later. Keep writing.

• Vary the documentation. Pick the material and the form of that material (quotation, anecdote, statistic, action, description) that are appropriate for the point being made.

• Answer the questions the reader will ask. The story is a conversation with an individual reader, even though only the answers to the reader's questions are printed.

• Remember: Shorter is better. What can be left out should be left out. A good piece of writing may be judged by the amount of good material that isn't used. Everything left in develops the *single dominant* meaning of the story.

PROBLEM: How do I edit my copy to CLARIFY the meaning and keep the story tight and interesting?

SOLUTIONS:

• The answers to what to add, what to cut and what to reorder are within the text. Ask what it needs, and it will tell you what to do.

• Cut what can be cut. Everything left must add to the meaning of the story.

• In revising, the effective writer builds on strengths as much as or more than he or she corrects mistakes.

• To make writing effective, we must realize that we cannot solve the problems of *language* until we have solved the problems of *structure,* and we cannot solve the problems of structure until we have solved the problems of *content.* Therefore, give your text the following three readings.

1. Read the text fast — at a distance, as the reader will — and ask the large questions of *content:*
  - Are all the reader's questions answered?
  - Is new information needed?
  - Is the piece built on undocumented assumptions?
  - Is the genre appropriate to the meaning?
  - Are there any tangents that can be cut loose from the piece?
  - Is there any section that should be a separate story?
  - Is each point supported by convincing evidence?
  - Is the piece long enough to satisfy the reader?

Problems and solutions

- Is the piece short enough to keep the reader involved?
- Can the dominant meaning of the piece be stated in one sentence?

2. Read the text a bit more slowly, in chunks, and answer the questions of *structure:*

- Does the lead catch the reader in three seconds or less?
- Does the lead deliver on its contract with the reader?
- Is each point in sequence: Does it both answer a question and ask one?
- How can I get out of the reader's way?
- Is there an effective variety of documentation?
- Does the piece carry the reader forward?
- Are the dimensions within the text — the size of each section in relation to other sections — appropriate?
- Does the end echo the lead and fulfill its promise?

3. Read the text slowly, line by line, and answer the questions of *language:*

- Can the piece be read aloud? Does it sound as if one person is talking to one person?
- Are the important pieces of information at the ends and the beginnings of key sentences, paragraphs and the entire piece?
- Does each paragraph make one point?
- Does each paragraph carry a full load of meaning to the reader?
- Do the paragraphs vary in length according to significance: the shorter the grafs, the more important their information?
- Are the paragraphs in order (are the reader's questions answered where they will be asked?), so that formal transitions are not needed?
- Does the reader leave each sentence with more information than when the reader entered it?
- Are most sentences subject-verb-object?
- Are the sentences shorter at the points of emphasis or clarification?
- Are the verbs active and strong enough to drive the meaning forward?
- Has the right word been found so that the meaning does not lie between two almost-right words? Remember that Mark Twain said the difference between the right word and the wrong word is the difference between lightning and a lightning bug.
- Are there sentences that announce what you are going to say or sum up what you have said and, therefore, can be cut?
- Are there dependent clauses that should be moved so that they come in a natural sequence within the sentence?
- Does the meaning depend on verbs and nouns, not adverbs and adjectives?
- Is there sexist or racist language?
- Can the writing be made more specific?
- Can people be put into the sentences?
- Are unnecessary "-ly"s, "-ing"s, "that"s and "would"s cut?
- Is every fact checked?
- Is each word spelled correctly?
- Is there anything I can do to make the writing
  - simple?
  - clear?
  - graceful?
  - accurate?
  - fair?

Chapter 3

Help or hindrance?

Complaining about each other is a favorite pastime of newspaper writers and editors. At one writing workshop, this antipathy was turned to advantage when Don Murray asked writers and editors to list ways they hinder each other on the job — as well as ways that they help each other.

Behind the shield of anonymity, the writers and editors came up with nearly 100 suggestions, which are listed below. Candid and revealing, they not only expose the tensions between writer and editor, but also hint at ways of achieving a lasting truce between these natural enemies of the newsroom.

By *Journal-Bulletin* writers and editors

What can an editor do to help a writer?

1. Confer. Communicate as much as possible with writers. Tell them what you want and don't want. Give them reasons.

2. Listen. Too often an editor gets into a fixed position. Open your mind and be willing to admit you can learn something.

3. Act as the first reader of the writer's material — a buffer between the writer and the reader.

4. Ask the questions and contribute the ideas that may stimulate the writer's thinking and reporting.

5. Be adjustable — willing to change your mind about a story as the writer brings forward new information.

6. Be supportive — not with fraudulent pats on the head, but with useful criticisms and compliments when deserved.

7. Check with the writer — not by nagging, but by giving reassurance that you are available for help. If you have a definite direction for the story, make sure you communicate it to the writer.

8. Don't judge in advance what the writer should produce.

9. Suggest approaches and techniques without demanding that they be used.

10. Offer a different viewpoint on the set of facts the writer has collected.

11. Challenge the writer's assumptions.

12. Find the holes in the story (the writer usually knows they're there, anyway) and demand that they be filled. Better: Ask the writer what he or she thinks are the holes in the story.

13. Help refine the story idea at the point of assignment.

14. Discuss editing changes with the writer during and after the editing process.

15. Provide encouragement for the use of unconventional techniques.

16. Talk over stories before they are written.

17. Make the assignment clear in the beginning. Insist that the writer produce what is asked for, when it's asked for.

18. Ask the questions a reader would ask — after the reporting and before the writing.

19. After thorough discussion, negotiate the length of the story. Give the writer an equal say in this, but when a decision is reached, enforce it.

20. Point out errors that are recurrent.

21. Ask first what the story is about; next what problems the writer is having; and last when the writer can have the story done.

22. Don't be afraid to read the writer's notes — but only at the writer's request. With our computers, that's not as difficult as it sounds.

23. Bring a piece into focus if the writer is struggling or off the mark.

24. Realize that some writers don't talk a good story but can write it.

25. Give story ideas in more detail than "How about a piece on . . . ?"

26. Let the writer come up with story ideas of his or her own. Better, tell the writer to come up with them.

27. Check with the writer before assuming that the writer is wrong.

28. Give the writer as much time as reasonably possible to write.

29. Point out breakdowns in the logical flow of a story, and suggest alternatives.

30. Suggest information that should be included but is not.

31. Change copy only if the change will make the story more complete, accurate and readable.

32. Remember that psychologically bad editing is far worse than technically bad editing. An editing mistake may be remembered by the writer for a week; a mistake in handling the writer may be remembered for a lifetime.

These suggestions show that writers know they need editors. They want editors who consult with them and listen to them, but who are also critical and demanding. In general, editors should be more open and consult more at the beginning of the writing process, and, while still listening, be more critical and demanding at the end of the process.

What does an editor do that hinders a writer?

1. Assumes. Makes changes on the basis of what the editor assumes the writer intended or the story means.

2. Issues inflexible plans for a story early on — without fully understanding all the relevant facts.

3. Sets unrealistic deadlines.

4. Leans too heavily on a preconceived idea of a story.

5. Fails to respond — pro or con — to story ideas.

6. Criticizes without factual support.

7. Misleads by being unsure about the writer's and editor's mutual goals.

8. Approaches the writer from an insecure position. Then the writer and the editor must deal with the editor's insecurity, as well as the story.

9. Doesn't listen to what the writer has to say in the planning of the assignment. This is a surefire way to ensure that the editor will be surprised — and possibly disappointed — by the finished product.

Help or hindrance

10. Tinkers with the copy — makes minute changes for no reason other than what words are pleasing to the editor.

11. Tells the writer exactly what the editor wants, and in precisely what order. This lobotomizes the writer and robs the writing of its zip.

12. Is both condescending and defensive in discussing the writing and possible changes.

13. Changes, rewrites, overedits without consulting the writer.

14. Ignores the writer until the story is in.

15. Disrupts rhythm for the sake of conciseness.

16. Suggests what the story is or should be before the writer has done the reporting.

17. Sets a story length before the editor knows as much about the story as the writer.

18. Pigeonholes the writer as a hard-news or features specialist.

19. Pushes for something that may not be there.

20. Insists on formula leads.

21. Inserts mistakes in the copy.

22. Fails to read the story carefully before writing the head.

23. Nitpicks to assert the desk's authority.

24. Makes changes without explaining why. If writers are to learn from mistakes, editors must point out the mistakes.

Writers seem most upset when editors prejudge the writer or the story, are rigid, or make changes for reasons external to the story. Writers and editors should focus on the story, and consult about what works in that particular copy.

What can a writer do to help an editor?

1. Leggo. Allow the editors time to do their job — to question, challenge, correct and revise copy where necessary; to cut stories in the most careful manner to fit the space available; and to consult with the writers.

2. Be thorough and accurate. The less time editors spend checking spelling, addresses and titles, the more time they will have to read, assess and edit in a substantive way.

3. Challenge. Editors need feedback from writers about the way their stories are edited and displayed.

4. Be clear and concise in early discussions of the story.

5. Give the editor information that is not included in the story but may be relevant.

6. Ask for advice.

7. Communicate. Tell the editor why you did what you did — and be open to his or her suggestions. Get to know the editor as a human being — what makes this person tick.

8. Understand an editor's schedule. Work with the editor to arrange talking time.

9. Be willing to take criticism, to admit that not every story is perfect, to make changes where they are warranted.

10. Be willing to get the extra fact that the editor thinks is necessary, or to re-answer the question that you think is already adequately answered — often it isn't.

11. Refuse to bend where bending isn't justified; sometimes the editor needs to be told when a change must not be made.

12. Keep stories to the length requested, or at least in the ball park.

13. Meet deadlines.

14. Be objective about criticism; try not to take it personally.

15. Tell the editor what the story is about before you write it.

16. Use a dictionary.

17. If you're having a problem with the length or deadline, tell the editor at once.

18. Ask questions about the assignment if you are unclear about what is expected.

19. Forgive. That is, fight the good fight to preserve the beautiful story, but don't harbor grudges or prejudices.

20. Proofread your copy.

21. Think through your proposal to modify an assignment and present logical arguments — not emotional ones.

22. Don't be resistant to reasonable suggestions or criticisms.

23. Keep a flow of ideas going to the editor; don't just wait for the editor's ideas.

24. Praise a good headline or layout. Editors need to be stroked, as well as writers.

Editors need consultation from writers. Editors also need a response. Collaboration is a two-way street.

What does a writer do that hinders an editor?

1. Procrastinates.

2. Argues unnecessarily over editorial decisions — battles should be chosen carefully.

3. Fails to challenge the editor's ideas.

4. Ignores the editor's requirements. Insists that the writer is the only one qualified to make judgments.

5. Calls the editor a butcher.

6. Lets insecurities get in the way of the writer-editor relationship.

7. Refuses to believe that the writing-editing process is give-and-take. Refusal to negotiate usually results in losing.

8. Rides deadlines, giving the editor too little time to do the editing.

9. Stays aloof — ignores the editor, not letting the editor into the writing process.

10. Expects the editor to do all the proofreading and to clean up sloppy grammar and spelling.

11. Hands in copy longer than the assigned length without consultation.

12. Ignores the assignment — leads the story in a different direction, without first consulting the editor.

13. Fails to check all the facts, or attempts to hide inadequate research.

14. Writes without a focal point.

15. Always second-guesses and Monday-morning-quarterbacks all decisions by all editors.

Writers make an editor's job difficult when they are unprofessional, miss deadlines, don't write to length, turn in sloppy copy. Writers need to accept editors as consultants and collaborators.

Chapter 4

Talk Talk:
Notes on the art of interviewing

In May, 1985, staff writer Berkley Hudson led a session on interviewing at a seminar for improving reporting skills at the American Press Institute, in Reston, Va.; this chapter is based on material Hudson assembled for that seminar. Part I, "Interviewers on Interviewing," offers words of wisdom from celebrated practitioners of the "art of listening." For Part II, "When All Else Fails: How to Get the Interview," Hudson provides an inventory of techniques gleaned from Journal-Bulletin *colleagues and from his own 12 years as a reporter. Chapter 9, "Bookbag," includes a bibliography to inspire interviewers.*

I. Interviewers on interviewing

The initial problem

The initial problem is always to approach total strangers, move in on their lives in some fashion, ask questions you have no natural right to expect answers to, ask to see things you weren't meant to see. — **Tom Wolfe**

The first essence of journalism is to know what you want to know; the second is to find out who will tell you.
— **John Gunther**

Follow the Scout motto: Be prepared

The preparation is the same whether you are going to interview a diplomat, a jockey or an ichthyologist. From the man's past you learn what questions are likely to stimulate a response. — **A.J. Liebling**

Before every interview I prepare a long list, a short list, and a "hello-goodbye" list of questions I will use depending on the person's reaction to my call.
— **Steve Kurkjian**

I read as much as I can to prepare for an interview.... If you could see the amount I read ... so much, it scares me.
— **Oriana Fallaci**

What I do is quite simple — homework.... Basically I must respect the person I'm interviewing: there's no point to it otherwise, life's much too short. — **Studs Terkel**

The art of listening

I must have done 7,000 interviews in the first 10 years of (radio's) "All Things Considered." My best interviews are the ones in which I listen most carefully: for new ideas, new perspectives, but also for slips of the tongue, slips of logic; for contradictions, enthusiasm, tension; for what's not being said; for silences, too, and what they reveal. Manic-depressive listening, a reporter once called it. — **Susan Stamberg**

Most men and women lead lives, if not of quiet desperation, at least of desperate quietness, and they jump at a chance to talk about their work to an outsider who seems eager to listen. — **William Zinsser**

I found that most people not only hunger to talk, but also have a story to tell. They are often not heard, but they have something to say. They are desperate to escape the stereotypes into which the pollsters and the media and the politicians have packaged them.
— **Bill Moyers**

There is an art of listening. To be able really to listen, one should abandon ... all prejudices, pre-formulations.... When you are in a receptive state of mind, things can be easily understood.
— **Krishnamurti**

I was ... trying to get deeper and deeper — so "deep" I would *really* understand.... To do so I was spending long hours listening, asking questions and watching.
— **Robert Coles**

The gentle art of interviewing is based on the principle of persuading the other fellow to do the talking. Just how to get him started is the reporter's problem.
— **John Hohenberg**

Part of the skill in interviewing comes from a sort of quiet observation all along: "Does this sentence, this statement, have an unquestionable meaning? Is there any certainty as to what this person means?"
— **Harry Stack Sullivan, M.D.**

I listen. I ask questions and I listen. I'm constantly overwhelmed at the number of first-rate reporters who spend their time telling the source what they think.
— **Hugh Sidey**

In their own words

Nothing so animates writing as someone telling what he thinks or what he does — in his own words. — **William Zinsser**

The challenge is to preserve the truth of that person without distorting what the person says. — **Studs Terkel**

The cruelest thing you can do to anybody is to quote him literally, with no selectivity ... particularly anybody who is prone, as (Hemingway) was, to feeling friendly with somebody and to relax and let his hair down and talk Indian talk and all that, never dreaming that it would come out any other way than the way he felt about it.
— **Arnold Gingrich**

Just because someone "said it" is no reason for you to use it.... Your obligation to the people you write about does not end once your piece is in print. Anyone who trusts you enough to talk about himself to you is giving you a form of friendship. — **Lillian Ross**

Play with the "quotes" by all means — selecting, rejecting, thinning, transposing their order, saving a good one for the end. Just make sure the play is fair. Don't change any words or let the cutting of a sentence distort the proper context.
— **William Zinsser**

What about quoting? You shape *all* writing, including whatever you quote. In the relationship you establish with a person you are writing about, it is up to you to find the quotations that get to the truth of what the person is. That does not mean you make up quotations. Somewhere along the line ... you will find the quotations that are significant — that reveal the character of the person, that present as close an approximation of the truth as you can achieve. — **Lillian Ross**

What hath God wrought? The telephone

Almost everyone is completely at ease on the phone and used to talking freely. It prevents them from seeing a tape recorder in action, which can cause even the sophisticated to change gears and begin to orate and talk artificially. The subject is not aware, even by the slightest visual clues, of the interviewer's boredom, embarrassment or indifference, and consequently will talk with the fluidity of a patient on a psychoanalyst's couch.
— **Denis Brian**

The telephone is journalism's most important tool. Phones connect reporters to sources, to facts, to information and verification. The phone took us to places we couldn't afford to visit and introduced us to people we otherwise couldn't have met. On the phone, I'm not distracted by the ugly tie or the nervous tic or the exquisite manicure.
— **Susan Stamberg**

To tape or not to tape

I tape, therefore I am. — **Studs Terkel**

Do not use a tape recorder. The machine, surprisingly, distorts the truth. The tape recorder is a fast and easy and lazy way of getting a lot of talk down.... A lot of talk does not in itself make an interview.... A writer must use his own ears to listen, must use his own eyes to look. — **Lillian Ross**

The act of taking notes is, however fragmentary, an act of writing. To bypass this process by having someone talk into a machine is to lose the subtle mystery of seeing words emerge as you put them on paper.
— **William Zinsser**

Interviewers today ... rely too much on the tape. They don't listen. They don't carry on a conversation.... Then, especially the younger generation are apt to treat words that come off the machine as gospel and feel they can't touch them when they transpose them to paper.
— **George Plimpton**

The moment you introduce a mechanical device into the interview ... you are creating an atmosphere in which the person isn't going to feel really relaxed, because they're watching themselves.
— **Truman Capote**

To give is to receive

If you're having a difficult time with a subject, you in effect change roles. You ... begin by making little confidences of your own that are rather similar to the things that you think you will draw out of them. Suddenly, they'll be saying, "Ah, yes, my mother ran away with five repairmen, too.... Ah, yes, my father robbed a bank and was sent to prison for 10 years." Then you're off to the races. — **Truman Capote**

What I do is to reveal a good deal of myself, my ... personal life. Sometimes I find that sharing experiences inspires a kind of confidence and gets them to reveal things ... I don't think they would have (revealed) ... if the interviewer hadn't been honest about himself. — **Gay Talese**

You know R.D. Laing, the Scottish psychiatrist? One of his points is that the psychiatrist has to be the fellow-traveller with the patient: He must reveal his own being to the person. That opens up the person and, in a sense, your own vulnerability. I'm pretty terrible with a portable tape recorder. Sometimes, (say) an old lady in a housing project will see my tape recorder isn't working. She'll say: "Hey, it's not working!" I say: "I goofed." My own vulnerability makes her feel more kinship.
— **Studs Terkel**

Getting to know you

If I'm doing a piece about a steel-mill closing, I go to the steel mill *and* to the union hall *and* to the church and whatever other place is part of the guy's life. I see little value to sitting across an office desk from someone, but even that can be revealing. Where does he sit or where does she seat me? How does she deal with the subordinates and superiors who come and go? What's on his desk top? What's on his walls? Books? Does he ignore the view? How does he or she speak to telephone callers?

I always try to see people at home, no matter where else I may see them. In their own surroundings, you can see them much more naturally, watch them interact with others, and, most important, see the choices they have made: pictures, books, music, tools, toys, kids' rooms, formal or informal approach to home life. I can learn something from where the TV is, whether the set of encyclopedias or bowling trophies is prominently displayed, whether the guy hugs his wife or touches his kids, what clothes he or she wears at home, what's on the refrigerator door.

— **Carol McCabe**

An interviewer without curiosity is as useless as a seasick sailor.

— **Denis Brian**

I'm curious about everybody. I think a good journalist is always a voyeur and a Peeping Tom.

— **Rex Reed**

Nuts and bolts

Keep your notebook ... out of sight until you need it. There is nothing less likely to relax a person than the arrival of someone with a stenographer's pad.

— **William Zinsser**

I have no other theory than I ask short, rather blunt, open, simple questions. Another, ... secondary theory is to not be afraid to ask about inconsequential things. I have wasted more hours by asking ... great sweeping questions of policy. ... it's never been below me to ask when (someone) got up, how he felt, how he treated his kids, what books did he read, what movies had he seen. ... These insights into personality prove invaluable.

— **Hugh Sidey**

It's a conversation, not a laundry list

I suppose I have been influenced by jazz since I was a jazz disc jockey and wrote columns on it. Jazz has a beginning, middle and end. The framework is skeletal; at the same time there is an arrangement. ...

So it is with a conversation. I have an idea in the beginning. I don't just shoot blindly. I have ideas but I make adjustments. You adjust. You change the sequence of questions. Suppose a person says something I didn't think he was going to say. He leads me to something else. It's like jazz: You improvise.

— **Studs Terkel**

If you go in with a laundry list of questions and you've got blinkers on, and you don't observe what's going on, you really are going to miss the guts of a story. You keep your eyes open. ... As far as relating to people is concerned, I hate the laundry-list approach. Sometimes I'll use it if all I'm interested in is a factual response. But most of the time I'm interested in an emotional response and I'm trying, even in the half-hour interview, to get a little closer to this guy than might ordinarily be possible. I do that by showing real interest.

— **William Blundell**

In the early days (my interviewing technique) was much tighter. I had a series of very sharply defined questions. I was in a hurry to put them across: bing, bing, bing. As the years went on I've taken to a much more relaxed technique, which I think is more effective, of letting the interview develop (at) its own pace.

— **Harrison Salisbury**

The impact of what we write

As soon as another human being permits you to write about him, he is opening his life to you and you must be constantly aware that you have a responsibility... to that person. Even if that person encourages you to be careless about how you use your intimate knowledge of him, or if he is indiscreet... it is up to you to use your own judgment in deciding what to write.

— Lillian Ross

The right stuff of New Journalism

I try to follow my subjects unobtrusively while observing them in revealing situations, noting their reactions and the reactions of others to them.

I attempt to absorb the whole scene, the dialogue and the mood, the tension, the drama and the conflict, and then I try to write it all from the point of view of the persons I am writing about, even revealing, whenever possible, what these individuals are thinking during those moments that I am describing.

This latter insight is not obtainable, of course, without the full cooperation of the subject, but if the writer enjoys the confidence and the trust of his subjects, it is possible, through interviews, by asking the right question at the right time, to learn and to report what goes on within other people's mind.

— Gay Talese

Catching people at off moments is the dream of any interviewer. Ava Gardner was quite loaded when I interviewed her. It was the most honest interview she ever did.

— Rex Reed

Simple questions for complex people

There's a certain knack to interviewing writers. It's not like a news interview, where the emphasis is on facts and information. In literary interviews, ideas and personalities are the real topics. I try to go in with a point of view about the author and his or her work, and a sense of what the focus of the conversation should be.

Then there's the matter of the questions themselves. Fancy questions don't work. In fact, sometimes the simple question "Why?" will produce the most intriguing answer.

Often I ask how the writer was feeling — what was in his or her mind when the work was created. That approach also works well with painters and dancers. It gets to the heart of the creative process.

— Susan Stamberg

Reporter's intuition

Trust the way you react to a person in the first few moments of meeting him.

— Lillian Ross

II. When all else fails: How to get the interview

- Say that your wife, your husband, your mother, your father, your boyfriend, your girlfriend, your son, your daughter, your brother, your sister ... wants to know what the interview subject thinks.

Saying that your editor wants to know or that you're on deadline doesn't usually get you too far.

- Call back later in the day.
- Call back the next week ... the next month ... the next year.
- Send a telegram.
- Enlist the help of the subject's friend, neighbor, secretary, mother, father, brother, sister, son, daughter, aunt, uncle ...
- Enlist a co-worker or former co-worker of the subject.
- Send a letter.
- Send a certified letter
- Advertise.

It worked for Jessica Mitford when she was doing an investigative piece on the Famous Writers School. It worked for me when I had problems finding homosexuals who would talk to me about the life of homosexuals in a small Oregon town; I ran a classified ad in the personals column and got plenty of solid responses.

- Take a plane trip or taxi ride with the subject.

I flew from Boston to New York with Randall Forsberg, a prominent anti-nuclear activist, after she had said she was too busy to see me. I interviewed her on the plane and then in the taxi on the way to where she was giving a speech in Manhattan.

- Drive the subject to the airport ... train station ... bus station.
- Drive the person home.
- Drive the person to prison.

It worked for *Journal-Bulletin* reporter Greg Smith, who drove a town-council president, convicted on federal fraud charges, to his first day behind bars.

- Call a mobile operator to reach the person on a ship, in his or her car, on a mountaintop.

- Go to Sunday school.

Truman Capote says he went for the first time in his life when he moved to Garden City, Kan., to investigate the killing that he described in his book "In Cold Blood."

- Jog with the person.

Here's a quotation that came after Christopher Scanlan, of the *Journal-Bulletin,* went on a morning jog with Providence's police chief; the jogging so relaxed the chief that he dropped his defenses and talked about how he really felt about crime and punishment.

"Nobody is going to tell me that you're going to stop crime by being nice to people. You have to push people around.... If you have to take a guy around the corner and give him a couple of shots, maybe that's what we should do.

"If a guy commits murder and we know he committed a murder, why don't they string him up the following day?"

The chief apologized for his remarks after the interview was published, and soon thereafter he was dismissed.

- Take a job.

Journal-Bulletin staff writer Bruce Butterfield worked in the Rhode Island jewelry industry.

- Take up golf, football, music, lion taming ...

It worked for George Plimpton.

- Intrigue the person.

Alex Haley researches people's lives from birth to age 15 — from before their fame — finding out tidbits; he uses the information to create a nostalgic point from which to start, dangling the nostalgia before the subject like an enticing carrot. He says, "That means more to famous people than the latest headlines on them."

- Meet the person outside his or her place of work.
- Scare the person.

That's worked for Pulitzer Prize-winning investigative reporter Elliot Jaspin, a *Journal-Bulletin* staff writer, who advises: On an investigative story, frighten the weakest link, if there is one, and tell that person that you have the goods on him or her. Be sure you do, and be very specific and accurate. Make sure you've checked your libel options with your libel lawyer.

By frightening the weakest link, you may be able to work your way up to the top person you need to interview in an organization.

- Offer to take the person to breakfast, lunch or dinner.
- Enlist the help of the person's lawyer.
- Give the person breathing room if he or she seems to feel crowded.

Say: "I've got lots of questions. If I ask a question that you don't want to answer, just say, 'Next question.'"

Or, to someone who says he or she won't talk, say very quickly: "I've got only one question and it's ..." This might get the person talking.

- Go to the person's house.

It worked well for Woodward and Bernstein.

- Send the person a cassette tape and some written questions, asking the person to record his or her thoughts by responding to the questions. Provide a stamped, self-addressed envelope in which the person can mail you the tape.
- Send the person a bottle of very good wine. It worked for *Journal-Bulletin* staff writer Dan Stets, who was covering General Dynamics official P. Takis Veliotis, who had a policy of not talking to reporters. It got Veliotis's attention — Stets got his interview.

Chapter 5
The Write Stuff
Sharing the lessons of good writing

Since the first edition of "How I Wrote the Story" was published, in 1983, the Journal-Bulletin's *writing program has attracted attention from newspapers and journalism educators around the country. This chapter is adapted from an article that appeared in 1984 in the first issue of* Style, *the journal of the American Association of Sunday and Feature Editors.*

By Christopher Scanlan

Hanging on the wall of the *Journal-Bulletin* newsroom is a cork bulletin board with an eye-catching drawing of a fighter jet. The nose of the plane is a quill tip and the banner above it says: "The Write Stuff."

"The Write Stuff" bulletin board is home to the *Journal-Bulletin*'s weekly writing contest, which entered its third year in April, 1984. Pinned to the board are the results of the contest, the winners' explanations of how they reported and wrote their stories and an envelope containing the next week's entries.

"The Write Stuff" board is also the most visible sign of a writing program that seeks to share the lessons of good writing by focusing on excellence and exploring the conditions that produce it.

Learning from one another. That is the guiding principle of all the work the *Journal-Bulletin* has done in the last three years to improve its writing. We've done it in a variety of ways, and any news organization, whatever its size, could easily adopt them.

Why bother?

"The major complaint I hear from most reporters is that no one ever tells them how they are doing. They don't get enough help, support or instruction," Roy Peter Clark, director of the Writing Center at the Poynter Institute for Media Studies and former writing coach for the St. Petersburg *Times*, observed in an article about writing coaches that appeared in *Byline,* Northwestern University's journalism review.

Those feelings were echoed by a group of new reporters who attended a one-day writing seminar at the *Journal-Bulletin* conducted by Don Murray, the newspaper's writing coach.

"It's helpful to talk about writing with other writers," one reporter said afterwards. "It's too easy being a working journalist to get locked into writing routines, forgetting about alternate styles and the issues of what newspapers should be attempting to communicate."

"I learned that perhaps the greatest thing we can give to one another as writers is our time and opinions," said another. "I learned not to be afraid to ask for the advice of other reporters."

In response to these voiced needs, our writing contest institutionalizes the newsroom practice of talking about how a good story came to be: how the writer went about reporting and writing it.

At the *Journal-Bulletin,* the author of the best-written story of the week is awarded a prize of $40. The contest is judged not by editors or the publisher, but by writers — previous winners of the prize. When the contest began, one story a week was selected, but then it was decided that deadline pieces were in unfair competition with long-term projects and features; so now the judging committee may select both a deadline and a non-deadline story as best stories of the week. (Although we haven't done it yet, other papers have discussed adding a Headline of the Week contest, to bring editors into the process.)

Members of all editorial departments are eligible to win the prize: people in news, sports, financial, arts, lifestyle. One week's prize was awarded to former *Bulletin* columnist John Hanlon, who was retired when he won for a story he filed on the 40th anniversary of the D-day invasion, in which he had taken part as a paratrooper.

Five winners of the prize serve for five weeks on the judging committee, which usually meets on Thursday afternoons to select winners from the preceding week's papers. The longest-serving member of the committee usually chairs the judging session. The winners are ineligible to receive the prize while they serve as judges, and for three weeks thereafter — a rule designed to spread the prizes among the staff.

Editors are eligible to win, but they are not allowed to serve on the judging committee. "This was done to make the contest the exclusive province of the writers," wrote Metropolitan Managing Editor Joel Rawson, in a report he prepared for an editors' convention. "No editor can use (the contest) to further his program or promote his own people (or hers). It is a chance for the people who report and write the newspaper to make their standards count and to recognize their peers."

Besides the judging responsibility, there is one other catch to the prize: Before they collect their money, winners have to write an essay explaining "how I wrote the story." These "stories behind the story" are posted in the newsroom and circulated to all editorial departments, the paper's 11 suburban bureaus and the Washington bureau — a process aided by the computer's "bulletin board."

Through the "How I Wrote the Story"'s, the contest provides a forum for the staff to share the lessons of good writing. At their worst, the "How I Wrote"'s sound like a bad Academy Award acceptance speech ("I'd like to thank my editor, my wife/husband, the guy at the next desk"). At their best, they are illuminating discussions of the news writer's craft, detailing reporting and writing problems and solutions.

As Rawson put it, "In this way techniques of the craft are shared. Questions such as How did you get that dialogue? How did you reach that source? Why did you lead with that? How did you select your material, decide on a focus?"

Rawson noted in his report, "You can tell how the program is going by looking at the list of judges at the bottom of the announcement of the weekly winners. Listed are those who attended and those who were absent. Sometimes only a single person will have judged the contest. Sometimes all five were present. Sometimes there was lively debate. Sometimes none at all. It is a barometer of commitment and morale. And like all barometers, it records both the highs and the lows."

In addition to the writing contest, the *Journal-Bulletin* has several ways of encouraging good writing.

Every Monday at 12:30, after the editors have had their morning news meeting, reporters clutching brown bags and soda cans file into the conference room for the weekly writers' lunch.

One week the talk is about ethics. Another week, about leads. Once the group watched a videotape of a "Frontline" show featuring Seymour Hersh reporting a story. Not all the discussions are even about journalism; one week we talked about the best new car to buy.

Setting an agenda beforehand usually helps the session, and the lunch hour has proved to be the best time for most people — the least disruptive of the workday.

Yet another aid to writers at the *Journal-Bulletin* is a section of the library devoted to writing and editing. Many of the titles are listed in the "Bookbag" chapter of this book.

To coach or not to coach

When the *Journal-Bulletin* hired Donald M. Murray as its writing coach, in 1981, it joined a small but growing number of papers that have instituted a system by which reporters, between deadlines, can work with someone to improve their writing.

"The writing coach is a phenomenon still in its infancy," Terri Petramala reported in the *Byline* article about coaches. "In a recent study conducted by Ray Laakaniemi, associate professor of journalism at Bowling Green State University, of 485 daily newspapers with a circulation of 25,000 or more, 30 had writing programs."

One of the first questions facing any paper that is starting a writing program is whether to hire a writing coach.

Writing coaches would perhaps not be necessary if more editors were able or willing to help writers improve their writing. Unfortunately, in all too many newsrooms the way an editor makes a story better is by rewriting it, instead of letting the reporter do it. Obviously, deadline pressure may rule out anything but a quick rewrite at the desk, but because of this situation, a writer may never learn how to rewrite well. So a writing coach is appointed.

There are, it seems, two types of writing coaches: the visiting fireman and the insider.

Don Murray is an example of the visiting fireman: an outsider brought in by management. Through an annual series of workshops, seminars and working lunches, Murray has introduced more than 100 *Journal-Bulletin* writers and editors to the "process approach" to news writing. And his visits have helped us keep alive the spirit of our writing program.

The outsider role that Murray fills has its advantages and disadvantages.

There may be initial suspicion when an outsider comes into a newsroom, but a major advantage to the outsider's role is that the coach doesn't have to worry about deadlines, budgets, meetings, personnel matters and the scores of other responsibilities that an editor faces every day.

Two examples of insider coaches are Alan Richman, who was assistant managing editor for writing at the Boston *Globe,* until he left the paper to write for *People* magazine, and Paul Salsini, who was the Milwaukee *Journal*'s state editor. An insider coach should be either an editor who gets along well with reporters or a senior reporter who attracts younger reporters eager to learn from an experienced hand.

The advantage to management of having an insider, as opposed to an outsider, as a writing coach: The person is already on the payroll.

Regardless of whether your paper appoints an outsider or an insider, the coaching should not be viewed by the staff as a trip to the woodshed. Asking a writer to work with a coach should express a recognition of talent, not lack of skill: Management thinks so much of this person's abilities and potential that it is willing to spend time developing them. If it looks as though the coaching is for problem writers, as a form of penance, the writing program is doomed.

Where can a paper find a coach?

Local colleges and universities, and on its own staff. The greatest editors are teachers. Consider this obituary that appeared in *The New Yorker* about one of its editors:

"The work of a good editor, like the work of a good teacher, does not reveal itself directly. It is reflected in the accomplishments of others. Bob Gerdy was a consummately good editor. He had the qualities that were needed. He was generous, he was sensitive, he was tactful, he was modest, he was patient, he was imaginative, he was unfailingly tuned in. He never suffered from the editor's occupational delusion that he is writing the writer's work. He found his own joy in helping other people bring their writings to a state of something like perfection."

Whether your newspaper decides to appoint a writing coach, start a writing contest, add a writing bookshelf to its library or publish a collection of its best writings, two ingredients will always be needed to improve the writing and editing skills of the staff:

Editors who care about writing and writers.

Reporters who care about writing, and who respect the crucial — but mostly thankless — role the editor plays in creating good writing.

Part II: The Process of Editing

Chapter 6
Consultive Editing

> *The main responsibility of editors is not only to exceed their best standards but to value good writing by insisting on quality. Writers are desperate to learn. Get into a teaching relationship with your young writers. Look for people on your staff who care about words. Care about words yourself.*
> — William K. Zinsser, editor, former journalist, teacher and author of *On Writing Well*

By Donald M. Murray

In April, 1981, the *Bulletin of the American Society of Newspaper Editors* devoted an entire issue to "A Special Report on Better Writing." Among the contributors was Donald Murray, who made these observations:

"Editors earn their pay. They have to deal with a flood of copy, much of it inaccurate, poorly organized and illiterate. Each edition of a newspaper is a miracle of executive decisiveness and editorial productivity, a refutation that Murphy's Law rules. Everything doesn't go wrong, just most things.

"We need editors who can produce newspapers and also produce writers, editors who can tolerate, manipulate and support the self-indulgent, anxiety-ridden people who turn out copy that isn't just up to standards, but is above and beyond newspaper standards.

"Most writers are non-organizational men and women, self-absorbed, self-doubting to the point of false confidence, exceptionally sensitive to their own problems and insensitive to their editors' problems. But if editors want good writing in the paper, they're going to have to nurture and support writers.

"Newspaper editors must find new ways to develop and retain writers if they want writing to improve. Newspapers must also find ways to develop editors if good writing is their goal."

One way to achieve that goal is Consultive Editing, a name for a style of editing that is based on the premise that the best editor-writer relationship is one of collaboration. "You edit people, not copy," is how Joel Rawson, a former Providence *Journal* editor, puts it.

Consultive Editing has four primary aims:

1. To make use of the knowledge and experience of the writer.

2. To give the writer primary responsibility for the story.

3. To provide an environment in which the writer can do the best possible job.

4. To train the writer, so that editing will be unnecessary.

Consultive Editing techniques

● Encourage the writer to speak. At first, questions will be necessary, but soon speaking will become the writer's normal pattern.

● Listen to what the writer is saying, not to what you expect the writer to say.

● Enlist the writer to help you diagnose the central issue at each stage of the writing process. (If the writer's syntax is confused, it may indicate lack of focus.)

- Recognize that an effective conference may take only 30 seconds.

- Find out, with the help of the writer, what works best, so the other elements in the story can be tuned to it.

- Get writers to articulate what they did when the reporting and writing went well. They will teach you, and themselves, so you both will have a resource of techniques to use when the writing does not go well.

- If you don't know why the story doesn't work, admit it. Get the writer to help you identify the problem. Neither you nor the writer is infallible.

- Remember that the writer knows the story — how it was reported and written — better than you do. You need to be trusted by writers, so that they will reveal the clues that help you help them produce good stories.

- Remember: You do the most editing when you do the least.

A method of Consultive Editing

When the assignment is given:

Ask the writer to suggest ways of reporting and writing the story. If your idea turns out to be the writer's idea, then you're ahead of the game. If the writer's idea is better, you're way ahead. If it isn't, then you have your chance to speak.

During the reporting:

Be available to the writer, so the writer can solve his or her problems by talking them through. Use your experience as a resource. Let the writer use you as a test reader.

Before the first draft:

Listen to the writer tell you the focus of the story, the approach and the length. Give the writer room, if possible, but if you have a strong problem with the focus or the approach, talk it out. Set a deadline and a length; listen to arguments against either, but then make a final decision and stick to it.

At delivery of the draft:

Encourage the writer to tell you what works best and what problems may exist before you read the draft. Your job is not to judge the writing but to collaborate on the production of an effective story. You need the writer's knowledge to help you read the story intelligently.

After reading the draft:

Confirm or modify or flatly disagree with the writer's evaluation of the work. If editing or revision is necessary, invite the writer to suggest how it will be done, and, if possible, let the writer do it.

After publication:

Get the writer to tell you the history of the story, if the story was particularly good, or invite the writer to discuss how a story that didn't work could have been written and edited more effectively. It's best to build on strength, though: Don't look for the weakest aspect, but the strongest. It's more helpful to reinforce what works than criticize what does not.

" A helpful editor should have the following qualities: understanding of and sympathy for writers; the editorial talent to recognize and appreciate journalistic and literary talent; an openness to all kinds of such talent; confidence and strength in his own judgment; moral and mental strength, and the physical strength to sustain these; energy and resourcefulness in helping writers discover what they should write about; literally unlimited patience with selfishness and egotism; the generosity and character required to give away his own creativity and pour it into a group of greedy and usually ungrateful writers. This kind of editor is a rarity. If you're lucky, you may find one. Avoid the following kind of editor: one who does not like writers. "

— Lillian Ross, in the introduction to *Reporting*

What do good editors do?

We are editors.

Some of us work with reporters. Some handle copy. Some deal with other editors. We bring to our jobs our own experiences, vanities, insecurities, goals and talents. We have different approaches and philosophies, weaknesses and strengths, and, yes, tricks up our sleeves.

In the following pieces, some editors at the *Journal-Bulletin* share their perspectives, each as different as the editors' personalities and the desks on which they work.

The result is a resource for editors anywhere who wonder what they can and should expect from themselves. And writers, we hope, will take heart from the theme that emerges from among these ruminations: that editors view themselves not as reporters' masters, but as their collaborators.

The inspiration for this effort was an editing seminar given at the *Journal-Bulletin* by Roy Peter Clark, of the Poynter Institute for Media Studies. Two of us compared notes afterwards and found we shared impressions and resolves:

• Editors, like writers, need an opportunity for self-evaluation.

• Any of us might be amazed to discover what we can learn from the editor working right by our side.

• Anything that can be done to share the collective experience of editing will strengthen a newspaper.

We then went to our fellow editors and invited them to write about editing — about what works for them, about what editing means to them. We invited "true confessions." We asked a simple question:

What do good editors do?

— **Tom Heslin and Alan Rosenberg**

Is this stuff interesting?

By Thomasine Berg

Writers often think editors are nuts for choosing to spend life parked at desks mucking through other people's words. Fact is, editors get to work with the fun part of the whole process: storytelling.

Most of my work at the *Journal-Bulletin* has been with developed stories. When it's your job to edit these kinds of pieces, the key questions are: Is this stuff interesting? Does it move, touch, anger, tickle, surprise, sadden or inform? If it does, you as an editor are in for a treat, a good read. If it doesn't, you get the satisfaction of working with the writer to make it do one of those things, or else you conclude it's a lost cause.

That's my argument for why editors aren't nuts and why, therefore, writers should consider them worthwhile human beings, not potato heads.

I believe in many of the standard editing commandments. Ideally, you have the luxury of time to do some of those high-minded things:

• Read a story through once all the way with hands in lap. Try to come to it as fresh as possible, as the average reader would.

• On the second read, make a mental or paper-pencil outline to pin down what's doing what in the story. Is the order logical — does it flow, make sense?

• Talk to writers about significant changes, particularly when moving sections around or making any changes in the lead.

• Talk to writers always. Before, during and after. My biggest frustration — the cause of most damage done to writers, stories and editors — is getting plugged into one another late.

• On last read-through, read letter by

letter. This is the tedious minutiae hunt that can be tolerable when the writer has done a similar check of facts and spellings. It's nasty business when the writer has sloughed this part off.

No surprises
By Alan Rosenberg

The question is, How do you make the newspaper a truly collaborative enterprise, making sure everyone is moving in the same direction and toward the same goals?

I try to employ the principle of "no surprises."

Before and during the writing, I try to talk to the reporter about what's coming, and how it will be structured. And I'll often look at the lead on a "read" on the computer — especially when heading toward deadline. Reading on a "read" avoids tying up the reporter's time while I look at the story, but ensures that the need for wholesale changes won't be discovered later, when there's no time to make them.

Once a story is done, my preference is to read it through by myself, for comprehension. Then I like to edit with the reporter by my side, so we can talk as we go through the story. This ensures that in changing things I don't make them wrong or lose a subtlety. It also ensures that the reporter will have no unpleasant surprises.

If possible, I like to examine a story level by level, from large questions to small — it makes no sense to resolve small questions of style and grammar if the story is incomprehensible. On deadline, though, I may be forced to look at all levels simultaneously:

• Sense. Does the story make any? If it's internally inconsistent or there are large holes, it's silly to go further.

• Structure. Assuming the story is comprehensible, is the lead the most effective one possible, or is there something buried in the copy that ought to be brought higher? Are all

• Finally, I like to have writers read their stuff one last time after I'm done with it. This catches any mistakes that can get edited in, as well as giving the opportunity to discuss grammatical or word-choice changes that writers may disagree with.

thoughts on the same subject placed together? If not, is the scattering purposeful, and does it work? Is there some trick — insertion of italic quotes, for example — that ought to be employed?

• Style. Is the story making full use of the senses — sight, sound, smell, taste, touch? Are there places where the story could be brought to life with details that the reporter may know or could gather through further reporting? Can the writing be made less verbose, stiff and jargonish?

• Mechanics. Are things spelled correctly? Is the grammar right? Is the newspaper's style observed? I never assume that anyone else will catch an error. It doesn't take long to fix them.

Once I've read and approved a story, it moves to the copy desk. "No surprises" applies here, too: If something is going to require adjustments by the desk, I say so in advance.

The result: No screaming fits by anyone; just a smooth process that gets everything into the paper in a logical and readable way.

One other thing I've learned came in recent efforts at writing, after two years as an editor. It's a lot easier to sit in a newsroom and make assignments than to try to get that elusive interview on deadline and then write the result in a manner surpassing hack work. I think editors should periodically be assigned to write stories — especially stories that involve reporting, not just think pieces — so that they can remember what it is like on the front lines.

Will this make it better?
By Phil Kukielski

I tend to view the question of what makes good editing from a reporter's perspective. So here are some of my thoughts about the kind of editing I think has improved my writing and reporting.

• Every good story has to start with a good idea. Nobody, no matter how talented, can turn a bad idea into a good story. The trick to editing, I think, is to put the best ideas in the hands of your best people.

I tend to rate story ideas on an A, B, C scale. An A story is one that people will read and remember: Typically, I think, an A story is one that involves drama, or a collision of interests, people, emotions; a sense of scene or place; and something unexpected or ironic. Exceptional reporting and writing can sometimes turn a B idea into an A story, but I have yet to see a C idea turned into an A story.

• Nothing counts as much as the enthusiasm of the reporter. Once a story is assigned, no one should be allowed to bad-mouth it. The reporter must start out with a positive attitude, believing that there really is a story to wrap around the idea. Sometimes it turns out there is no story there, but that should be a decision reluctantly made by the editor after a good-faith effort by the reporter.

• Editors should have some prescience but harbor no preconceptions; they need to have good instincts about a story, but should not confuse instinct with information. The worst experiences I have had as a reporter have been when editors have told me what the lead to my story should be before I've had a chance to make a single phone call; they were seldom right. I was then put in the position of writing a story that ran against what the editor believed in his heart to be "the real story." And if the editor turned out to be exactly right, I felt as though I had been robbed of the thrill of discovery.

• Editing the reporting is as important as editing the writing. The role of the editor is critical at the point when the reporting of a story is near the end and the writing is about to begin. A good editor will then listen a long time to the reporter's ramblings, and try to react as a reader would. The conversation should be considered a working draft, in which the reporter tries different approaches to the story, and sorts through the information for the key facts. A good editor, therefore, needs to be a good listener.

• Editors should treat drafts as drafts: They should read the first draft for such broad considerations as organization, approach and voice — not to make spelling and grammar changes. I've always found it annoying to go to an editor with a concept problem and get nitpicking instead of advice. Copy editing is the last step in the process, not the first.

• Making it different doesn't necessarily make it better. No story I have ever read as an editor has been written exactly the way I would have written it; but before making a change to a story, I think every editor should ask, "Will this make it better?" Turning a 28-word sentence into a 25-word sentence that says exactly the same thing is not my idea of constructive editing.

• Knowing what's wrong is not the same as knowing what's right. It is the job of the editor to spot what's wrong with a story; it's the job of the reporter-writer to fix it. Editors can improve a story only by taking something out if it. The reporter is the only person who has more information to add.

• A writer's job is not finished until beads of blood appear on the forehead. Reporters should not be allowed to dump a problem story on an editor's desk and wash their hands of it — rewriting is the essence of writing. Ideally, an editor should take over a story when it is 90 percent done, and then push it that critical final 10 percent that represents the difference between good and great. Every great story is as much the result of great editing as it is of great reporting and writing.

Editing the developed story

By John Granatino

A very talented reporter once accused me of treating her differently from other reporters. Of course, I answered; I couldn't imagine treating every reporter the same. Each reporter needs different amounts of listening, encouragement, constructive suggestions and reinforcement.

But having said that, let me add that there are some techniques that I generally use on all developed stories. By "developed," I mean nearly every story written ahead of time and held for publication, as opposed to reactive stories, written on deadline.

1. Know the story

First I read the story through once or twice without touching a key. It's absolutely vital to know all of the content before talking with the reporter.

Editing is a collegial process, based on mutual respect. If you've shown that you've taken the time to understand the story and the reporter's problems, the reporter is more likely to be interested in what you have to suggest.

2. Change the turf

Presuming some work is needed, I take a printout of the story. Taking a printout brings the story discussion out of the editor's turf — the computer system — and into the hard-copy turf more familiar to the writer. I think that's an important psychological concession that says to the reporter that you're more interested in the content of his or her work than in the process of expediting type. There'll be time enough after the story is completed to expedite type.

On the printout, in pencil, I identify what I take to be the major theme of the story. I underscore sections of the story that address this theme particularly well, and I bracket sections that seem tangential.

3. Meet with the reporter

After my printout is ready, I meet with the reporter, preferably in an open-ended conference designed to allow all questions concerning the story to be aired.

My first question — if I was not the originating story editor — is to ask what the assignment was and how the reporter set about fulfilling it. I ask around the edges of the story: Did the reporter think this or that aspect was important? Did the reporter have reporting difficulties that twisted the content? Did the reporter have lingering questions? My aim here is to develop a shared approach to the story, even before the story is "edited." If both the reporter and the editor agree on the story's theme and its side issues, the editing is much easier. I guess what I'm saying is that a whole lot goes on even before sentences and paragraphs are discussed.

Also, I make a point of asking, "Is this a good story?," which seems to have a galvanizing effect on reporters. More often than I would ever have suspected, the reporter will tell you right away that he or she thinks the story needs help.

Ideally, after all these questions, any suggestions I might have for the story become superfluous, because the reporter will see where the story has departed from the theme. But if there is still some question, I go over the story with the reporter. I make sure to point out the parts I enjoy, saying specifically how I reacted: To say, "I liked this part" is to say nothing; I try to say, "This part angered me" or "This part made me smile" or "This part made me cry, but then this part puzzled me." Finally, I point out questions of fact that I have, and the parts that don't work as well as the good parts.

4. Let the reporter finish the job

After the meeting, it's up to the reporter to rewrite or reorganize where necessary. I believe strongly that it's not the editor's job to rewrite. This is especially important in any story in which the reporter has taken the trouble to develop a natural, nonjournalistic voice. The difference between the reporter's voice and the editor's will be immediately apparent in the story, and will surely distract the reader.

And nothing will anger a reporter so much as some editor's arrogant rewriting of the original copy. It's as if the editor is saying the reporter is not capable of finishing the job.

Doing one thing well

By Tom Heslin

When I was a regional bureau chief, I directed the daily news report from two offices serving nine communities. Our newspaper's bureau structure is traditional: The beats are carved up geographically, key municipal meetings are staffed, the cops and courts are part of the routine, etc.

The typical story-to-reporter ratio usually comes in at about 30 to 1, a fact that I found myself pondering while I made the hour drive each morning to the Newport office. By the time I'd parked my car I'd be in a cold sweat, babbling to myself and running to the office.

And then the voice of reality:

"You can't do everything."

I know, heavenly Muse, I'd say. But how much can I do?

"Unknown, but maybe you can do *one* thing well ..."

Yes, that's it, I'd say. Today, I'll do one thing well.

The next step was to find that one thing.

I tried to talk with each reporter as early as I could. I tried to find out what was still in their notebooks, what their priorities were. We talked about their ideas; we talked about my ideas. We kept it light. We laughed. We thought. We figured out what interested us. We settled on an informal list of stories: to do, to check, to work on for the future. We set our priorities, acknowledging that they'd probably be overtaken by events.

Gradually, I got a feel for the potential of the next day's report. I knew where it was strong, weak. I'd talk to my boss, the state editor, and tell him what was real, what was not, what was possible and what was probable. I got his reaction, tried out ideas on him, got a sense of what he liked or didn't.

It was a process that brought me to a point where I said, This is it: This is the best we've got today — this is what I'm going to do well today.

I'd then go back to the reporter to get a better grip on the potential. Was it real? Could we take it for a ride? What kind of reporting would it take? Did the reporter need help? What did we need for graphics, photography? What could we do with the reporter's 29 other stories?

Well then, I'd say, let's do it.

The process was never this clean and orderly — you can't hear the phones ringing and the sirens screaming. But we tried to apply this process, in some degree, to every story we dealt with.

The point of all this is that I saw my challenge as an editor as talking with the reporters, listening to them, helping them establish their priorities and making them feel comfortable with their commitment to a given story.

If I could, I tried to give some input into the writing, at least the lead — to work as a co-conspirator in settling on an approach to the story. Rarely did I see the finished story before I left the office for the day; the editing was done by the desk.

The next morning, before I started my trek to the Newport bureau, I usually stopped in at the downtown office to take a look at the morning paper to see how things had panned out. If we were on page 1 or page 3, I figured we'd won.

Gifts

By Charles McCorkle Hauser

A writer gives, and an editor takes. That's the stereotype.

Certainly a good writer gives. He gives his all. His creative juices. His heart. His soul.

But the good editor — anonymous, unbylined, unsung, even unappreciated (it goes with the territory) — has a great deal to give, too.

We've spent a lot of time in recent years putting the writer under the microscope — isolating, identifying, labeling and analyzing his attributes. Let's do the same for the editor. While the list of things a good editor gives to a writer is long, I'll focus for the purpose of this short piece on four that I would rank right at the top:

1. The gift of time

Good editing takes time, and the most important time of all is spent not with pencil or cursor, but in conversation with the writer. Sometimes deadlines press, and stories must be railroaded. But when possible, push other matters aside and give the writer your undivided attention.

Yes, I know you have 50 other things competing for your attention, but the story the writer is working on at that moment is, for him, the most important story in the world. Make it, for that moment, the most important story in the world for you, too.

If you really don't have the time, be honest with the writer; don't shortchange him by giving him a quickie discussion and a fast kiss-off. Make a specific appointment for when you do have time.

2. The gift of tolerance

Let the writer make mistakes; let him risk failure. Let him try a different organization, an unusual voice, an unorthodox approach. First person? Why not? Second person? Let's see what happens. Tell the story from an unexpected point of view? Give it a whirl.

We all should have the right to learn from our failures. And sometimes, instead of failing, we succeed handsomely with an offbeat approach.

3. The gift of focus

As an editor, you're sometimes better able to see the true dimensions of a story than the writer, who can be too close to it. But you'll be making a mistake if you say, "No, this is all wrong. I'll tell you what the focus of the story should be." Instead, help the writer find the focus for himself.

The best way I've found to accomplish this is to make a simple request: "Tell me what this story is about." Then listen. In the oral telling, the writer will often zoom in on the heart of the story. You probably won't have to say, "Yes, that's it." He'll know.

4. The gift of empathy

I never had an editor I didn't learn from, and perhaps the finest I ever worked for was Tom Fesperman, managing editor of the Charlotte *Observer* in the '60s. I was his state editor.

I remember going to Tom one day to discuss a Sunday story idea — the emergence of the Republican Party as a new political force in South Carolina. It would take a week of a reporter's time, and I wanted to borrow a particular city staffer for the assignment.

"Why don't you go down to Columbia and do that one yourself?" Tom said.

I began to protest about all the projects I had piled up and the demands on my time, but he cut me off.

"How are you going to be a good editor," he asked, "if you forget what it's like to be a reporter?"

And he was right. Every editor who works with writers should be given the chance now and then to abandon the desk and get his teeth into a story at ground level.

Those are my top four. You may have your own, and you may rank these differently. But if you're an editor, they should be on your list.

Chapter 7

Editing people, not copy: An interview with Joel Rawson

> *Even if what you've got is a piece of copy, don't sit down and start working on the copy. Start working with the people who created it.... The end result may be ink on paper.... But you don't get a good result by fixing it with a pencil. You fix it with your mouth and your intellect.*
>
> — Joel Rawson, former *Journal-Bulletin* editor

Most of "How I Wrote the Story" is devoted to the process of writing newspaper stories. In this chapter, an interview with an editor provides an insight into the editing process.

Joel Rawson, now executive editor of the Lexington (Ky.) *Herald-Leader,* was metropolitan managing editor of the *Journal-Bulletin.* He was interviewed by staff writers Barbara Carton, Brian Jones and Christopher Scanlan.

Q: In several "How I Wrote the Story" accounts, you are mentioned as a guiding force behind the story. How do you see the editor's role?

A: I try to help people do what they need to get the job done. I'm here to help my boss, I'm here to help my subordinates.

I see myself as mostly a producer. I am the person that goes out there and makes sure that things happen.

Q: What's the difference between a writer and an editor?

A: As an editor, you represent the organization. The publisher has certain things that he wants the editors to accomplish for him. The editors also have a responsiblity to the survival of the organization — whether or not it's around in five or ten years, whether or not it's published tomorrow.

Q: At the story level, what's the difference?

A: Once again, the editor's job is to assist, to be the producer. The reporter's job is very direct: The reporter has a much more direct responsibility to the sources of information and to the actual content of the story than the editor does. Editors who think they should control the content of every line of every story are making a mistake. They should know what it is, they should help evaluate, but they're not there to sit down and say what it should be.

Q: What are the qualities of a good editor?

A: If I were writing, what would I want? Somebody who gives me good assignments, makes good use of my time. Somebody who sits down and says this is worthwhile and who can convince me it is worthwhile, and if it isn't really worthwhile, is at least willing to say, "OK, guy, we're going to do this because we're going to do it, and don't give me a ration of grief to go along with this." We're all smart enough to know when we're doing something because we've got to do it.

I'd want somebody to listen to me. Somebody backing me up. "I went out there and did an honest, good job. Now you back me up."

I'd want somebody who wouldn't blow it, who's sensitive to what I've done, so when I read the headlines in the paper, they don't embarrass me. They help me sell my story, and they're accurate and true to the flavor of the story, as well as the facts.

What I'd want, then, is just good support from an editor, and I think that's what a good editor does: He supports people and the product.

Q: What does it take to be a good reporter?

A: First of all, (being) thorough, really thorough — people who want to know all there is to know about it. The people you have to say, "Stop reporting this. Lay off (to)." People who come up with ideas and angles that I could never think of. If you bring me back something I didn't know, it surprises me and delights me. That's what makes a story interesting. That's reporting. If you tell me no more than what the TV gave me last night, what do I need you for? They did it in color.

The other thing is fairness. I want you to be fair with my ideas, give me a chance, but I also want you to be fair with other people. If you go out there and you're saying to somebody, "All right, talk to me," you're asking somebody to put a lot of faith in you. You can't necessarily say you can make them look good, but what you can do is give an accurate representation of what they're trying to communicate. You must be very fair to everybody you're asking to confess into your tape recorder.

And I want you to respect writing and this craft. I don't demand that you be slick and I don't demand that you be facile. But I want a reporter to want to transmit that information clearly. I want you to think about the reader, feel for the guy who has to read the story, and say, "Am I organizing this material in a way that he can get at it? Am I using language that he can understand?"

Then the last thing I want you to do is join in the rest of the newspaper. I want you to care when that first edition comes up. Do you look at it to see if somebody has bollixed the whole story or there are typos that can be fixed, or there are inaccurate facts that you forgot to correct from the draft?

When I was a kid, I was on a wrestling team. A wrestling team is a funny thing, because it is not a team, it's just a bunch of people who go out and wrestle and what's important is whether you win or lose, not whether the team wins or loses. I'd rather have a newspaper that *isn't* like that, isn't a bunch of individual players going out and saying, "Did I win or lose today?" but, "Is this paper good today?"

Q: What's the most important part of the story process for you?

A: Recognizing the idea. I can have a good idea and transmit it, or I can recognize your good idea and go with it. It's not always when you assign the story — it may be way down the line when you hit the idea: This is what's going on here. You've got to be receptive to the central idea, the thing that the story is about, and you can recognize that from Day One or you can pick it up far into rewrite. And you have to be sensitive to it in others, whether the photographer on the job saw it, or a casual reader of a draft.

Q: How do you discover it?

A: I try to figure out what in the story appeals to me. I've got this theory that the human being as a basic animal hasn't evolved much in 2,000 years. That's why they say all the plots are still the same, boy meets girl, etc. So you sit down and say, "What appeals to me as a human being?" There's love, there's fear, there's greed, there are basic motives. There are stories that appeal to a person's intellect.

It doesn't always have to be an emotional peg. But I think that the stories that really stick with you, the ones that become worth a great deal of space and effort, are usually those stories that have emotional appeal.

Q: This emphasis on discovering the human appeal of a story: How did you develop this?

A: I come at this business like most of you guys do. I went to journalism school. I was trained to find out what the news was, what the lead should be. I went to work on the night desk at the Providence *Journal.* I would see a story and I would say, "That's not what this story is about, that's not what's going on here at all."

The one that got me the most was the story of the policeman who shot a woman on Route 95. A couple with their two children coming home from Warwick — for some reason, the cop stops this guy in Providence. This man is going a little fast. His kids are asleep in the back seat, his wife is sitting beside him. A young police officer jumps out of the cruiser, runs up there with his revolver drawn, grabs the driver of the car, pistol goes off, kills this guy's wife. There's a lot of breaking news on this story. There were a lot of issues — Should policemen have guns? Should they be drawn? Etc., etc. The thing that kept hitting me was that the woman was dead but the cop's life had ended, too. The old collision of forces, the Bridge of San Luis Rey. It always seemed to me that we were trying to report the issues and we weren't reporting the people. And that's when I started to say, "What's really going on in the stories that we're doing?"

The point to that story is that Mike Stanton and I are working on the suburban desk too late at night, ranting and raving, and I'm saying, "You've got to do the people, you've got to do the people, not the issues — the people are the issues. What happens to people is the news." That was the beginning of what I'm trying to do now.

Q: Is what the story is about what you call the spine of the story?

A: No, a spine is a device to carry the reader forward. The subject of the story may be about a parent's love for a child and the sacrifices they make and the joys they take in his progress. The spine of the story might be a narrative thread about taking the child to Disneyworld or getting the child ready for school. The spine gives the reader a sense of organization and purpose about a story.

Q: How important is talking about a story before the writing and during the writing?

A: I'm talking so that I know everything you know. I'm trying to get out ahead of you, because I will frequently get copy that doesn't include salient points about what you know. And if I'm to effectively edit copy later on, I've got to find out what's going on.

Q: Do you think talking about a story before or during is important for the writer?

A: It depends on the individual. There are people that I won't talk to, simply because if I talk to them, that's the end of the game — their need to communicate is what's going to compel them to write something. And that's OK. There are different ways of working with different people.

Q: What's the most important question for a writer working on a story?

A: "What's this story about?" It's the first thing I want to know as a reader. You don't have to tell them right off. You might make them work to find out what it's about. I'm not one of these people that thinks that every story has to tell you by the fourth paragraph what the story is about. There are times I've read down to the last lousy line to find out what a story was about, and been captivated for the entire route.

Bob Chiappinelli had a column the other day and the whole column was in the last line. He told an engaging tale and he got me to the last line and it was a nice piece of craft. But he knew what the story was about when he sat down and wrote it.

Q: How important are endings?

A: Ends do two things for you. They ultimately set the tone of the story. They're the last thing the reader is left with, whether it's a happy story or a sad story, a mean story, whether it's a "gotcha" ending. They should leave the reader with what you set out to do.

And they should also signal to the reader that the thing is over.

Q: Regarding the distinction between reporters and writers: How can you be one without the other? How can you report something if you can't get it across, and how can you be a writer of nonfiction and not know how to report?

A: There are people with strengths. There are some people who are better at talking and getting the facts and the color than they are at writing, and there are other people who can put sentences together much more gracefully and still have a hard time thinking of the next logical question and forcing themselves to go be a total idiot, which sometimes being a reporter demands of you. But the business is now demanding that you be able to handle both. We're not interested in just plain competence; we want excellence on both counts. There are fewer and fewer newspapers and more and more people going through journalism schools. We're going to end up with people who can do both.

Q: How do you read a story for the first time?

A: If it's a fairly long story, I'll print it out, put the pencil aside, and start to read it from top to bottom. If I get interrupted, I go back and start over again, because I want to get from top to bottom in one sitting. I am asking a reader to do that.

Then I ask, "Does this story work?" Never mind the story I'd expected to see. Does *this* story work? Then I'll go over it to see if there is something obviously missing.

It's about the second reading that I'll sit down and start making notes on copy. If I'm reading a printout, I'll block areas by subject matter.

The second reading is usually organizational, figuring out what each section of the story does. When you do that, you'll find stuff that doesn't have anyting to do with this story, or you find that there's stuff so scattered it loses its effect.

By that stage, I'm beginning to really understand what is in the story and what's out of it. As I'm going through the blocking, it's beginning to occur to me, "Gee, there was that great stuff she told me about and it isn't in here. Where did it go? Should it be in here? Yeah, of course it should."

Now you've got something to talk about.

There should have been previous talking at least to understand what we're reporting. Now we can go back and start talking about the words on paper.

The last stage, the final run through the story, will be the actual copy editing — names, places, dates, Are you sure about this, sure about that?

Q: What do you mean when you say you edit people, not copy?

A: You try always to make your influence and your decisions felt from the assignment, from the conception, from talking all the way through the reporting, writing and editing of the story, so that everything meshes. A lot of editors like to begin with fixing the copy. They don't try and fix the reporting, they don't try and fix the idea, they don't try and fix the previous editing of the story. They say if I rewrite this paragraph, it will be better. Some cases, that's true; some cases, that's the only time available to you. But in the ideal circumstance, what you do is you go back and you talk to the person who wrote it. If you're dealing with a subeditor who's seen a story through, talk to the subeditor: "What were you trying to achieve?"

Even if what you've got is a piece of copy, don't sit down and start working on the copy. Start working with the people who created it — you're always working with people. The end result may be ink on paper — that's what we're all striving for. But you don't get a good end result by fixing it with a pencil. You fix it with your mouth and your intellect.

Q: How do you keep yourself from rewriting the writer?

A: I don't always. But I want you to do it yourself. Nag, goad, plead, kick, scream, holler, praise — whatever it is to make you do it yourself.

Q: Why? Other editors are just as happy to rewrite.

A: Did you ever read your own stuff and it's the fourth graf before you recognize a sentence you put together? I didn't like that when it happened to me.

Number two, I've never seen anybody happy with how I rewrote them — even if I was better than they were. So what I do now is we sit together at this terminal. Terminals are marvelous, because you just pass that keyboard back and forth. I'll rewrite the paragraph, the writer will say, "I think I got the idea now," and he'll take it and put it in his words, and then he'll go away happy and I'll go away happy.

Q: What mistakes do people make most frequently?

A: The thing that I resent most is sloppiness. I resent getting a story with misspellings in leads and errors of fact, and I resent getting a story that I know somebody didn't sit down and reread. Even on deadline I expect somebody to go back and reread that story and fix up what is obviously wrong with it. You're taking up a lot of people's time and you're also ruining your credibility and mine if work like that goes through the copy desk or other editors on this newspaper. And if somebody else doesn't catch (the mistakes) and they go into print, it hurts us all.

Q: What literature do you think a writer should be familiar with?

A: I go back to the turn of the century right up to the '30s, when there was a tremendous explosion of the American style and the American idiom and a love for a language that was vigorous and curt and full of swagger — language that was a departure from the English prose of Hawthorne or James. Everybody else always starts with Mark Twain, but I start with Stephen Crane and the story I read is "The Open Boat." "The Red Badge of Courage," too. And then Sherwood Anderson and Hemingway and Carl Sandburg.

We're talking about some evolution of prose style, some method of communicating very directly what people want to know, or need to know, or care to know, to live with or to be entertained by.

What should you read? You should read everything. You should read short stories and you should check them out and say "Why did they move me?," if they do. I go back and try and take them apart for their construction, their word choice, their timing of material, the kinds of verbs they use. You know you're going to become a writer or an editor or spend a lot of time messing with this craft when you start taking it apart, figuring out how it works.

It's like little boys with their car engines — you know: "I'm really fascinated, Daddy, so I went out and took a wrench and started to take your car apart." Well, some of us sit down and start taking prose apart. I started taking prose apart when I was 18, 19 years old. Read "Up in Michigan," by Ernest Hemingway, and said, "How did he do that?"

My father, who is an engineer, and I would go to Washington, and I would go off to the Smithsonian and look at the steam locomotives and airplanes, all these marvelous machines batted out of aluminum and machined out of block steel — engineering marvels, from the shape of their wing down to the oil galleries in a piston engine. And my father, who had lived with this all his life and was an expert on the internal-combustion engine and thermodynamics, would go over to the National Gallery and he would look at Monet. And he said the thing that always amazed him about men is that they would spend their lives to create things of beauty. There is that in us. It's not wrong to want to create beautiful things with words.

Q: Is one of the drawbacks of emphasizing writing and writers that you have to put up with writers' moods: cockiness, despair, wanting constant massaging and —

A: Reassurance. One of the most frequent complaints I heard when I was in the United States Army was that no one paid any attention to us. It's the same everywhere. What I'm doing now is trying in my small way to manage a creative enterprise, which is writing. It's pretty tricky, it's a lot different, but the human animal is the same, and what you're doing is working with people who want recognition, who want help, who want time, and whether they're flying airplanes for the United States Army or writing prose for the Providence *Journal,* what they want is some recognition. It's the same animal, and any good manager or leader is going to know that, no matter what they're doing.

Q: How do you fan the spark in a writer?
A: There's always a point when you're reading what somebody wrote and you say, "I like that." It's the 13th graf, the 12th graf, sometimes it's even the lead. You wander over to the desk and you say, "Who did that?"

They say, "We didn't touch that bozo's copy, we were in a hurry."

Then you walk over to the person and you say, "Gee, that was pretty good. I really like graf number 13. I liked what you did there. Tell me about that."

And you give a little time and praise.

The biggest problem in this stuff is knowing the difference between what is good and what is not, and there ain't a whole lot of people in the world who really do.

That's what you look for in editors: whether they really know the difference.

Part III: How I Wrote the Story

Chapter 8
How I wrote the story

The stories in this chapter are organized by the date of publication.

Maine budworm war:

What poisons pests may poison people

By Carol McCabe
The Providence Sunday Journal, May 27, 1979

WYTOPITLOCK, Maine — Thick clumps of old French lilacs are blooming beside the cellar holes and barren barns here, and the fields are moist and green. The barn swallows are back from Brazil and if the ones up at Blair and Ruth Yeomans's house would stop their crazy swooping around, they might eat a few of the black flies. Meadow Brook and Little Meadow Brook are full of trout. The goose at Jim and Rita Potter's place, the one that lost its mate, is no longer in love with its own image reflected in the bumper of their pick-up since they gave it a mirror to adore.

Jim Potter takes off his boots outside the trailer after a day working in the woods. The boots are mud-crusty because the woods are full of runoff. The ridges are alive with water this time of year.

Potter, who was born on this place, has been in the woods for 30 years. He started out when he was seven or eight, working with his father, yarding logs with horses. Nowadays, he works with a skidder, cutting pulp for a contractor who sells his logs to a paper company.

Northern Maine is upholstered with eight million acres of spruce forest, trees from which the mills will make toilet paper, paper towels, newsprint and enough other products to account for about one-third of what economists call the "value-of-manufacturers" in Maine.

By contrast, the total value of all fish, raw forest products, potatoes and other agricultural products together account for only 16 percent of the total, and the tourist business to only about one-tenth.

"The truth of it is: The paper companies own this state, pure and simple," Jim Potter says as he pushes up the visor of his Johnson Chain Saw cap and goes inside.

There, his wife, Rita, is working in her housecoat after bathing off the dust of the potato field where she works.

Rita, the mother of Victoria and Bret, is a beauty, with ash-blonde hair and eyes that are the light-blue shade of full-skinned blueberries. Down at Augusta, she thinks, they probably call her that crazy broad in Wytopitlock.

She's the one who has people all stirred up about the fact that again this year, as for the last decade, the paper companies, with the help of state and federal governments, will spray millions of acres, including sections in this area, with poisons designed to kill the spruce budworm.

The budworm, a hungry larva that feasts on the new growth of spruce trees, must be sprayed, the state Department of Conservation says, or it will destroy $30 million worth of spruce and fir this year alone.

Mrs. Potter got mad about the spraying last year and circulated a petition door-to-door in this end of vast Aroostook County to stop it.

The reason why Rita Potter and increasing numbers of other Maine residents have begun to fuss is that they wonder whether the spray might poison people as well as pests. Environmental activists are convinced that it might, and a federal environmental-impact statement, issued early this year, expressed some concern that the pesticides might produce health hazards.

For the first time, the state this year admitted that the pesticide-spraying posed a health risk and it ran advertisements urging that young children, pregnant women and breast-feeding mothers leave the spray areas.

"Spray Advisories" appear on letter-sized sheets tacked up in forest areas to be sprayed. "Conclusive scientific evidence is lacking that any of the spray materials being used in Maine this year are the cause of human disease when applied as proposed," the advisory reads, but the state suggests: "Since effects on health remain under study, we recommend that persons who need not be in the spray areas, and particularly those who may be especially susceptible to health risks, avoid the spray areas during the period of May 20 to June 20 .... Persons who plan to be in the spray area and who are concerned about possible health hazards may wish to consult a physician for advice."

THE ADVISORY lists steps that campers, woodsworkers and others in the area being sprayed should take, including changing clothes and washing skin with soap and water.

Gov. Joseph E. Brennan has defended the program, saying, "It's not a major, major risk," but concedes that the spraying is a trade-off between the need for wood fiber and the danger to public health.

Rita Potter wryly says she thinks she'll send her son Bret, who's nine, down to stay at the governor's place until the danger period is over.

At the trailer alongside Route 171, Jim slides his lunch pail onto the kitchen counter. "What I base my argument on is this: They say there's no proof it is harmful. Well, by the same breath, they have to say there's no proof it isn't, don't they?"

"The state said last year that this would be a good place to test a new chemical because there were so few people here," Rita said. "Sometimes I think people hadn't protested before because they didn't realize for a long time that they were being polluted. Finally, last year, they began to see, and they signed my petition even though everybody around here works for the paper company — there's nothing else to work *for* — because, they'd say, 'My car got covered in oil and that must mean we're getting covered in oil,' or they'd say, 'My flowers all died.'"

"BUDWORM CITY," they call the project center at the airport in Millinocket, near Mount Katahdin and Baxter State Park. Here, officials from the Maine Forest Service direct the activities of about 100 persons involved in the $11-million program to spray an area of forest larger than Connecticut.

Six million dollars will be paid to chemical companies for the four insecticides to be used; four million dollars will pay for the aircraft and the pilots to fly them. A token $175,000 has been earmarked for environmental-monitoring projects to study effects on humans, brook trout, aquatic insects and birds.

At an opening meeting of the pilots and chemical crews last Monday, Ernest Richardson, on loan to the budworm project from the Maine Division of Human Services, talked about the chemicals to be used and precautions to be taken.

"Sevin (Carbaryl) has been under study by the Environmental Protection Agency since 1976, when it received evidence that the insecticide, which is sprayed over Maine forests in a kerosene solvent, causes birth defects in dogs.

"Orthene — well, in short, I'll tell you — it stinks terribly," Richardson told the spraying assembly. "It's pretty raunchy to work with, but pretty darn safe .... Dialox is moderately toxic .... Matacil is being used on an experimental basis, and it is the most toxic chemical we have the experience of using this year. We're gonna send sound plumbing in 'em. The only thing that makes a guy shiver is having a plumbing failure in flight."

THE PILOTS had been coming in from the south and west for nine days before the start of spraying last week, waiting for project director Ancyl Thurston to give the go-ahead and release the "blocks" of the map for spraying as the budworms reached the moment in their maturation when insecticides would be most effective.

At the motels in town, where the sauerkraut smell of the paper mill is a constant presence, suntanned men in cowboy hats and boots, Californians in sandals, bearded Vietnam vets and veterans of other wars paced the lobbies and fed the pay phones.

The Alabaman was there, the pilot the others say is at least 60. He still eats, sleeps and dreams airplanes even though his war is history to most of the other guys. One of the planes of his war was there, along with a couple of Connies, a flock of C54s, PV2s, a couple of TBMs and helicopters, and five Thrush Commanders, the small crop-dusters that have been touted as useful in controlling spray drift. They've had some problems with that.

Last year, an elementary school was sprayed, and many individuals have reported spray drifting beyond buffer areas around settlements, highways, waterways, and the property of those who have asked not to be sprayed.

MITCH LANSKY, who lives in Bancroft, raises bees. In 1976, he followed the procedures to request that his property not be sprayed, then went out and put markers at the tops of his tallest trees.

"Within a week I got sprayed with Sevin," he recounts. "It was really early in the morning and I was going to work at a sawmill. I was standing right there when they flew directly over me. I could see the stuff descending around me and I was kind of crazy, standing there shaking my fist and shouting at them. There was white stuff and dead insects all over the place." Lansky received a $5,000 out-of-court settlement from the spraying contractor.

Efforts are made to prevent spray from drifting. Flights are made only in calm weather and at low speeds. The same precautions that make spraying safer for the people below, however, make it less safe for the pilots.

No pilot has ever crashed during the Maine spraying program, but there have been close calls, particularly in a case last year in which two planes designed for anti-submarine warfare had to return to base fully loaded. The planes were not designed to land loaded.

One observer reported seeing one PV2 bounce on the runway, then watching its pilot hit full throttle in an attempt to remain airborne, barely missing three aviation fuel trucks. According to the observer's report, the pilot landed on the next pass and later reported that he had nearly released all of the insecticide in the plane.

PROGRAM OFFICIALS readily admit that the flights are hazardous. Project director Ancyl Thurston says that the pilots are well-paid. "They'd have to pay me well to fly 110-165 mph at tree-top level."

"Lobotomy cases," one of the pilots at Budworm City terms his colleagues. Glenn Lemler of Flagstaff, Ariz., who runs a ski patrol in winter and sometimes works budworms in the spring as a navigator or guide-plane pilot, stood near the flight line in sandals and hiking shorts.

"Those planes are graveyard relics that come alive in May. I don't mean they aren't in good mechanical shape. You can bet they're not going up until they're in good shape. But these guys are crazies. If they were to go down and the crash didn't get them the juice (poison) would."

"There will be no dumping or spilling in any airport," Richardson told the pilots. "The storm drains (at the field in Millinocket) drain toward a potential outlet for their drinking water. You will catch all spills in buckets and pails . . . . Let's make a steadfast decision that we're not going to spill." Tanks would have to be washed out between different chemicals, he said. "Nobody today wants responsibility for the dumping of toxic wastes. Most places ship the stuff to New Jersey, but someday even New Jersey won't want it. When it's time to flush your tank, fly your flushings somewhere out on the block (spray areas.)"

THE PILOTS were told how the chemicals work and what to do if they became contaminated. (Pilots are, obviously, exposed to a higher concentration of the toxin than anyone on the ground would be.) The chemicals, Richardson said, are essentially nerve poisons. "Overexposure inhibits the enzyme that allows the muscle to relax. That's how it kills the bug."

A contaminated pilot, he said, would first have some vision trouble. "That's the bad one — you lose your depth perception."

Then, he said, there would be stomach cramps, partial paralysis of arms and legs, some breathing distress. Each flight crew, he said, would receive a bottle of atrophine tablets as an antidote.

"They are to be taken only if you feel you are becoming symptomatic. If you have a plumbing failure, pop one of these and come on home."

Each crew, he said, would carry an agricultural respirator. "If you get doused, someone will take you back to your barracks or motel. Do not go alone. Change your clothes and wash by normal means."

Flying graveyard relics filled with nerve poison may be a high-risk job, but the pay is good. "Most of the pilots come away from this with seven or eight thousand dollars for about three weeks' work," Lemler, the navigation pilot, said. That's just about what Jim Potter the logger brings home from the woods in a year.

"THE MEN in the woods have to go in, spraying or no spraying, or not get paid," Rita Potter said.

"Timber crews operating in the area may not have phones" (and therefore could not be notified that an area has been sprayed), a public-relations woman for the project said at Budworm City. "Of course most of them couldn't care less." They say "We've been sprayed before and we'll be sprayed again.

"One thing made me mad," Jim related. "There was one area we cut half of, one year. The next spring they sprayed it, and we went in to cut the next day. We cut everything. Somebody should have known all along we was going to cut there and there wasn't any point in spraying."

Jim Potter works with a machine called a skidder. "There's *no* way you can cut with a skidder and not knock down the young trees. They got one worse than that called a harvester that doesn't leave anything standing.

"THEY USE softwood for pulp and they'd like to do away with the hardwood in these forests and have only softwood, farm it like a hayfield. They think they know more than nature did when it put hardwood there in the first place. The paper mills are increasing production every year, and they keep trying to think of how to grow more softwood.

"Well, if you start eating the chicken, you will be getting less eggs. They are lulling people into a false security by saying it's good for the economy to cut more wood and make more jobs. They're creating jobs, sure, but what's going to be left when they ge' done?"

Potter is an amiable man with a Maine accent as thick as the woods around Blunder Pond. He says he has been radicalized by what has been done to the land around him.

"Any kind of radical there is up here, I guess I am now," he says.

Rita is English; they met when he was in Edinburgh in the Navy. "Her father — I guess he thought that Rita and I were goin' a bit on the radical side. He came to visit and he hadn't been here in five years.

"I said, 'Come in the woods and see.' He took a look around and he said 'Bloody hell.' Just like that. 'Bloody hell, it looks like an A-bomb hit.'"

THE BARN SWALLOWS at Blair and Ruth Yeomans's house are swooping around, Blair says, because "we pulled down a barn pole this morning and they had to get out and find a new place. All the old barns is gone. The swallows have been down to Brazil all winter and they come back and go half crazy because there's no barns to nest in."

Blair is in his 70s and has lived on this place near the fire tower for 50 years, since he married Ruth. Ruth was born here, and so was her father. Blair is sitting this morning at the table that used to be full at haying time.

"It's an awful thing to see a town die. Once there was five farms up this road. It was the lack of market that killed them." Blair says. "All these farms was poor annaway. They had these farms up here to grow hay, horses to eat the hay, and boys to work the woods with the horses." When Blair says "horses," it has a special Maine sound: "husses."

"Well," he goes on, "it was in the first war that they started growing potatoes, and then pretty soon the market went and they were hauling potatoes out of here and dumping 'em. Then pretty soon the Federal Land Bank owned half the town of Drew."

BLAIR WORKED the woods. "Working the woods, we didn't make a third of what the men in the mills made. Every time they'd get a raise in the mills, the price in the woods would drop. They were unionized. There weren't any unions in the woods. They called us the last independent people, and I guess we was. We paid for it."

"Now," Blair Yeomans says, "they're trying to build the woods over so it will be all stands of spruce and fir, no hardwoods. Cut everything down at once, and the first thing that comes back will be your balsam fir, which is what the budworm loves best of all.

"They're making what I'd call budworm heaven in the woods, and then they want to spray people with poison to kill the budworms. I told them that once on the television news, and they asked me what were my credentials. They wanted letters after my name. I said I got letters after my name — DDT."

"The book *Silent Spring* is going to come true if they keep on," Ruth says.

Blair says the changes in the woods began ... "Well, how old's Dennis?"

Ruth says Dennis is 27.

"WELL, DENNIS, used to help me in the woods, peeling logs, when he was 14, 15, still in high school. I was one of the last ones to peel logs. They weren't clear-cuttin' yet. Even after that, it was a while, then they began saying, 'Cut, cut, cut, cut.'"

"I preach husses," Blair says. "With them, you could keep the mills goin' and keep people working in the woods. One man on the

Harvester takes the place of 15 men in the woods, and when they ge' done, it's all tore up."

Ruth is sitting nearby on a stool, thinking about the spraying that's about to start. "The governor came on TV and said the paper companies were important and there weren't many people here anyway.

"Isn't it awful to get a governor who puts paper companies before people? I should think his conscience would bother him when he tries to sleep at night. He gets on the TV and thanks people for conserving gas and leaving it for the tourists. What tourist wants to come to a state that's spraying poison all over them?"

"That big green dollar is gonna kill this state," Blair says. "I don't know how they'd get such a product, but if they'd take this money for spray and buy some truth serum and spray it all over Augusta, it'd do more good, I think."

THE YEOMANSES signed a request form to have their property, where they do organic gardening, exempted from spraying. "They have a line on there that asks what you are concerned about," Ruth says. "They give you examples like bees, cattle, and so on. I wrote in 'People.' They didn't have people on their list.

"Well, I don't say this to be morbid, but we know we don't have a lot longer. We're not worried about ourselves in this. My first thing is children, because we know so little about what it's going to be like for them in 120 years. We have three great-grandchildren and they are so adorable ...

"Sometimes I wonder why we're still here when everyone else is gone. My father almost sold this place two times, and we've had fires start. But we stayed. It just seemed we were meant to stay. Maybe something my granddaughter said is a kind of clue. 'Hold onto it, Granny,' she said. 'The way the world's going, we may all be back up there with you.'"

"BLAIR YEOMANS is a true rebel," says Rita Potter, down the road near the one-lane bridge. "He says he'll be out of there with a shotgun if they try to spray him, and he says he's going to teach the women to shoot. Says women shoot all wrong."

It sounds like war. "Yes, it is like the war," she says. "First the spotter comes in, and then there are two or three planes coming in right behind him, spraying poison. You can see the pilots' faces."

She has been with Jim in Wytopitlock for 21 years. "I have been all over the world, and this is the most beautiful place. I felt so lucky to come to this place. But even in 21 years, I have seen it devastated, and it breaks my heart because while my daughter may leave here my son may want to stay where his father's family comes from."

IN A FEDERAL COURT in Portland on May 18, a group of citizens and environmental activists tried to stop this year's spraying program, arguing that the sprays may be dangerous, that they are ineffective anyway and that better forest-management programs could eliminate the need for poisons.

The judge ruled that the effort came too late, because the planes, the pilots and the poison had arrived in Maine and would have to be paid for.

"By the time this case could be properly heard on its merits, the case would be moot," he said.

In the meantime, however, the federal goverment announced after seeing the Environmental Impact Statement that this is the last year that it will participate in the spraying. The state has also served notice that it wants to get out of the spray project by 1981, leaving the effort to the paper companies, which now pay two-thirds of the cost.

Winds caused delays last week, but on Tuesday evening, as the sky turned golden behind blossoms in the old apple trees behind the dead barns of Wytopitlock, the Alabaman and the rest of Quebec team were in the air, flying out of Old Town airport, laying down a heavy spray on the spruce trees of Aroostook County.

Just about that time a trailer truck pulled out of the yard of a vast paper mill a few miles down the road heading south. The lettering on its side read: "Soften the Blow. Vanity Fair tissue."

Carol McCabe

How I wrote the story

Some general observations.

The spruce-budworm story, datelined Wytopitlock, Maine, ran in the Sunday *Journal* on May 27, 1979. It was one of five pieces I wrote that year around a central theme of man's manipulation of nature. (The similarity of theme and the connections between one story and another did not become clear until after all five were done. They came up one by one as events developed, and were never planned as a series.) The others included pieces on an Agent Orange victim, a herbicide-spraying incident, a community whose water was poisoned by a chemical dump, and the uneasy life of a nuclear neighborhood.

The five stories, submitted together, won the 1980 American Society of Newspaper Editors awards for deadline and non-deadline news writing (combined that year) and a series award from the New England Associated Press News Executives Association.

I have picked out the spruce-budworm story for examination because I think it may illustrate certain techniques that are typical of the way I work on out-of-town stories.

The assignment

Like most assignments for Sunday news, in which reporters are given considerable freedom to develop a story from an editor's lead, this one was open-ended. Joel Rawson, who was then Sunday editor, sent over a two- or three-graph wire story clipped from the *Journal*. It said that a group of residents of northern Maine was trying to stop the state-directed annual aerial spraying of pesticides over pulp forests, fearing damage to human health.

As I remember it, the item had caught Joel's interest because, as a pilot, he was aware that a large fleet of spray planes and mad pilots converged on the Maine woods every spring for this event. The best stories that I do come from ripples of intuition, either mine or an editor's. That's probably true for most of us. The handwritten note on the clip asked if I wanted to check into the story, and I did.

Joel and I agreed that there was enough there — if only color — to make a Sunday piece. I was intrigued by the scale of the program and by the fact that questions had arisen about possible hazards.

Setting up

My notes don't show when I first got the suggestion but I think it was midweek. I called a writer friend in Maine to ask if she had read anything on the subject in the state papers. She hadn't, but referred me to Peter Cox, editor of the weekly *Maine Times,* which does a superb job of covering environmental issues. Peter filled me in quickly over the phone on the background of the protest, gave me names of two or three people who might have additional information, and told me that a hearing was scheduled in Federal Court in Portland on Friday, he thought, on a request for an injunction to halt that year's spraying until effects on human health could be studied.

One of the names I had been given was that of an attorney who told me that the hearing was scheduled for Friday morning at 10, and outlined the legal points involved. I made arrangements to go to Portland.

(Note: Being a reporter is like being a Moose or a Rotarian. There are brothers and sisters wherever you go, waiting to help you. I get my first, best help on most out-of-town stories by going to the local papers and seeking out the person assigned to the story or beat. Those reporters are as generous with time and information, plus the vital introduction to the keeper of the files in the library, as we would be to them in our town. In addition, I never hesitate to call personal friends in an area where I'm going. Their advice can save many hours.)

At the hearing on Friday, May 18, I learned that the headquarters of the spraying project was at Millinocket, at the base of Maine's northern thumb, and I compiled a list of state officials concerned with the program. A federal official's testimony gave me a clear picture of the shared responsibility of the two governments and the paper companies, and other testimony gave me background on hazards and past accidents. The request for an injunction was denied, the judge stating that, since the program could begin as early as the following Monday, the question would be moot before it could be considered. The only citizen publicly opposing the program who was present — Portland is at a considerable distance from the northern forests — was a businessman. I talked with him at some length and made extensive notes as a backup, but hoped to find the central figure or figures for my story somewhere in the woods, on the scene.

After court adjourned, I went to lunch with *Maine Times* reporter Lucy Martin, who filled me in on background and gave me the name of Larry Lack, who would be covering the spraying from Millinocket.

While no date had been set for commencement of the spraying, which is tied to the maturation of the budworm larvae, I had learned in court that the planes were already arriving for work that could begin as early as Monday, May 21. Since spraying once begun could be interrupted by poor weather conditions such as high winds — an interruption that could cause delay in getting the story — I decided to be in Millinocket on Monday. I called the *Journal* from Portland to ask that a photographer be scheduled for two days beginning Monday morning and to enlist Joyce Olson's aid in making plane and rental-car reservations. (Joyce is one of the great assets of our newsroom; she can find airports that aren't on your map and charter a plane to drop you there, and be back to you in four minutes.)

At Millinocket, I would find planes, pilots and poison. But I knew by then that the story would not be about a protest, because the denial of the request for an injunction had ended any organized activity. The story would have to come from what I heard from people in the spraying area.

I love maps, read them like Ouija boards. I got out the Maine highway map and examined the area around Millinocket. When I saw the name Wytopitlock, I decided that my people would be there. A hunch.

(Note: I don't know how to deal with this subject helpfully to others, but much of what I do is based on luck and intuition. I have unaccountably good luck on stories. The only useful observation I have to pass along is that luck gives me confidence, and confidence often gives me the story. I know it's going to be there, because it always is, so I don't shrink up.)

Getting the story

Photographer Bryce Flynn and I arrived at Millinocket about 3 p.m. on Monday afternoon and went to the largest motel in town, where I thought we'd find pilots who could tell us where the center was. I asked the registration clerk if there were any pilots around, and she directed me to a banquet room, where, she said, they were just about to start a meeting.

I went in a side door and sat with the group, just in time to hear that this was the initial organizational meeting for the program. The geography and schedule were explained and rules were set down. A pesticide expert outlined the properties and hazards of the chemicals to be used, as well as which chemicals were to be used in which "blocks." Pilots were taking notes, and I did too, accumulating within minutes a great deal of invaluable information on specific substances to be sprayed over precisely identifiable areas. I was able to quote these experts on the hazards of contact with chemicals. The breeziness of the language, contrasted with the seriousness of the message, worked in the story.

(Note: Finding the pilots' meeting was luck, but not entirely. You can usually assume that something will be taking place at certain locations, and you go there and ask around. I talk a lot, to clerks, cab drivers, maids, gas-station attendants and anyone who might have noticed things. I do not interview them; I gab and listen. This seems to me fairly standard procedure:

"What's that tremendous building down the street? Is that a paper mill? Yeah? There must be a lot of pulp grown around here — saw a lot of logs going down the highway. That much? Wow. Isn't this where that big spraying project is going on? Do the pilots stay here? They must be an interesting bunch, from all over the country. Oh, yeah? In there? Really?"

Another point that the pilots' meeting illustrates is that anybody can fit in anywhere with the proper confidence. If a middle-aged mama can move into a group of pilots in Aussie hats and shorts, anybody can fit in; it's all in acting as if you belong. People who saw me at the meeting later accepted me without question on the airfield and around the motel lobby as I hung out and grinned and listened to stories.)

After the pilots' meeting, I located Larry Lack of the *Maine Times,* who was already in town, and he was typically helpful in introducing me to several project officials who gave me useful quotes. Larry also provided me the name of Mitch Lansky, a newcomer to Maine who was operating a small organic farm in nearby Bancroft and had been paid a settlement when he was sprayed in a previous year.

Then Bryce Flynn and I went to Wytopitlock, traveling through gorgeous countryside along the back roads, looking for the people I wanted to write the story about. I didn't know them yet. The beauty of the land began to enter the story inevitably, and I took notes on what I saw without yet knowing I would use: lilacs blooming out of cellar holes, apple blossoms in abandoned orchards, sagging barns. It was spring, a time when the life was surging back. I learned later that the economy of the area had changed from an agricultural base to a forest base in one generation, and the lilacs and swallows searching for barns where they could build nests became symbols of displacement that I used in the lead.

The Potters' trailer caught my eye because of the "no spraying" signs on the roadside nearby, giving an excuse to stop and ask about the budworm project. (Note: Oh, Lord, it's hard to knock at that first door.)

Rita Potter opened the door and invited us in. Her husband, Jim, came home from work in the paper company's woods and the two of them began to talk about the changes in the land and the life of rural Maine. Jim had been born on the place and lived all his life on the farm and the woods, and they had children whose future they worried about. They were angry at the paper companies for what they saw as greed, an overweening eagerness to take every cent of profit they could get from the countryside and a callousness toward the harm being done to the natural balance. Still, the Potters' own income came from the paper companies, the pulp woods. When we left, I had two hours of good quotes and, I thought, the central characters for my story.

Good people lead you to others. The Potters said we mustn't miss Blair and Ruth Yeomans, but since the light for photos was about gone, we decided to wait until morning.

Very early on Tuesday morning, we went to the small airfield, where the planes were waiting for orders to take off. We were able to wander freely on the field, talk to pilots as the planes were loaded with pesticides, picking up quotes on the hazards of such flights, anecdotes of earlier flights, information about the planes. Later, inside the headquarters for the project, I talked with officials I had met on Monday at the motel, and filled in details of the program.

Late in the morning, we went back to Wytopitlock to visit Blair and Ruth Yeomans, whose house is at the end of a road near a fire tower. We happened to arrive just as another guest, Mitch Lansky, was preparing to leave. By luck, he was there to ask Blair some questions about bees, and I was able to ask him about the time he had been sprayed.

The Yeomanses changed the story, deepened it. Blair is the old Maine farmer who has lived his life by certain rules that seem to have changed. As we talked that day, the story in my notes became the story of a changing America, with the spraying of pulp forests serving as a metaphor for America's increasing emphasis on money and commerce: Blair's "Cut, cut, cut, cut," and Ruth's ". . . People. They didn't have people on their list." If I had quit the night before, knowing I had enough for a story after talking to the Potters, I would have missed the best. Blair and Ruth represented to me the dignity of the old, hard rural life in which nature led and man followed. The Potters were a middle generation, depending on the new, man-directed ways, but longing for the old. The spray planes and pesticide people and the Vanity Fair truck were the new wave, producing more disposables and waste.

By the time we left the Yeomanses, less than 24 hours since we had arrived in Millinocket, without a single appointment, I had a story that I liked about people who mattered.

We still had some work to finish. That evening, we learned, the first planes were to cover certain blocks nearby. We went to a patch of woods in there and sat on a logging road, consumed by black flies while waiting for a plane to drop poison on us. I copied the instruction sheet posted in the woods, warning nursing mothers and young children to get out.

We were back in Providence on Wednesday, May 23. I had been gathering the usual 11-foot sack of source material from newspapers, government officials and paper-company public-relations offices. I had Xeroxes of clippings, government publications and news releases. I combed them for relevant facts and figures, and prepared the notes in categories.

I couldn't touch the piece on Thursday because of longstanding appointments for interviews on another story, but on Friday I got to the terminal and wrote for Sunday. I wrote 3,300 words in about six hours — about top speed for me.

The writing

This was not a piece whose construction was a challenge. I used a few devices — natural, local allusions wherever possible, as in blueberry eyes, accents thick as the woods at Blunder Pond — and let the voices of my central characters dominate. Blair's speech, in particular, is American poetry.

I didn't have to push and tug the material; I just had to let it out. I just sat there and listened to the voices in my head while I let them use my fingers.

(Editor's note: Writers often talk about their characters "dictating" a story, about a story "writing itself." Clearly, there has to be more to it than that. Asked to elaborate on the process of writing the piece, McCabe produced the following sequel.)

1. The fugue state (somewhere near Utah)

The time just before I begin to write is the most important time I spend on a piece. By now the piece is there, waiting inside the notebooks, tape transcripts, clip files and photos, like a sculpture waiting for release from a block of limestone. I just have to figure out how to get it out of there.

As I begin, I turn on my own switch before the machine's. I put myself into a "fugue state," a sort of hypnotic trance in which I am sensitive to blips of idea and memory, receptive to the voices of my characters, whom I begin to hear as I write. I cut off all but minimal consciousness of the room around me, and often practice ritualistic behavior of an embarrassing sort, rattling my fingers or doing curious things with the musculature of my face. (It is probably best to avoid looking at me at such times.)

In the case of this story, the time lag was short and so it was easy to return to the necessary scenes. The impressions had been strong, and sensations rolled back into place immediately.

2. Is it a story?

Not every account in the newspaper is a story; the news story is just one possible form of journalistic prose. Before dealing with this piece, I had to decide at some point whether I wanted to write a story or present information. We have battled back and forth over the ground of pyramid versus story too many times to do it again here. I am obviously in the camp that believes that if you can do an honest news *story* with the material you have, you stand a chance of affecting your reader, as well as informing him.

A news story, by my definition, has plot; that is, the organization of incidents into a narrative. A good plot, according to Aristotle, ought to have a beginning, a middle and an end, and be constructed so that no incident can be displaced or omitted without destroying the unity of the whole. Aristotle never had to cover the closing of a rubber plant.

Still, I think he gave us an ideal to aim for, even though as nonfiction writers dealing with balky facts, we'll never be able to produce the tidy stories of fiction writers. As Joan Didion said, life does not take a narrative line.

The journalist storyteller needs the sense of drama that's essential to a fiction writer — drama whose essence is that man cannot walk away from the consequences of his own deeds. Whatever its structure, plot usually depends on conflict as the basis of action. Characters move from incident to incident. In the "unified" plot, they move to a classic climax; in the "episodic" plot, they simply come to an end, a moving end if we're successful. Sometimes the end is just that human beings persevere, as Dostoevsky's characters persevered to triumphs that were never complete.

OK. Dostoevsky aside, I knew that my Maine material had all the elements of a story, from setting to characters to conflict to the end in which the people were neither victorious nor defeated, but simply persevered. It was up to me to supply the structure — the organization of elements — and the texture or style.

3. What's the story about?

I know it's obvious, but it has to be repeated. The most important question as you approach a piece is "What's this story about?"

I've skipped it, and so have you. And the result can be a story that's too long or too vague, or races off in several directions at once, softening its impact with irrelevant information.

Once you have decided on the subject of the story, the structure suggests itself. You can see what is needed, not needed. You know what sort of lead to write and what kind of ending you need. (I often find the end before the lead. More about that later.)

This wouldn't be the definitive story of the spruce-budworm project; I had no such assignment or intention. My assignment for a long time has been to write about the people of America, particularly the people of our region, to tell how we live now. In these stories, events, trends, politics, the economy, etc., serve as background to people.

The subject of this story had been obvious since the first day in Maine. We were surrounded by the color and fragrance of new grass, new leaves, blossoming lilacs, by the flight of birds and the misery of black flies. Life was returning to the land after the death of winter.

The event that would provide the conflict was the poison drop, designed to kill one form of life. That the program was undertaken for practical reasons or that it could ultimately benefit many people did not change the story. This was a story about the most familiar subject in literature, as in journalism: the struggle of life against death.

4. The lead

Now that I had the subject, the lead made itself known immediately.

(A digression. Once I'm in the aforementioned fugue state, snapping my fingers endlessly and rocking like a catatonic, my subconscious takes pity on me and types me a few grafs. They're not perfect, but they give me the general idea, so I can take it from there. I do not understand this process, but I do not dig at it to find out how it works; I walk very softly around that place and say, "Thank you.")

I found myself describing life, contrasting the lilacs and grass with the dead barns and empty cellar holes. The first graf set the scene for the conflict to come. The swallows — their energy, mobility and confusion in the face of death (the barns) — were chosen as a recurring symbol.

The landscape happened to be especially important in this story, but I usually include some description of place in any story. I believe that the sense of place — a place as broad as New England or as narrow as a room in a Providence neighborhood — is a great device for achieving intimacy with the reader. In it, we have something that TV cannot do as well as a local or regional publication can: *We* know the territory.

5. People

Good news writing is not the use of words. It's the use of people.

During the time I'd spent in Maine, I had been collecting people, as well as information, and the people would be infinitely more important to the story. They, and not facts about papermaking or chemical properties, would bring readers into the story.

If I could make readers care enough about those people to want to know what happened to them, the story would be read. I don't have any tricks for accomplishing this; I just believe that if the writer cares about the people, the reader will, too. (I don't mean "care" in the sense of being soppy about a character, but in the sense of caring enough to present him or her as whole and human as much as I can within the limits of the story.)

I think I'm fairly careful about selecting major and minor characters, trying to leave out those whom I don't need, who contribute nothing to the forward motion of the story, but including enough people to convey the conflict at the heart of the story and provide voices for the narrative. I try to let the voices of the characters provide most of the exposition. The narrator is the storyteller, a worthy figure who goes back to the Babylonian epics, and up to the "connexion man" of Riddley Walker, but I believe the narrator should hide. I try to do what Uncle Remus did and let Br'er Rabbit tell what happened to him.

However, there is some material only a narrator can present, for reasons of fairness, overview or ellipsis. I try to wrap such material around the live quotes wherever possible, in order to maintain a human presence. Where that's not possible, I may use language that recalls a character's voice, as in "The reason why ... Maine residents fuss...." Let the narrator take on the flavor of the characters.

I try to get my people onstage as fast as possible. In this case, the landscape was important enough to come first, but I brought the folks on in the second graf.

I chose the Potters to lead with because

they — through a combination of Jim's history in the woods, Rita's activism, the overview of change provided by her father and the presence of kids to represent the future — provided an excellent framework for the narrative.

The Yeomanses, older and reflective, accepting of natural death but angry at technology's failures, were deliberately saved. I wanted to use them for the kind of antiphony that I like for the end of a story like this.

6. Dialogue

Each individual, with a personality of his own, has his own manner of speech — rhythm, inflection, accent, emphasis, tone and the shaping of sentences. Writers since Chaucer have written for the ear. I think that the careful reproduction of people's actual speech is one of the best ways we have of describing a character in a story. The reader can't see him, but it's possible to hear him.

I try to quote exactly, and to explain when a quote is strange. (Jim Potter asks, "What's going to be left when they ge' done?" The narrator explains, "Potter is an amiable man with a Maine accent as thick as the woods around Blunder Pond." I have set the stage for him to continue speaking in a Maine accent and reassured readers that I am not making fun of Jim Potter.)

I think American regional speech is poetry. I'm not fond of jargon, copspeak, inflated official rhetoric, valspeak and so on, but I believe that they, like regional speech, reveal more about the speaker than long grafs of explanation. Speech reveals education, temperament, aspiration, pretension and other secrets, as Professor Henry Higgins knew.

I use speech for contrast. In this story, the cool voice of the government man listing the properties of the poisons to be sprayed was in contrast to the passion of the local people's arguments about the chemicals.

On this business of speech, I don't think anyone has put it better than (of all authorities) the writer of the *National Enquirer*'s guidelines for writers: "If someone says, 'Never has so much been owed by so many to so few,' don't change it to 'We owe a lot to the RAF.'"

One more word about colloquial speech: I handle language as sound when I'm trying to show character in a story like this, but in a news account that aims at fast communication of information, I treat language as written words and use standard spelling.

7. Structure

This piece is episodic, building in cinematic scenes. (I think that most of us have been so influenced by films that we write in scenes, moving within a given scene from long shots to close-ups.)

The story begins with the peaceful landscape into which the characters are introduced. The background of the controversy is filled in — exposition.

Then there's the scene of the planes waiting and the pilots being briefed — a scene to create tension.

The people in Wytopitlock wait at the Yeomanses' farm, where talk about the immediate situation is enlarged into a commentary on the major changes that have degraded the quality of life in the Maine woods through profitable technologies. Options are discussed.

Through Ruth Yeomans, the reader hears that the governor has decided to go ahead. Rita Potter, resigned as she waits, says her heart is breaking at the devastation of the land.

The climax is inevitable and fast: The planes take off, the spraying begins. But the failure of the persevering humans has not been total; governments are reconsidering future poison programs. The ordinary people in the woods have achieved a small human triumph.

8. The ending

The end seems as important to me as the lead, the two of them balancing the weight between. Sometimes the end stands out from the material and I can work backward from it. In this case, I had put aside material for several possible endings. The ending I used was the only thing salvaged from an evening of standing in the woods under the spray planes. It had seemed important to be there as the woods were sprayed, but finally, there was nothing much to say except that the poison was sprayed and the black flies bit.

Not until I decided what the story was about did I see the value of a note I had taken as we were driving out of the area that night. There had been something troublesome about that message on the side of the truck about our national need for throwaway paper. When I saw the truck again in a fugue state, I read it as a message from Ecclesiastes. It seemed to fit.

Breakfast with the President:

Selling the New Beginning

By Charles McCorkle Hauser
The Providence Sunday Journal, February 22, 1981

WASHINGTON — The city is warm and muggy, canopied with a mottled overcast, heavy with the hint of rain.

Inside the White House, as if to compensate for the gray dullness outside, the East Room sparkles with spring — centerpieces of yellow lilies at each of the dozen breakfast tables covered with matching yellow linen, polished silver, china emblazoned with the presidential seal in a royal purple border.

And on this Thursday morning following Ronald Reagan's unveiling of his economic program before the Congress and the great American television audience, more than a hundred newspaper and broadcast editors from around the country wait expectantly for the President to arrive.

THE MENU consists of orange juice, scrambled eggs, bacon and sausage and sweet rolls and sauteed mushrooms, topped off with a generous serving of salesmanship for "America's New Beginning: A Program for Economic Recovery," the title of the thick briefing book at each editor's place.

This is a target group in one of the great public-relations blitzes of our time, organized to put pressure on Congress by selling the public on the most significant turnaround in the role of the federal government since the administration of Franklin Delano Roosevelt.

The phrase — "New Beginning" — comes trippingly on the tongue from all sides. The Washington *Star* banners "Reagan's 'New Beginning'" across the top of its front page. Clearly, the words are designed to take their place in history beside the "New Deal" and the "New Frontier" and the "Great Society."

THERE'S A STIR at the center door, and an aide announces, "Ladies and gentlemen, the President of the United States." Everybody stands and Ronald Reagan strides in briskly and sits down in a reserved place at one of the tables. He's wearing businessman's gray-blue, with just a touch of red in his tie to match the healthy glow of his cheeks.

After the scrambled eggs, the business of the morning begins. The first speakers, mercifully brief, are Donald Regan, Secretary of the Treasury; David Stockman, director of the Office of Management and Budget; and Murray Weidenbaum, chairman of the Council of Economic Advisers.

Regan and Stockman both mention that they will be departing shortly to go "up on the Hill" to testify before a congressional committee about the program. The words "the Hill" seem to constitute the second most popular phrase on people's lips in Washington today, because everyone knows that Capitol Hill is where the Reagan program will live or die.

Weidenbaum finishes his pitch and introduces "the number one economic communicator of our nation — the President of the United States."

THE PRESIDENT steps up to the lectern, delivers some introductory remarks about his program and then takes questions.

He is relaxed this morning, responding in measured cadence, unlike the rushed delivery of his speech the night before. "We believe people are ready for a great change," he says, and he uses his hands to illustrate two lines on a graph — the hands criss-crossing to show budget deficits turning into surpluses.

The questions are not hostile, but the editors are looking for more detail about the program. The answers are couched mostly in generalities, echoes of the previous evening's speech. This is not a man who deals in specifics.

The sense of humor shines through. Responding to a question about the opposition to his program by the AFL-CIO, currently meeting in Florida, Mr. Reagan says, "Sometimes they're out of step with their own rank and file." Then, smiling: "They certainly were in the last election." Zing.

The sound of a helicopter landing on the south lawn penetrates the room. "They're waiting for me," the President says, and takes his leave, headed for a long weekend in California.

ON THE SIDEWALK in front of the White House in the mist march 50 demonstrators, some wearing miners' helmets, and carrying placards protesting budget cuts in the federal program to eradicate black-lung disease.

Another picketing group shows up across the street on the edge of Lafayette Park. White House police escort the black-lung group to the other side so the new marchers can have their turn on the stage.

The new arrivals carry signs protesting budget cuts in welfare programs. The rain drifts down more persistently. The watercolored letters of the signs begin to streak so it's hard to tell what they say.

How I wrote the story

I used to think my practice of taking notes on everything in sight when I was on a story reflected some sort of basic insecurity, but writing coach Don Murray says it's just sound reporting. You really don't know what you're going to need until after you get into the writing. You may think you do — you may think you have the focus of your story firmly in hand — but a story has a way of taking on a life of its own, and the material you ignored as irrelevant may turn out to be essential to the piece you wind up writing.

I really think we're both right. A full notebook is a security blanket. In addition to ensuring your readiness to pursue various turns and twists in the story, it permits you to peruse your entire collection effort to look for patterns that can suggest the focus and voice of the story.

The piece I did on a White House briefing for editors is a good example.

I flew to Washington on a Wednesday evening with no idea of what sort of story I was going to write. I knew only that I was not interested in doing a spot story for next-day publication; I was aiming at the Sunday paper.

I woke up the next morning at the Hay-Adams House, across Lafayette Square from the White House, reached for a notebook, and started my day by jotting down the weather forecast (rain) from the early TV news. Over coffee I made notes on what the headlines in the Washington papers said about President Reagan's speech to Congress the night before ("Reagan's New Beginning"). On the short walk to the White House, I noted the feel of the air (muggy), the look of the sky (mottled). Right through the morning's activities, nothing was too minor to record in the pocket steno book I was using.

At one point I had no trouble recognizing that I had a usable item. That was when I left the White House after the briefing and stood in the mist to watch the demonstrators with their picket signs. I knew that the symbolism of the streaked signs would be my ending.

On the noon plane back to Providence, I flipped through the pages of my notebook and shaped the story in my head. It would be a chronological narrative, starting with the feel of the city and ending with the pickets in the rain. Back in the office, I sat down at a terminal and let the words flow.

In the absence of a close deadline, I'm not a fast writer; I usually rewrite and polish each sentence and each paragraph as I go. I spent about three hours on the piece before I was satisfied with it. I had no problem with length; I like to write tight. Judy Stark, in charge of the Sunday paper, did the editing, and suggested some changes that helped the pace.

Later, reading the story in print, I realized I had done a couple of things that are interesting because they did not stem from conscious decisions: First, I had used the present tense, which tends to give an immediacy, a you-are-there feel to a story. And second, although I had felt as if I were writing a first-person story, I had never used the first-person pronoun.

And there's no question that I wound up using a lot of that "irrelevant" stuff that I had compulsively crammed into my notebook.

Having a baby:
'In sorrow thou shalt bring forth children'

By Christopher Scanlan
The Evening Bulletin, March 25, 1981

In the labor room at Kent County Memorial Hospital, Jackie Rushton rose from the stretcher, her face pale and smeared with tears. A nurse pressed the fetal pulse detector against her abdomen, a taut mound stretched by seven months of pregnancy. The detector was blue, the size and shape of a pocket flashlight with earphones attached, and Jackie Rushton's eyes fixed on the nurse who strained to hear the bird-like beating of her baby's heart.

"Here's the heartbeat," the nurse said after several moments of silence, "It's 126 and it's fine."

If there's a heartbeat, why isn't she giving me the earphones so I can listen? Jackie thought. That's what the doctor always does when I have my checkups. First he listens, and then he says, "Here's the heartbeat. Listen." She didn't say, "Here's the heartbeat, Listen."

I've lost the baby. The baby's gone.

JACKIE AND ROB Rushton's daughter, Lola, was 18 months old when they decided to have another child. Jackie went off the Pill. Nothing happened. By the time Lola started kindergarten in September, 1979, her parents were convinced she would be their only child.

Then last June, Jackie, 25, missed her period. "Don't be silly," Rob said, "you're not pregnant." But one day early in July, Jackie went to the drugstore and bought one of those home pregnancy tests, and when Rob came home for lunch she was waiting with champagne.

THE FIRST THREE months Jackie was tired all the time. She dragged herself around during the day. She went to bed immediately after dinner. She woke up tired. Her parents visited from England and she drove them to the beach often. She lay on the warm sand at Bonnet Shores in Narragansett and slept.

Autumn came to Pawtuxet Village, the neighborhood where the Rushtons have lived since they immigrated from England in 1978. Breezes carried the leathery smell of dying leaves. The air turned colder. Jackie felt fine again.

In November, the Rushtons bought their first house, a summer cottage on Warwick Neck that needed work. Rob, 31, is a building contractor, and he began spending all his free time getting the house in shape. In the meantime, they moved out of their apartment on Post Road to stay with their friend, Marge O'Hara, who lived a few blocks away on Spring Garden Street.

Winter arrived. The air in the village was tangy with woodsmoke. The baby began to kick.

Shortly before Christmas, the temperatures dove below freezing. In the Rushtons' new house, the pipes burst. At the time it seemed like bad luck. A few weeks later, it turned out to be very good luck that they were still living with Marge, a delivery room nurse at Kent County Memorial Hospital.

IN THE EARLY hours of Jan. 22, six weeks before her March 4 due date, Jackie's water broke, a normal beginning of labor. A doctor at Kent County Memorial told Jackie that morning that labor might still be a week away. He advised her to go home and wait.

That afternoon, Marge drove to the Zayre's on Warwick Avenue with Dawn, her 13-year-old daughter. They bought a turquoise nightgown for Jackie and a yellow quilt with ducks and teddy bears for the baby. That night, they held an impromptu shower. They didn't have time to wrap anything, so they let Jackie open the bags. They talked about names. Joel for a boy. Zoe or Leah, if it was a girl. Maybe Hannah. Marge, who had to work the next day, went to sleep around 9.

AT 10:15 that night, Jackie went upstairs to the bathroom. When she pulled down her pants, she saw the blood. She yelled for Rob, who came running with Dawn behind him. Dawn took one look and ran into her mother's bedroom.

"Mommy, Mommy," Dawn cried, "You've got to help. Jackie's bleeding." Marge shook herself awake and went into the bathroom. Jackie held a bloodsoaked towel.

The bleeding, Marge knew immediately, meant one of two abormal pre-natal conditions: *placenta praevia,* in which the placenta comes out before the baby, causing loss of large quantities of blood; or *Placenta abruption,* in which the placenta separates from the uterus. Either way, Marge knew, Jackie and the baby were in serious trouble. The placenta is the source of a baby's oxygen. If the infant wasn't delivered quickly — by Caesarean section probably — it could die. It might be too late already. Marge didn't tell any of this to Jackie or Rob.

"Get your bag, Jackie," she said. "We're going to the hospital. Get the car, Rob. I'll call the doctor."

ROB'S TOOLS filled the back seat of the station wagon. The three of them squeezed in front, with Jackie in the middle.

Rob speeded up when they turned onto Post Road. There were only a few cars on the road. He wished a policeman would pull them over and give them an escort to the hospital.

"What's going to happen?" Jackie said. She began to sob.

In the blackness of the winter night, the streetlamps shone like moons. Marge shivered with cold and fear. Should she just make small talk or try to prepare Jackie for what to expect at the hospital? Once they arrived, she knew, things would happen fast.

She tried to sound breezy. "Well, you've missed your shower, Jackie, but that's all right. We'll have one later. And don't worry about not having any baby clothes. I'll see to that."

"What's going to happen?" Jackie said.

Rob glanced at Marge. She looked worried and that made him even more afraid. He had never seen so much blood. He thought about Susan Gilbert, a friend from England. She had started to hemorrhage before her second baby was born. The doctors couldn't stop the bleeding. Susan died. Rob gripped the steering wheel with both hands, grateful he had to concentrate on the driving. He wanted to scream.

"Everything will be all right," he told Jackie. "Keep yourself calm. If you're calm, the baby will be all right." *Come on God, he thought, you've got to be with us now.*

The light at Warwick Avenue was about to turn red. Rob slowed, looked both ways and shot through the empty intersection, horn blaring. "Be careful," Marge cried, "We've got to get there in one piece."

They passed a shopping plaza, a string of one-story shops. Behind the plate-glass windows, the night lights shimmered.

They turned onto Route 95.

"Rob, the petrol tank is on empty," Jackie cried.

"It's all right. There'll be enough to get us there."

We're going to stop in a minute, and I'm going to be stuck on 95. I'm bleeding, and I'm going to be on 95 flagging down cars.

Off the highway now, turning up a long straight road lined with tall trees. Doctor's shingles hung from signposts in front of several houses. They climbed a slope and saw the hospital. Rob slowed by a cluster of signs and followed an arrow marked "Emergency Room Entrance."

"Don't worry," Marge said. "We're just going to get out here."

"Don't even tell me where you're going," Rob said. "I'll find you."

"Marge," Jackie said, "I'm frightened."

MARGE TOOK Jackie's arm and led her up the ramp to the emergency room. They walked through the first of two sets of glass doors. Marge hurried ahead to grab a wheelchair.

Suddenly, at the door to the waiting room, Jackie felt intense pressure in her abdomen. Then it passed. "Marge, help me," she cried. "I've delivered the baby. I've had the baby."

Marge let the wheelchair go and ran back into the doorway, grabbed Jackie and pulled her inside.

Jackie was dimly aware of the crowd in the waiting room, a large airy room with vinyl couches and chairs set in rows. A gray-haired man in a leather coat turned and stared at her.

Fay Masterson, Marge's supervisor in the obstetrics ward, appeared. Like an angel, Marge thought. She and Fay picked Jackie up and laid her on a stretcher.

Above her, Jackie saw only the white ceiling and fluorescent lights. She felt disconnected, unable to see what was happening. She sobbed hysterically. Everything had gone horribly, horribly wrong. She could feel herself bleeding. She felt exposed and alone, aware of people around her but not really caring. There could have been a crowd of 10,000 and it wouldn't have mattered.

Marge heard the squeak of screens being placed around the stretcher, blocking the view as she and Fay pulled Jackie's red corduroys off.

"It's all right, Jackie. It's not the baby," Marge said. "It's just a blood clot."

She's lying, Jackie thought. I felt something come out of me. I've had a baby. They're just telling me that to keep me calm so they can get me to a room and try and get the baby breathing.

ROB HURRIED into the emergency room and saw Jackie on a stretcher, crying hysterically. Before Marge whipped a white sheet over her legs, he saw the blood between them, a splash of scarlet. Marge and the other nurse pushed the stretcher through a set of swinging wooden doors and disappeared. He dashed after them. They were racing the stretcher down a narrow passageway with green walls and round convex mirrors high up in the corner.

"I've had the baby," Jackie was crying.

"No, you haven't," Marge said. "It's all right."

Rob tried to catch up. *This is really serious,* he thought. Susan Gilbert's face rose before him. No, she's not going to die. Don't think negatively. Just go, man.

"Get out of the way, Rob," Marge cried. "We've got to get her upstairs."

They took a sharp right, pushing the stretcher through another set of doors.

AS THE DOORS slapped back and forth, Jackie saw Rob's bearded face, framed by a small square window of netted glass.

They rode up in the service elevator to the maternity ward on the third floor. Marge held Jackie's hand and rubbed her head. She thought of Dawn and of Jonathan, her nine-year-old son. They had been so excited about the baby.

IN THE LABOR ROOM, Fay Masterson and the other delivery room nurses alerted by Marge's call converged on Jackie, inserting an intravenous needle in one arm, taking her blood pressure. They wore sea green and flowered surgical clothes. A mobile of one-dimensional red apples hung from the ceiling.

Dr. Thomas A. Vest, an obstetrician, came in. He drew Rob aside and told him he would try to deliver the baby normally. If that was impossible, he would perform a Caesarean section.

The nurses were having trouble getting Jackie's sweater off. She lifted herself up so they could pull it over her head. She felt blood pump furiously from her body. There was blood everywhere.

Now they couldn't get her bra off.

"Let me do this," Rob said, stepping in. He tried to make a joke. "I can do it with one hand." Nervously, he struggled with the clasp. "I've lost my knack," he said, and then worked it open. They put a gown on her.

Jackie didn't understand. *Everyone seemed so calm. Rob was managing to crack a joke. It was like he worked there, like he'd done this every day of his life. Marge is so cool and confident. I'm the only one who's feeling this hysteria.*

THE HEAVY BLEEDING, Marge knew, posed a serious threat to the baby. She took the fetal detector and pressed it against Jackie's abdomen, listening intently through the earphones. She was silent for several moments.

"I don't hear it, Jackie," she said.

Marge tried to make her voice carefree. "But I'm not too good at it. Let me get Beth." She walked out of the labor room into a small office used by the delivery team and stood there, taking deep breaths. What are you going to say? *"There's no heartbeat"?*

She's lying, Jackie thought. *I know she's good at this.*

Another nurse, Beth Graziano, took the detector and listened.

"Here's the heartbeat," she said finally. "It's 126 and it's fine."

Rob looked at Jackie. She was still bleeding. "Just think of yourself," he said. "Pull yourself through."

Jackie didn't say anything. *I can't. I can't just say, "Oh well, you know, the baby's gone, but I'm going to try to fight to live." I don't want to.*

"You've got to keep calm," Rob told her. "Because the baby's still inside you."

For the first time, Jackie was afraid of dying. She remembered Susan Gilbert's sister telling her how much blood the doctors gave her. The more they gave her, the more it poured out. *Please God, let the baby be alive. Let the baby be alive.*

"Say a prayer," Rob said. "Say a prayer."

Dr. Vest returned. He told Jackie and Rob that they were going to take her into the operating room now. Because of the bleeding, he was going to wait until then to examine her.

"Right," Rob said. "I'm ready then."

"No," the doctor said, "you're going to have to sit this one out."

Jackie spoke up. "Could you give me something to put me under?" she asked the doctor.

I want to be put out cold and not wake up for three days. They're going to wheel me in there, they're going to take a dead baby from me, and I'm going to be awake the whole time, and I'm going to know all about it, and I don't want to know. I want to be unconscious. I don't want to know anymore. I don't want to face it.

"Give me a kiss," Rob said, leaning down to kiss her.

The nurses wheeled the stretcher out of the labor room into the corridor. Jackie turned around and looked at her husband.

"Goodby, Rob," she said. *Why did I say that? It's so final, so flat, so ending. Not like I'll be back in a minute. Like I'm leaving him.*

"Say a prayer," Marge told Rob. The nurses pushed the stretcher through a door marked "Delivery Room." "Take good care of her, Marge," Rob said.

ROB SANK into a chair in the hallway. The floor was black and speckled tile. In the next room, a young woman in labor screamed. On the wall facing him, the bulletin board was crowded with hospital memos, an ad for a childbirth class and a large photo of a nurse cradling a naked baby. *Hey man, grab hold of yourself. Nothing's happened. You've just got to say a prayer. Just shut up and say a prayer. Please, Jesus, don't let either of them.... Please let them both live.*

JACKIE FOUND herself in a large, blue room. Freshly washed surgical clothes were stacked on cabinets lining the wall. The nurses pushed the stretcher into another room. It had green walls. She saw the operating table, a narrow black cushion wrapped in white sheets. They lifted her off the stretcher and onto the table. The sheets were cool.

Above her hung two immense lights, like huge ice cream scoops. She could see her reflection in the shiny metal. She wanted to ask them to move the lights. But then the lights went on, and her image disappeared in the brightness.

They gave her a shot and she could feel her legs tingle and then she couldn't feel them anymore.

The anesthesiologist was asking her about England. She looked up at his masked face. She knew he was trying to take her mind off the situation, but what she really wanted to say was "Why are you talking about that?"

A nurse attached the bottom of Jackie's gown to a metal stand in the center of the table, blocking her view of the operation.

Both of her hands were strapped down. *I feel like I'm crucified. I can't feel my legs.* She stared into Marge's eyes and gripped her hand. Marge looked so calm.

But Marge felt helpless and scared.

Dr. Vest made an incision in Jackie's abdomen and began to cut through the layers of skin and muscle. He took bandage scissors, with one blunt end, and cut into the uterus. Marge held her breath. *Please God, please.*

IN THE HALLWAY, Rob was praying. In his mind, he could see the operating table. The doctors and nurses in their gowns and masks stood over Jackie. Then something strange happened. Rob isn't a churchgoer, but he believes in God. And now he imagined he saw Jesus standing in the operating room. Rob watched Him move His hands over the table. A blessing. Rob let out his breath in a long, deep sigh, suddenly calm.

IN THE DELIVERY ROOM, Marge saw the little head emerge. It was pink. Marge looked at the clock on the wall for the precise time of birth. "Eleven-eleven," she called out.

The doctor lifted the baby out. He could see that the placenta was in the path of the birth canal, *placenta praevia*. They had gotten to the baby just in time. Another few minutes and the baby would have suffocated without the placenta's source of oxygen.

"We're all right, Jackie," Marge said. "You've got a daughter, and she's fine."

She can't be normal. It's still not all right.

"I've got to tell Rob," Marge said and ran out of the room.

Rob saw a nurse running toward him. "Rob, you've got a daughter, and she's fine," Marge said. "Jackie's fine. I've got to get back." Marge's face was half-hidden by the surgical mask. It would be a week before he realized it was she who had given him the news. He jumped out of the chair and then sat down again.

JACKIE FELT as if she had been lying on the operating table forever. A nurse walked to the head of the table. She held the baby in her arms. Jackie could only see the top of her head. She was tiny and wrinkled. When Lola was born, she felt so high — a "Wow, look at what I've done" feeling. She didn't feel that way now. Somehow it still wasn't right. *The baby's alive now, but in five minutes she's not going to be all right."*

The nurse took the baby away to be weighed and measured, to have her footprints taken.

ROB THOUGHT of Dawn, waiting back at the house. He lifted the phone at a desk in the hallway to call her. He heard the dial tone and then put it back down. His head was too fogged to dial.

A nurse walked by him, pushing a metal incubator with a glass top and side. The baby was inside. *She's pretty, but so small. Everything's all right.*

IN THE DELIVERY ROOM, Marge also was thinking of Dawn. She didn't want her daughter to remember only the frightening part — Jackie bleeding, rushing out of the house. She went to a phone outside the operating room.

"Dawn," she said, "it's a little girl, and she's fine."

"Mommy, I've never prayed harder in my whole life."

IN THE RECOVERY ROOM, Jackie drifted in and out of sleep. In the middle of a sentence she would doze off. Rob sat beside her bed and held her hand.

"I'm sorry you lost your sleep, Rob."

"Don't be silly."

She fell asleep again. When she woke, Rob said: "How do you like Hannah for a name?"

"Yeah, that's nice."

"Well, let's call her Hannah."

"Okay. I really like Hannah for a name."

IT WAS almost midnight. Marge had to work in the morning. She went into one of the small bedrooms set aside for doctors and lay down on the narrow bed. She wanted to cry, but tears wouldn't come.

ROB KEPT nodding off as he sat by Jackie's bed.

"Why don't you go home?"

"No, I'm fine here." His head slumped.

"Please, Rob, go. I'm fine. Go home and get some sleep and come back tomorrow."

The doors were locked when he got home at 3 a.m. Normally, he would have been upset, but he didn't have an ounce of anger in him. He stood on the porch, calling for one of the kids. He waited almost a half-hour before Lola came to the back door.

"You've got a sister," he said, hugging and kissing her.

AT 10 A.M., Marge came back into the recovery room, carrying a pink bundle.

She placed the baby in Jackie's arms. Hannah was asleep, nestled in a blanket. Around her neck was a blue and white necklace with her last name. She wore a diaper, and the soles of her feet were still smudged with ink used to take her footprints.

Jackie looked down at her daughter. She was so tiny. She looked at her face. *How pretty she is .. and how normal. Maybe everything will be all right after all.* She counted the baby's fingers and toes. There were 10 of each.

"Marge, look at her." Jackie said. "How beautiful she is." Jackie didn't feel a great surge of joy. That would come later. Now, she was in awe. She didn't touch Hannah. She didn't want to wake her. She could have held her forever, just looking at her.

How I wrote the story

For much of 1980 and on into 1981, my beat on the *Bulletin* was not City Hall or courts or the economy, but a single Rhode Island neighborhood.

Pawtuxet Village, straddling Warwick and Cranston, was to serve as a sounding board for what was going on in the state and nation that election year. Photographer Anestis Diakopolous and I did stories about people's attitudes toward the coming presidential primary, the 1980 census and pollution in the Pawtuxet River.

Joel Rawson, managing editor of the *Bulletin* at the time, was also interested in stories on people's daily lives. So Anestis and I reported on the first day of school from the point of view of the mother who must let go. We did a piece on loneliness and how a women's center in the neighborhood tried to help women with it, another on the courtship and wedding of a young couple. There was some resistance in the newsroom when these stories began to run — the "Is this news?" debate that always seems to arise when a story has no obvious peg.

One day, Mark Patinkin handed me a piece of paper with a quote on it from philosopher Will Durant:

"Civilization is a stream with banks. The stream is sometimes filled with blood from people killing, stealing, shouting and doing the things historians usually record; while on the banks, unnoticed, people build homes, make love, raise children, sing songs, write poetry and even whittle statues. The story of civilization is the story of what happened on the banks. Historians are pessimists because they ignore the banks for the river."

So are journalists, I decided, and stopped worrying about the criticism about the Pawtuxet stories.

Using the "banks versus river" as a guidepost, I think the most effective story in the Pawtuxet series was "Having a baby: 'In sorrow thou shalt bring forth children.'" It's about people's lives, and it's also what Rawson — who wants news writers to return to the storytellers' art — likes to call a "story story": It had a beginning, a middle and an end. The New England Associated Press News Executives Association named it best written feature for 1981 in a paper of more than 60,000 circulation.

The story began in February, 1981, when *Bulletin* City Editor Merrill Bailey, who lives in Pawtuxet and gave me many good tips, came up and said there was a hell of a story in the village. He told me about his friends and neighbors Jackie and Rob Rushton and Marge O'Hara and their mad rush to Kent County Memorial Hospital for the emergency birth of the Rushtons' daughter Hannah.

Merrill's description of it — the race to the hospital, the nearly tragic outcome — sold me in a minute. It was such a good story, and it even had a happy ending.

A few nights later, I sat in the living room of Marge O'Hara's house, where the Rushtons were staying. Jackie fed the baby, and then she, Marge and Rob told me the story of that night as my tape recorder whirred.

I tried to get them to tell it in chronological order. I knew I was going to reconstruct the night, and I wanted to hear how it had happened. I knew I could come back for details, but I wanted to have the story told to me as I knew it had been told to Merrill, and how it had spread around the neighborhood.

The Rushtons and Marge O'Hara were very open. The baby had come home just a few days before, and their memories of the night she was born were fresh. They remembered every moment, it seemed, and I was able to stop them and ask what each had said at a particular moment, and even what they were thinking. To describe her interviewing technique, Barbara Carton uses the metaphor of painting a portrait: You have to get people to sit still long enough to get every wrinkle. That's what I was trying to do, and I pumped them for specifics: What happened then? What did it look like? What did you see? What did you say? How did you feel? What were you thinking at that moment?

I stayed for almost three hours that night. The next morning I began transcribing my tapes, which took me a couple of days. While editors sometimes get annoyed by reporters plugged into earphones for days on end, there are times when the machine can't be beat. For someone like myself, who can't take shorthand, it means getting every word, accurately, and all the nuances, as well as being free to take notes of a different sort — what people look like, their gestures, their setting — and jot questions that pop up.

Actually, I think the tape recorder can be a time saver. If you've done the interview right and you've asked all the questions, the answers are on the tape, and you don't have to keep going back.

I began by separating the material chronologically, and then by setting — breaking down the night into — scenes: the ride to the hospital, the labor room, the delivery room, the hallway where Rob waited.

I realized I couldn't reconstruct the night solely on the basis of interviews, so I arranged to visit the maternity ward at Kent County Memorial Hospital. In the labor room, I saw the fetal detector and noticed that it looked like a pocket flashlight. I got a lot of good details — the color of the room, the wall decorations — although I would only use a few, so this visit was crucial. Once I saw the setting, I felt I could convey it. I could also ask Jackie questions about what I had seen. Were the sheets cool? Could she see herself in the overhead light?

I had a lot more to do:

I drove along the route they took that night, and noted what stores they drove by and the doctors' shingles on the road to the hospital.

I wrote a draft that showed me what I still needed to know. I went back to Marge O'Hara's house one weekend morning, when Anestis went to take a family portrait for more details.

For facts on the medical problems that night, I borrowed a book on pregnancy from Peter and Nina Perl, who were the parents of two babies. I questioned Marge, the nurse, closely.

I knew I had the whole story there; the question was how to tell it.

Joel Rawson had taught me several stories before that there had to be a "spine," something to drag the reader along to the end. I decided that the question I wanted to set up immediately in the reader's mind was the one that keeps every storyteller going: What next?

Don Murray advises that stories start as near the end as possible. I asked myself what the moment was where the story could have gone either way — where the baby could have lived or died. I realized it was when Jackie thought the baby had died and the nurse was lying about hearing the heartbeat. That was my lead, since I figured readers would want, need, to know what was going to happen, and I could make them read until the end to find out.

But how to write that lead? At the time, I was studying Carol McCabe's stories, because I was really impressed with the way she immediately got you into the dramatic action of a story.

In 1976, she wrote a series based on visits to the 13 original American colonies, which won the Ernie Pyle Award. I noticed that in most of these stories, she always began with a scene and an action. Her verbs were always active and vivid: "Cold rain *spattered* on the sand outside the gray house where Worthe Sutherland and his wife, Channie P. Sutherland, live." "The Bicentennial tourists *flowed* through Paul Revere's Mall...." "Three trailer trucks *growled* impatiently as a frail black buggy turned onto Route 340...."

My lead-off scene, then, was the labor room, and the action was Jackie lifting herself up as the nurse listened to the baby's heartbeat. That set up the tension I wanted, and I felt I could step away to give the necessary background and still keep people reading.

I switched immediately to the day Jackie learned she was pregnant. Then the pregnancy. But this had to be dealt with quickly; I used the weather to convey the passage of time. Other details — like wood smoke in the cold night air — told a story about the neighborhood I'd come to know.

My big problem was cutting, since the participants had given me a wealth of detail. The story was so powerful that I tried to understate as much as possible. Short sentences. Dialogue is action. Keep it moving.

Using the three viewpoints — Jackie, Rob and Marge — kept the perspective changing. Marge's job allowed me to talk about the medical problem without having to change to an intrusive reporter's voice. The different characters also bring a different tension to the piece. Marge tells the reader that the situation looks bad, something Rob and Jackie could only wonder about.

(There's a question about reconstructing dialogue. I think if everybody agrees on the dialogue, that's the memory they have; and since all agreed, I accepted it. I also let them read the final draft. Some people might be aghast at this tactic, tantamount to letting your sources edit you, but I thought it only fair, since I was going to reveal some very intimate details. As it turned out, I had made a few minor errors, which they caught.)

Once Jackie's water broke and the mad dash to the hospital began, I just followed the night through. I used italics for interior dialogue, making a point of writing "Jackie thought" the first time I used this device. I jumped from my three characters.

A major question was where to end it. I had material about their return home with Hannah, but Joel said cut it when she has the baby in her arms and sees that everything is all right.

Merrill Bailey gave it a close reading and showed me that every editor is a reader and vice versa. He liked the dying-leaves image, but thought it wasn't precise enough. OK, what do autumn leaves smell like? "They've always smelled like leather to me," he said. Perfect.

Joel taught me another lesson I won't ever forget. The story was almost finished and I was pretty pleased with it, but he had a problem. There was something missing, he said. "You've got to paste some wafers in there," he said.

Huh?

The Red Badge of Courage, he said. Stephen Crane ends Chapter 9 with this line: "The red sun was pasted in the sky like a fierce wafer." Immediately, the reader is on that battlefield, staring up at the sky. You are there, in that place, in that time.

I had to find "wafers" in my story and paste them onto the narrative to give that sense of place, to make people "see." I had to go back for some, like the description of the shower gifts. Others were already in my notes, while some came from my own experience — I think streetlights hang like moons and the overhead lights in the operating room looked like an ice-cream scoop. These are just little things, but they are the details that I like the best, because they make me feel I was there the night Hannah Rushton was born.

Burning wire

By Barbara Carton
Sunday Journal Magazine, **May 3, 1981**

The Trident submarine built by Electric Boat at its plants in Groton, Conn., and Quonset Point is at the center of a controversy among the Navy, Congress and the company. The question is whether a quality submarine can be built on time for the contracted price.

Reporters have not been allowed inside Electric Boat. This story was written from interviews with one of the 4,000 persons who work at Quonset. It reconstructs from his memories what a typical night is like at the plant. The names of the worker and his friends have been changed at his request.

The submarine prowls the depths, sliding over drowned mountains and canyons of the ocean floor where all is black, empty.

She is 360 feet of steel death. Armed with 24 intercontinental missles, Harpoon rockets and MK-48 torpedoes, she can kill a city or sink a ship. Inside, 127 warm, pink and brown bodies are playing gin rummy, talking in the control room and reading in bunks. One walks down the center aisle with a cup of coffee, munching on a doughnut.

Cold, heavy water presses violently on all sides — 6,900 displaced tons of it, leaning against the metal hull with 536 pounds of pressure per square inch at 1,200 feet. Holding back that pressure are 2.24 million inches — 35 miles — of welds joining the submarine hull plates.

If those welds should fail, the water would burst into the aisles and bunks with a force greater than if the Hoover Dam let go.

THE ROAD INTO Quonset Point looks like the final stretch of Indy. Screeching tires. Weaving cars. The red necks, the blue collars, the country boys, the discos — all these guys escaping work, climbing the curbs and howling obscenities out the windows.

Tony is driving in the other direction, going in with the new shift. He drapes one arm over the truck's steering wheel. Stevie Wonder's *Hotter Than July* album plays from the tape deck. He wheels into the parking lot and pulls up close, across from the guard shack.

He gets out and walks past the guard stand, flipping his coat back to reveal the green-striped security badge clipped to his suspenders, then through the break in the chain link fence and into a corrugated metal building the size of a football field. He turns left inside the door, walks to the time clock near the locker room and pulls his card from the slot.

Click.

Another night at Electric Boat.

THIS IS WHERE submarine hulls begin, like towering steel tanks.

They line the perimeter of the room, perched on the laydowns, waist-high I-beam scaffolding. Nine on Tony's side of the room and beyond the pillars, nine more. Brown for Hy-80 steel. Green for high-tensile. Yellow for mild steel.

The building rocks day and night with the scream of grinding tools, the dentist-drill whine of the burr tools, the bap-bap-bap of pneumatic wrenches and the sizzling bacon noise of the welding rods, which means the boys on the floor have their heat right.

It smells of rust, burning leather and electricity. The smells hang in the air, especially near the gougers. Blue-white sparks cascade off welding rods. Lines and leads trail across the floor and over forked metal struts, like tree branches, and disappear into the tanks.

TONY CROSSES THE FLOOR, looking for Fox and waving to friends.

"How's it doin', Jim?"

"How ya doin', buddy?"

He stops midway out to pick up a coiled air hose. You have to grab them quick beause there never seem to be enough. He unclips his security badge from his left suspender, puts it on the air hose and continues.

Fox sits on a swivel chair at a tilt-top desk sandwiched between the tanks, munching a Rolaid. His red supervisor's vest is balled up in the desk with pens, paper and vouchers for wire.

Tony drops his tool box, welding hood and air hose in front of Fox's desk and walks out back to get a cup of vending machine coffee. Then he stands with his welding teammates sipping coffee, smoking cigarettes and waiting for Fox to give him a job.

The Fox is "an average Joe, a workingman's boss, a jeans-and-flannel-shirt man." He wears his vest only during inspections and lunches occasionally with the team.

Foxy hounds some of Tony's teammates but Tony says they deserve it. They are whiners, the guys that take five coffee breaks a night and call in with flu three times in the same week. There are four or five on the 17-man team.

One by one, Fox calls them forward.

There is Stevie Zingarelli, Tony's best buddy. Dark. Short. Tough. Speaks his mind. Interested in welding, his wife, his baby and one-liners. The undisputed vertical man on the team, an excellent stick worker.

Dana Parillo. Bold, brash, dresses like Aspen — down vest, bandannas and fisherman sweaters. "He's God's gift to women." Tony says. "We all know that. We're out to lunch and we see a girl walkin' by the truck or something. The girl could be really nice, real pretty. He spits on the ground. A lot of guys at work got pinups on their lockers. Don't say anything about Parillo's pinups, like 'She's not pretty.' Oh no, don't say that. Parillo's got all the best."

Sho' Hot. "One day he was sitting in front of his job. He had been sitting there a long time, staring at the metal. Me and Stevie were walking by. Stevie said. 'Hey, what's the matter?' Hot, he said. 'This metal's sho' hot. I *cain't* wayld it.'"

Arnie Weed. "He doesn't care too much for Electric Boat. He wants to be a dance teacher. He's a step-out on the weekends. Dressed. That's all he talks about is his clothes. 'I just picked up a leather,' he'll say, 'a nice, full-length leather for the summer.' He tells me, 'You oughta see me on the weekends. I get out of this place and I scrub all the dirt off and get myself clean, feeling good and I get my alligators on and my three-piece suit and my cashmere and I step out. I go down to Providence.' I say, 'Arnie, you do all that to go to Providence? I put on gym trunks and a T-shirt to go to Providence.'"

Kirby Peckham. "I first saw Kirby from the back," Tony says, "and I thought she had a pretty nice lookin' rear end. His hair is as long as my wife's. He's got a little waist, little hips and a cute little bottom. Kirby comes from money. He says he's only at Electric Boat to 'experience the working world.' He's experiencing it, all right. He wears his hair in a ponytail. When he takes it out, he gets at least four or five offers a night. I do it all the time too. I walk right up to him and say, 'Oh Kir-bee, I can't resist you. 'He says, 'Oh c'mon you guys. Jesus Christ, leave my hair alone.'"

Nick Aprans, he is one of the best mechanized welders around, but he never talks about how good he is. Nick is quiet.

Fox calls Tony and hands him a voucher for wire, a chit.

"Go over to 30, check Q.A. 54 — there's a repair between station eight and nine."

Tony picks up his air hose and plywood tool box and sets off across the floor for Tank #30.

He climbs 10 feet up the birdcage that hangs on metal claws off the tank top. He stands on the platform and surveys the seam — a thin, silver stripe running up the tank side, except for a seven-inch gash between stations eight and nine. First shift gouged out the impure weld, like a tooth cavity. Now, Tony will spend an hour filling it with clean wire.

He climbs down and plugs one end of the welding lead into the six-pack. He rummages in his tool box, between temp sticks, slag pick and wire brushes. He pulls out the stinger and screws it into the free end of the welding lead.

That done, he plugs one end of the air hose into the pig and threads the other through his tool box handle and knots it. He takes the badge off the air hose and puts it back on his suspender.

Tony checks his pockets for the wire chit and, leaving the rest of his gear at the job, heads to the wire room, near the locker room.

Micky is at the counter in a pair of patched blue jeans and a beard. A wire baker is on the back wall, like a pizza oven, and the holding ovens are on the side walls.

The flux on the 110-80 wire Tony needs is sensitive to moisture. It has to be baked, then stored under heat until use. It can be kept on the floor for only five hours before it soaks up too much moisture from the air.

Tony stands in line and when his turn comes, hands the chit to Micky.

"How much wire you want, Tony?"

"About three pounds."

Micky writes "three pounds" on the chit, looks at the clock, marks the take-out time, pulls the front sheet off and gives Tony the receipt.

He pulls an oblong, plywood box of wire off the shelf, writes Tony's badge number on the metal top plate with a grease pencil and slides the box down the counter to Freddie yelling over his shoulder, "Three pounds for Tony."

Tony carries the box of wire next door to the tool crib. It looks like an auto-parts store with shelves of tools. He reaches into his khaki pants pocket, pulls out a metal key chain, opens it and takes off two bronze tool chits that look like dog tags, stamped with his badge number. He puts them on the counter.

"Wire brush and a burr tool," Tony says.

He picks the tools off the counter and walks back across the floor to Tank #30.

There are many different kinds of welding, but arc welding, which Tony spends most of his time doing, fuses metal to metal with an 11,000-degree zap of electricity.

The arc is enough to dry hands and bake faces red, even when the welding rod is held at arm's length and the welder is wearing leather gloves and a hood. "It's quite a shock the first time you strike an arc," Tony recalls. "It's hot and violent and there are sparks all over the place. Sometimes you forget and do it with your mask up. That can be pretty shocking, too. Some people in my training class were so utterly scared they quit."

A WELDER moves his rod, with the arc flashing at the tip, up the seam, melting small puddles of metal from both sides. The rod is like a mechanical pencil — it has filler wire in it, which melts and drips into the puddles, strengthening the weld.

The air can contaminate a sensitive weld and make it brittle, so the filler wire is coated with a protective flux. The flux also contains a gas that burns, shielding the new weld from any contaminants.

Tony speaks of "flux" and "arcs" and "six-packs" as if he were born to weld. Five years ago though, he was a carpenter nailing asphalt shingles to cold roofs in West Barrington, his hammer hand red and raw from the winter wind sweeping off the bay.

A high school friend called one night about a welding class at the Electric Boat plant in Groton. The class was sponsored by the Comprehensive Employment and Training Act (CETA).

They drove two hours south to the plant in Tommy's 1966 red Mustang one December afternoon, wondering what Electric Boat does, exactly, and whether welding is bad for your health.

Tony spent 13 weeks in a yellow metal CETA training booth. "Alls I can do is teach y'all the basics," the trainer had said. "After that, y'all jes gotta barn waar. That's onliest ways y'all gonna learn. Y'all gonna git your butts in those booths and barn waar. Don' come askin' me no stupid questions. I already told y'all that stuff. Jes git in the booth and barn waar."

Tony burned wire. He graduated second in his training class and took a first-shift job at Groton. "I was doing junk. Garbage welds. Little tiny pieces of metal that had all been cut wrong and I had to build them back up. They'd sit me down on the ground in the middle of all this smelly oak scaffolding. I'll never forget that smell. It was like a bathroom."

HE QUIT, burned out and disgusted, during the strike in 1975. He tried carpentry again. He welded boilers. When the plant went out of business, he hauled his welding leathers out of the closet and reluctantly applied for work at Quonset.

Compared to Groton, Quonset was "a country club." It was smaller. More efficient. People called him "Tony," not "8654," when they handed out the paychecks. In Groton he was a new boy, welding tiny struts nobody would ever see. At Quonset, he aced the application test. The woman in personnel after glancing at his test results had called him "some hot-shot welder." The instructor who tested him gave him the inside track to the Fox, and the Fox gave Tony good jobs.

"I remember the instructor asking me about 20 questions about working on Hy-80 steel. I breezed right through. He held his hands out to form different types of joints and asked me what they were. 'That's a butt' I told him. 'That's a tee.'

"Then he gave me a test plate and had me run some horizontal beads and a couple of vertical beads. It all came back, like riding a bike. He had me run a 3/8-inch overhead fillet. We call them 'fillet of welds.' I hadn't done that in a long time, but it came back. When I first brushed it, it looked great. Real nice. Cherry. A good weld. Pretty. He put the 3/8-inch gauge to it and my heart was pounding. But it was perfect.

"I kept my modesty about me, but inside, I was going crazy."

Tony studied the EB manual and told Fox he knew how to do everything, even if he did not. At first, Fox checked his work three or four times a night. Tony burned wire. His welds improved. It was attitude, as much as anything.

"When I came to Quonset, I told myself, 'I don't care how bad it is, I don't care what the situation is, I'm going to look on the positive side of every single thing that happens to me.' Because the bad side doesn't do you any good. And that's the trouble with a lot of these guys."

Tony finds a ladder near the tank and leans it up against the birdcage. He unties the air hose from the tool box, clips his badge back to his suspenders and carries his gear up the ladder to the staging board, which hangs off the birdcage like a window-washing platform.

First the tool box, the welding hood and the wire box. Then, the air hose and welding lead. He spends some time arranging his tools where he wants them. "What a lot of guys will do is start right away. If they're in the tanks, they won't take time to get set up right, with respirators, blowers and suckers to draw the hot air out. Then they'll complain, 'God, it's sickening hot in there. Jesus Christ, you can't breathe.' The company supplies the equipment to make a job comfortable but these guys will wait until they make themselves dizzy and miserable before they set up. I tell them: 'If you don't want to use it, okay. But quit then. Stop making the rest of us miserable.'"

He reaches into his tool chest, puts on his gloves, his green Snoopy hat liner, and his leathers, which cover his chest and arms. He slips the welding hood over his head, with the mask in the flipped-up position.

Then he reaches his right hand up and tightens the plastic screw on top, until he can feel the headband press against his forehead.

TONY GETS HIT once or twice a week with flying slag.

He has purple and white burn scars on his arms and chest and burn marks in his shirts. He tries to lean back, out of the way, when he chips the 800-degree slag off the top of the new weld, but he is not always fast enough. He gets hit more often in the summer, when he opens his leathers at the neck.

"What got me last night," he says, "is I was in kind of a tight spot. Not something I could jump out of quick. And I hit that slag with my chippin' hammer — boy, you know it. It just goes psst. It sticks. For a second it will just stick. Then it will start to drop down your shirt. It will start rolling.

"Everything went flying. I pulled the leathers off, threw down my welding rod, threw the lead one way, knocking my wire box over and all the wire dumped out all over the place. I'm not screaming because I don't want to look like too much of a fool. What you do is lean forward and pull your shirt out, so the slag rests on the shirt, not on your chest. You stay like this for maybe 15 or 20 seconds to give it time to cool off. Then you sit up and hold your breath — wait to see if it's still hot.

"Then you feel it. Maybe it rolled down over here somewhere. But it's cool. Ahhhhh."

He remembers a woman in his training class who was welding one day in a blue Dickey shirt, without leathers. "She must have dropped a bunch of it because we hears all this screaming from the next booth over. We jumped up on top of our booths so we could look over, and there she was, ripping her shirt off, because she was getting burned.

"I feel bad for her now, but at the time, the poor girl was burning the hell out of her chest and we're all screaming, 'Take it off.' She didn't want to take her blouse off, but she had no choice because once the slag gets in, you gotta get it out or it just keeps burning you."

TONY SCREWS A WIRE ROD into the stinger at the end of the welding lead. He leans his head back and nods sharply. The hood falls over his eyes, enveloping him in black.

Inside the hood he hears the trapped sound of his breathing.

There is a strip of glass in the mask, but it is so dark he cannot see the tank. If he looks up to the ceiling, he can see dim, faraway specks of light. He can not see the welding rod, although he can feel it in his right hand. Tony strikes the rod against the side of the weld-scarred birdcage.

The arc erupts with showers of sparks.

Now he can see, but only straight ahead to the tank seam. The seam looks green. It is like wearing an underwater mask. Sparks bounce off the welding hood and land on his leathers. He sniffs at the smell. His mask flashes white. Inside, Tony can see his nose reflected in the glass.

He pushes a bead of weld up the gouged-out metal as if he is sending a trickle of water through a V-shaped canyon. Tony cradles the rod gently, weaving slowly back and forth. Inexperienced welders grip too tight. They undercut, they leave porous metal and they count to keep the rhythm as they wing the bead. Tick. Tock. Tick.

But welding is, as Tony like to say, "a thinkin' man's trade. Once you get good, you got all the time in the world to think."

Sometimes, if he is welding next to Stevie, they talk.

"I had a fight with my wife like you wouldn't believe," Tony will say.

"Yeah?" Stevie might respond.

"Jean calls me a slob. 'You're just a slob, Stevie,' she says."

And they will laugh.

THERE ARE WOMEN welders, but men own the floor in the same sense that the old Keno players, with their green work pants and cigars, owned the pool tables at the Portuguese American Club, or Tony's high school beer buddies owned the stone wall outside Lenny's house. EB workers have *Hustler* pictures in the locker room and they endlessly debate the merits of Susie versus Julie versus Bo Derek versus wives.

"There are guys at Electric Boat will tell you they still believe a wife has to be hit," Tony says. "You know what I mean, 'They want it. They need it. I gotta give mine a whack once a month to keep her in line.' I say. 'Oh, man, what do your wives do? They put up with it? 'She loves it, man,' they say.

"It makes it tough because I gotta stay on top of myself all the time and make sure this doesn't rub off on me, because it's an environment I'm in for a third of my life. I'm better off, if a guy mentions slappin' his wife, to just fade into the background. Sometimes, I've said, 'You guys are crazy.' But it makes it worse. The guys say, 'Who's this ass? Where's he come from?' "

TONY BURNS 20 overlapping beads and finishes the weld with three cover beads.

Then he stands back and flips up his hood.

The boys have different styles. Pete, for example, goes with the old-style, the high, small bead. Nick goes with pretty, fine beads. Textbook beads. Tony likes the way Stevie does it. Flat. Smooth. Wide. It is all personal preference.

He looks at the weld, smiles and climbs quickly down the scaffolding. He sticks his head up inside a hull section several feet away, where some welders are. "Stevie?" he yells. The tank is an echo chamber. Stevie. Stevie. Stevie. "He's not heeeeeere."

Tony finds Stevie in another tank. He taps him on the shoulder. "Come with me, buddy," he says, beckoning with one hand. "Come check this out."

Stevie puts down his tools, flips his hood and walks to Tony's job. They climb the scaffolding together and look at the weld.

He follows it up the seam. He leans in close to look at the beads. He runs his finger up it.

Then he looks at Tony.

"All *right* buddy," he says.

He extends an outstretched palm.

Tony slaps it.

"We're the best," Stevie says.

"You're damned right," says Tony, patting him on the back.

TONY SPENDS the next three hours working gravy jobs on the outside tanks — fixing other guys' screwups.

He stops for two coffee breaks, but he notices whenever he pulls up his hood, the same people are at the machine.

About 8 p.m., Tony begins checking his watch. At 8:28 p.m. exactly, he hangs up his tools and climbs down from the tank. He stands around near his job, looking for Stevie, Nick and Parillo.

Stevie comes over.

"You bring a lunch?" he asks.

"Nah, I didn't."

"Where ya wanta go?"

"I don't care."

"D'Angelo's?"

"Okay."

They look around the room at the guys crawling out of tanks and from laydowns until they spot Nick and Parillo standing outside their jobs.

Tonight as every night, Tony stares at the time clock until it registers 8:29 p.m. Then he hits the second-hand button on his digital watch.

Precisely 25 seconds later, Tony and Stevie skip towards the door. Ten feet from the door, with the supervisors opening their mouths to complain, the 8:30 p.m. lunch horn blows.

Electric Boat employees are not allowed to run on plant property. Tony and Stevie run, trailed by Nick and Parillo, 50 other guys and several supervisors. They careen into other guys running from the building next door.

Tony looks up and sees the big, electronic chain-link entrance gate click shut. Sometimes with everybody running, the guards fear theft. They shut the big gate and force everyone to crush through a small one, only wide enough for two.

"Hey Stevie," Tony screams over his shoulder, "the gate's shut."

"Oh Jesus," Stevie says. "Hurry up."

"I'll block."

They bolt for the little gate, like cattle stampeding a chute. The guard sits in his stand with the window open, looking down on the galloping herd.

Tony is the first to reach the van. He fumbles with his keys, unlocks it and reaches over to unlock the door for Stevie, Nick and Parillo to tumble into the front seat too, because the back door does not work. Several times, in their hurry to get out of the parking lot, they slammed it and it fell off the hinges.

"Put the window down," Parillo yells, trying to climb into the back seat as Tony starts the truck and screeches out of the lot, down the access road. "I gotta have air. Air. I need air."

Parillo leans into the front seat and cranks WBRU to the top volume, while Tony presses the accelerator and the speedometer climbs to 55.

The light is red. Tony punches the brakes. The light changes, but the car in front does not move. Parillo rolls the window down further and leans out, shaking his fist. "Let's go," he yells. "Waddya waitin' for, another shade of green?"

They roar into the D'Angelo's lot and jump out of the truck. By the time they hit the counter, another 25 Electric Boat workers fall in line behind them. Tony orders a Tab and a small Italian with hot peppers, oil and vinegar. Parillo orders a special ham and cheese. "And I want about that much mayonnaise on it," he says, measuring with his thumb and forefinger. "On each piece of bread. I don't want a dry one. You gave me a dry one last night. A lot of mayonnaise, and I want it on both pieces of bread, and I want onions on there, too."

When he first started at Quonset, Tony brought his lunch and ate it at the locker room picnic table. Pete was a regular there. He was a Navajo Indian and his lifelong ambition was to urinate on John Wayne's grave. Mention The Duke at lunch and Pete would wave his arms and bang his Thermos cup. "That jerk," he would say. "That idiot." Some people called Pete "Chief" and he seemed to like it.

At 8:50 p.m., Tony slams the truck into drive. Back up the access road. Into the parking lot. Through the gate. Three minutes to spare.

The 9 p.m. horn blows as they run in the door.

After lunch, Tony does more repairs, except for a short time near the end when Fox asks him to work with new boys.

"If you like living in New England," he tells them, " Electric Boat is the best place to work, because you got steady work — or, you could have, if some of these guys would get off their butts. Because look at how high the current administration is on defense. We could have work for years.

"And the opportunities are unlimited. If you stick with it and show a little bit of gumption and professionalism, it will take you four, maybe five years to get top rate. But it *should* take you that long. These guys are spoiled. They all want top rate after a year and a half. And if you're good, who knows? Like the night-shift superintendent of the plant — he started off 20 years ago as a shipfitter with General Dynamics. Here's a chance for me — for you — to gain an executive position without a college education."

TONY ALSO WARNS about peer pressure. "Most of the team is pretty much run-of-the-mill," he says, "Like everybody else, they get their jobs, they do what they gotta do to get by and they go home. Any company has the same situation. Nine times out of 10, the real complainers are at the lower end of the pay scale. But, like I say, I don't have any sympathy for these guys. Most of them came in off the street with nothing. No trade. No nothing. Busboys. Waiters. Real nowhere jobs. Gas station attendants. They came to EB, and EB gave them a trade.

"You hear people say, 'I want to change things.' They want to do it, but they don't do it at work. A lot of talk. But it takes courage. You know the sad part? It takes courage these days to be a good worker."

Too many EB workers, Tony says, have been told all their lives they are unskilled workers, that they can never be professionals. They resent anybody who thinks welding is a profession and is proud of it.

"I'm the one that has to put up with all the peer pressure. I'm the one that has to go to the bathroom and look at pictures of myself. Or find the front of my locker spray-painted. Or go back to my job and find that my welding hood is smashed in a million pieces. And these guys think it doesn't hurt. It hurts, all right. I'm a person, too."

ONE NEW MAN has promise. He works hard, asks questions and burns good wire. Tony tells Fox to "put some time into him." Another is what Tony calls an "I-know."

He had too much oxygen in his burning torch.

"You got too much air." Tony said. "It's just blowing the flame and it's poppin'."

"I know, I know."

"Well, if you know, why the hell are you poppin' it?"

"Listen, man, I used a torch before."

"If you know, how come you just popped it six times in a row?"

"Aaaw, it's a lousy torch."

Tony tells Fox the man is an "I-know." Fox rolls his eyeballs.

"Not another one."

AT THE END of the shift, Tony takes his time returning his gear to the wire room and tool crib. His wife is at work, and he doesn't feel like going to the bar for last call.

He goes into the locker room where Stevie is leaning up against a row of gray metal lockers, rubbing his eyes.

Tony knows from looking at his eyes that Stevie has spent part of the night on the Mighty Lift doing MPA — mechanized pulse arc.

"Hey, Stevie, have a good night?"

"Yeah, but my eyes are sore and I've got a dry throat from all that argon."

"C'mon Stevie, you like it."

"Yeah, I like it, but I still got my sore eyes."

Tony reaches in his tool box and hands Stevie a bottle of Visine. Stevie tilts his head back, but the drops land on his eyelids.

"You do it, Tony."

Tony pulls one of Stevie's eyes open with his thumb and forefinger and lets the Visine drip in. Stevie blinks. The excess Visine runs down his cheeks. Tony bathes the other eye.

They stow their gear. Tony reaches in for his coat, takes his sunglasses from the top shelf and shuts the door. He walks with Stevie past the picnic table and into the bathroom, to wash off the soot.

The gougers stand at the sink with blackened faces, except for little circles around their mouths where the respirators were. Other guys are dripping with sweat from working in the tanks. Some slather Noxzema on their burns. Some complain. Some are silent.

TONY WAKES UP the next morning at 10. He takes a shower and sits at the oak kitchen table, drinking coffee with his wife.

He looks out of the window, across the marsh reeds, to the glinting ocean beyond. His sleeves are rolled up and he has burns from the night before.

In the distance, a tug pulls a barge with a big, brown cylinder on the back, a submarine hull section headed from Quonset — where it was welded — to Groton — where it will be assembled and, eventually, launched.

Tony watches as it steams down the bay, slips under the sun and over the horizon — to where the ocean is cold and black, thousands of feet down.

How I wrote the story

The assignment

Joel Rawson was, I'd say, rabid to get a behind-the-scenes story on General Dynamics, the Electric Boat submarine division.

The company was having a lot of trouble delivering Navy Trident submarines on time and for contracted costs. It also had problems with poor-quality construction, including faulty hull welds.

Electric Boat had also been notoriously uncooperative with the press. Joel decided that if we couldn't get in through the front door to see what the place looked like, we'd get in through the back door, by asking workers to tell us about it.

The subject

Specifically, Joel wanted a story on a day in the life of one Electric Boat welder. Find a guy and walk him through his workday.

In the end, I found Tony by accident. I had thrown out feelers to everyone I knew who had friends or relatives working at the plant. I also mentioned the story to Dan Stets, the paper's Electric Boat expert.

It took a while, because I was pretty choosy about the subject. We never intended that he represent all Electric Boat welders but I wanted a middle-of-the roader — neither a chronic complainer nor a company man.

I had been looking for about three weeks when Dan called me. "I've found your man," he said.

He painted Tony as a very believable guy — someone who enjoyed his work but had gripes. Gerry Goldstein, Dan's bureau manager, also knew Tony, and thought he would be a perfect specimen.

Interviewing

This story demonstrates the way I interview for longer pieces. I've learned to do this through trial and error. That's not to say it's the best way; only that it seems to work for me.

First, I tape-record everything. That makes it possible to get long and accurate quotes. Also, I enjoy looking at people when I talk to them — I'd rather have them feel as if they're talking to a friend, not a reporter bent over a note pad.

Second, I always try to do the interviews at the person's house. It's an instant introduction to what the person is all about. Tony, for instance, had stacks of rock records, lots of best-seller fiction, pictures of his large Italian family and a closetful of flannel shirts and work pants.

Third, I prefer to have the person's husband or wife present. Tony's wife remembered some details he had forgotten, such as driving to his first Electric Boat interview in Tommy's red 1966 Mustang. She knew what he liked most about the job, what he liked least.

I try to break the interviews into three sessions:

1. I spend the first session asking lots of seemingly irrelevant questions that allow me to get close to the subject, and allow him or her to feel comfortable with me. I ask about parents, childhood, goals, dreams — the whole ball of wax.

Lots of times, I get only one or two details from several hours of this type of interviewing. But they're the details that add depth to the story. For instance: "There are women welders, but men own the floor in the same sense that the old Keno players, with their green work pants and cigars, owned the pool tables at the Portuguese American Club, or Tony's high school beer buddies owned the stone wall outside Lenny's house."

2. I spend the second session reporting the actual story — in this case, walking Tony through a typical workday. Before starting, I had Tony draw up a floor plan, so I wouldn't have to interrupt him with a "Wait a minute, is the tool crib near the water fountain or the door?"

3. The third session is mop-up. I'm generally writing by now, and know what direction the story is taking — what details I can forget and what scenes need to be flushed out.

I always tell the person what I'm trying to do, and that writing this kind of story is like trying to paint a portrait. That way, the person understands why I'm constantly interrupting for more detail.

The writing

Organization isn't my strong point, but I had an easy time with this story, because it started and ended with Tony's workday.

I had a much harder problem getting the mood. I wanted to write it the way Tony might — as if I were "one of the boys on the floor" and knew about slag burns, orange sparks and long hours at the bottom of dark tanks.

For me, the mood is everything. If I know what perspective to take, I get a big surge of confidence. It's the same feeling I periodically get waiting at a tennis court baseline for the ball and knowing, absolutely, that the racquet will connect with a solid "whump." I wish I could figure out why I sometimes have this feeling and sometimes don't. I think — but am not sure — it has to do with interest in or sympathy for the story.

The weekend before the writing, I happened to spend a long Saturday night at a dockside bar with some fishermen friends. That's important only because I came home with that sense of male camaraderie — the flannel shirts, the back slapping, the roaring pickup trucks — which I needed to tell Tony's story, and I'm not sure I could have done it otherwise.

The technical details were a problem, too. I had books on welding, but they didn't tell me what it looked like, felt like, smelled like. In desperation, I called a contractor friend, who let me try on his leathers and hood. He struck an arc, ran a weld bead or two, and generally made the whole experience come alive. This gave me the confidence to write casually about an art I knew nothing about.

I also used a lot of Electric Boat slang and ransacked Tony's brain for the welding war stories, as well as the little victories, like doing his first "cherry weld."

Hindsight

I suppose nobody's ever happy with old stories, and I'm no exception. I can see the seams. It starts, stops and starts up again, like a hesitating car. I also should have interviewed some of Tony's friends and family to round out my impressions of him.

But each of these stories is an experiment: I want to learn from them, to do a better job next time around.

Working in jewelry:

Behind the glitter lies a tarnished world

By Bruce D. Butterfield
The Providence Journal and The Evening Bulletin, June 22, 1981

PROVIDENCE — Carl Pfanstiehl sits on a weed-covered stone wall across from a complex of jewelry shops in the old Riverside Mill, two packs of Camels bulging from his breast pocket, a lunchtime bottle of Coke in his hand.

The sun is warm this summer day and Pfanstiehl has come out to sit in it a few minutes until a factory bell calls him back to his job inside.

He is a skinny man, with thin arms and a chalk-white complexion. His left hand and index finger are heavily bandaged from a work accident a few days before. It hurts when he moves it, he says, but he can't afford to stay away from his job another day.

Pfanstiehl is a jewelry worker.

For the last eight years, since he dropped out of high school at 16, he has worked in jewelry shops and manufacturing houses in and around this Olneyville Square neighborhood.

It has not, he says, been an easy life.

"The jewelry business is a tough business for the worker," he says. "Very tough."

"You work a year or so, sometimes just a few months, business gets bad, they lay you off. You go to another place, the same. You never get benefits, holidays — like that."

"If I could change it ..." he says. "But jewelry's all I know."

The long, deep sound of the work bell comes from inside the mill complex. Pfanstiehl gets up and walks toward it.

THE MILL BUILDING at 50 Aleppo St. that Pfanstiehl disappears into this day is home to 16 jewelry firms.

Over three months last summer and early fall the *Journal-Bulletin* visited each firm, observing work practices and conducting interviews with owners and employees.

In many ways, the complex is the jewelry industry in miniature.

There are polishing, plating and soldering "job shops" here that employ three or four people, small manufacturing firms that employ a dozen to 50 workers, and one large manufacturing company where more than 100 people work.

A few companies have since moved or closed.

But the conditions found in the shops last fall are representative of the conditions at hundreds of shops in the state. Many, like those at 50 Aleppo St., are tucked away in old mills, out of public sight and largely out of public scrutiny.

This mill, a long series of old brick buildings running beside the debris-strewn Woonasquatucket River, was the home of the American Woolen Company before World War II. Last fall its grounds were dirty, its corridors dark and its myriad buildings chopped up into factory space.

Inside, each day, nearly 300 people earned their living making jewelry.

The House of Borrelli

The way to Carl Pfanstiehl's job is through a loading platform in Building 2 and up two flights of narrow, wooden stairs closed off and dark even on this bright summer afternoon.

On the second floor, he walks by signs with peeling letters pointing down an unlighted corridor toward a place called Double B Industries and, farther down, a place called Loupal Originals.

On the third floor, past the locked and windowless door of a company named DVM, he arrives at the House of Borrelli.

Twenty-five people work inside, making what its owner calls a "specialty line" of cheap costume jewelry.

Lately, Pfanstiehl has been assigned to the casting room, where the dust of industrial talcum powder sometimes covers virtually every surface, and where alloy "white metal," mostly lead, is melted in pots with no fans to remove fumes.

This is where he tore his finger open on a casting machine, and where he lost an afternoon's pay because he didn't go right back to work after hospital doctors sewed up the wound.

A week from now — saying he doesn't want to "hassle" with his employer about a return to the accident room — he will remove the sutures himself in the Laban Street tenement he shares with his mother.

But Pfanstiehl doesn't think any of this is unusual. "It's just the way it is," he tells you.

FOR MOST who have worked there, the "way it is" at the House of Borrelli is minimum wages, weekly layoffs and poor if not unhealthy working conditions.

Large chips and little flakes of paint constantly peel from the ceiling, falling into workers' hair and onto their workbenches. At night, the assembly work is covered with old plastic because of the paint chips and because, when it rains, water drips constantly from the roof.

The bathrooms are dirty and smell of urine. The windows of the factory are covered with yellowing plastic, rolled up a few feet because it is summer and workers want air.

There is a sprinkler system in the factory and throughout the mill complex. But Borrelli's — whose aisles are littered with cardboard boxes — shares the floor of its mill building with two other jewelry shops and there is only one exit for the three — the dark, narrow stairway at the front of the factory. Workers at Borrelli's and the owner of DVM next door talk of their constant fear of fire.

At Borrelli's, there is no ventilation in the casting room to remove talc dust or metal fumes. In the spray room, workers say they must buy their own surgical masks to keep from inhaling paint mist. Basic first-aid equipment such as bandages, three employees say, is available only when the employees buy and pay for them themselves.

When it's lunch time, workers often eat at their benches. When they are sick and cannot work and even sometimes when they are injured, they get no pay. Holidays for most workers are payless days off.

Workers who have been in the factory a year get a week's paid vacation, the owner boasts. But more than 200 people a year fill just 25 jobs at Borrelli's. Fewer than 10 qualify for paid vacation.

Carl Pfanstiehl, who has worked eight months by vacation time, isn't one of them. Like thousands of other jewelry workers in Rhode Island, he will stand in line at the unemployment office for his "vacation" pay.

SIX CURRENT and former production employees interviewed by the *Journal-Bulletin* complain of these and other conditions at the small factory.

Mildred Vaughn, 20 and married to an ex-Marine out of the service only a few weeks, and Doris Vaughn, her 16-year-old sister-in-law, have just walked out of the plant, final paychecks in their hands. They were benchworkers for a month, but quit because Borrelli's stopped issuing payroll stubs with the checks.

"How are we supposed to know what we're being paid?" Mildred asks. "They just give you a check and a little piece of paper with some numbers on it." The numbers, she says they were told, are payroll deductions and wages, though without a breakdown of hours or what the deductions are for.

Back at their homes, they show a reporter several pieces of adding-machine paper they say they were given by Borrelli's as a wage statement the last few weeks.

There are several numbers on the tapes, but no indication of what they represent.

The unexplained deductions, the Vaughns declare, were the final straw. Both talk of the dirty shop conditions, unclean bathrooms, paint chips in their hair and water dripping from the ceiling.

"There's another thing," Doris says. "The shouting. They were always shouting. Not so much at people, but at things that always seemed to go wrong in there."

There is a lot of swearing some days, George Menzivarz nods, and always there is yelling. "They shouldn't yell at people like that all the time, but they do. I think they're very nervous," he said.

He is a 22-year-old native of Honduras hired early last summer as a polisher at $3.25 an hour. Despite the low pay and shouting, he says, he liked his job and hoped it would be permanent. Ralph, Borrelli's chief polisher, who asked that his last name not be used, said Menzivarz was a "good kid" and a hard worker.

Still, Menzivarz was laid off after five weeks with only a day's notice.

OUTSIDE BORRELLI'S, a permanent help-wanted sign is attached to the factory wall. Inside, in a paneled office with pretty displays of pins and bracelets, Melvin Bunson explains that a steady supply of new labor is needed to keep the shop running smoothly.

Bunson, Borrelli's plant manager, complains that jewelry workers are unreliable, often lazy, and frequently walk out on their jobs. Hard times in the jewelry industry, he says, are correcting that.

"My crew's getting better all the time. They realize they have to work to keep their jobs," Bunson declares.

Many of his workers, he is told, complain of layoffs and of supervisors who yell and treat them without consideration or respect.

He waves his hand in the direction of the factory. "Most of these people aren't ready for a personal touch," he says.

PERRY BORRELLI, the owner, is less harsh in his appraisal of jewelry workers. A husky man with dark, bushy eyebrows and a full beard, he began as a jewelry worker himself, became a model maker for Imperial Pearl, and opened his own shop in 1962.

"I know what it's like to be a jewelry worker. I know it's hard," he says. "That's why we try to give everybody a break."

He agrees that factory conditions "are not the best." But he blames much of it on the building, which he does not own, and insists that his work practices violate no laws.

Masks are not needed in the spray room, he says, because the fans in the spray booths are "adequate" to remove all fumes. While he has stopped issuing pay stubs with his checks, he says, his office staff will readily answer any worker's questions about deductions.

Borrelli confirms the lack of casting-room ventilation and admits that the casting room is often filled with talcum powder dust. But the dust, he says, is not harmful.

"You ever see somebody standing all day pounding bags of talcum together? It's dusty. Sure. But it's only talc. There's nothing in talc that will hurt you," he says.

He adds that there is no need for ventilation over the casting pots either because "it's just white metal" that's being melted. "There aren't any fumes that amount to anything anyway," he says.

Borrelli says that three years earlier, when he rented the entire second floor as well as the place on the third floor, he had fans in the casting room and exhaust hoods over each casting pot. But he said workers complained "of drafts and getting bursitis and that sort of thing." So he took the fans out, and when the operation was moved to the third floor, "We didn't bother hooking any of the stuff up."

Five years ago, the federal Occupational Safety and Health Administration inspected Borrelli's and cited it for more than two dozen violations of health and safety codes — including lack of protective equipment in the casting room.

For more than a year, Borrelli fought the fines attached to the inspection; he paid them only under threat of court action. OSHA revisited Borrelli's a month after its initial inspection and reported no evidence of protective equipment having been ordered or purchased for the casting room.

Despite this, OSHA records show no further inspections.

Double B Industries

Double B Industries is the kind of place people never just happen by. One floor below Borrelli's, signs direct you down a dimly lighted hallway of half-painted bricks.

A left off the hallway puts you on a wooden landing, overlooking the entrance to the shop. It is unmarked except for a dozen or so old chemical barrels in front of a solid wood door, and a note scribbled in red ink on a wall beside the door that advises: "Ring Bell."

There is no bell beside the sign. A hand-drawn arrow running 10 feet across the wall points to the bell. Pushing it brings someone to unlock the door.

Inside, Rose Jamgochian, a stout woman who has spent 40 years in jewelry, is busy sitting at a bench stringing heart-shaped lockets onto a metal plating rack.

Another woman, the one who opened the door, takes a seat across the bench from her and begins doing the same thing. They are alone.

"We got employees," she explains, "But they drift in on Mondays, you know. They had a bad weekend and it takes them time to get over it. So Mondays they just drift in."

Double B is what is known in the industry as a "job shop" — a jewelry firm that specializes in one process. Double B's specialty is electroplating — putting a gold or silver finish on white-metal jewelry pieces created by other firms.

The shop is owned by Mrs. Jamgochian's brother, Sarkis Bedrosian, and by Perry Borrelli. It is a large, L-shaped room with the plating operation along a back wall and the racking and stringing benches near the front door.

Mrs. Jamgochian takes a reporter past a stack of chemical barrels, some with cyanide markings on them, but most with no visible markings at all. "Everything's stored right," she says.

There are no fans or vents over the electroplating tanks, although there is at least one huge fan on one wall. There are fire escapes along the back of the shop, but only one staircase exit. Like Borrelli's, that exit is the dark, narrow staircase entrance.

During a later visit to Double B, a reporter and photographer watch as a plater gingerly steps over broken floorboards around the heated tanks.

The plater, Javier Gomez, said the holes had been there since he started working nearly six months before. Though he agrees it would be simple and inexpensive to nail new boards into place, he concludes: "I guess nobody thought of it."

Gomez, 27 and a native of the Dominican Republic, says he would like to see the floorboards fixed. "It's dangerous," he nods.

But he has few other complaints.

"I like my job because it keeps me moving. It's good for my health. It keeps me in shape," he says.

GOMEZ' VIEW of Double B Industries is not widely shared by others who have worked there or in neighboring shops and factories.

Indeed, the owner of one neighboring firm, a half-dozen employees in another firm, the landlord of the mill complex and a former Double B supplier all tell of a constant stream of profanity and shouts coming from this plating shop.

Estelle Sylvester, a former employee with three children to support, says she was hired to rack and string jewelry at $2.90 an hour — minimum wage at the time.

"I used to rack, but mostly it was unracking jewelry and dipping. I had to take the racks and dip them in the tanks just like the men did. They were heavy and the fumes were awful. They didn't give you any gloves or aprons or anything. I ruined every pair of pants I wore there," she says.

Miss Sylvester says the workers used to "get high all the time" from working over the degreasing tank, where jewlery pieces are lowered into the heated tank of trichloroethylene.

A former Double B plater, now chief plater at one of Rhode Island's better known manufacturers, insists the shop was the most marginally-run plating operation he's been in — with stringers called on to do plating chores and a lack of protective equipment such as rubber gloves and aprons.

"They had girls doing work on the line. They were supposed to be stringers, but they were plating. None of them knew what the hell they were working with. From that point, it was dangerous, too," he said.

Mrs. Jamgochian and her brother, Sarkis Bedrosian, denied these and other charges in an interview late last summer. "The safety and health of our employees is important to us," Bedrosian said. "I'd never ask anyone to work in conditions I wouldn't work in myself."

What about all the stories of a constant stream of profanity coming from the operation?

"There's some shouting from time to time," he says. "There may be some swearing from time to time. It's a factory."

Mrs. Jamgochian also denied charges of poor working conditions.

On two visits to the plating shop, however, a reporter saw stringers using old barrels of cyanide as trash receptacles — a move Health Department officials say is extremely dangerous for health and safety reasons. Another cyanide barrel was filled with discarded pieces of metal on the landing by the front door. The missing floor boards near the bubbling tanks of acid and cyanide were a blatant safety hazard.

On one trip to the shop, a reporter observed two young children at the benches. One, a red-haired boy in a colored T-shirt, appeared to be stringing jewelry. The other, a slightly older boy who appeared to be about 12, was carrying a rack of jewelry from the benches to an area where it was stacked for plating.

The two were again observed sweeping the floor of the factory on a return visit later that same day. At quitting time, they left the plant together.

"We weren't working or anything. She's our mother," one of the youths said when questioned by a reporter.

Rose Jamgochian said the two are the sons of a longtime employee.

"They weren't working," she said. "They were spending the day here because their mother couldn't get a babysitter for them. They're better off here than alone at home, aren't they?" she said.

Loupal Originals

Liz Florio, in her mid-20s, sits at an electric welding machine inside Loupal Originals and demonstrates how bangles should be sealed together.

Expertly, she slips pieces of curled steel into the machine, presses the cut ends together and melts them together with a quick jolt of 250 volts of electricity.

Five seconds a piece. Twelve pieces a minute. She does it fast and with such precision that the weld leaves barely a mark on the jewelry.

Occasionally, the operation leaves marks on people. Every time Miss Florio seals a bracelet, sparks fly from the machine and smoke curls up to her face.

"A lot of people are afraid of it," she says of the job. "If you don't do it just right, the sparks fly all over. They burn your slacks. I've ruined slacks. And every once in a while they'll hit your face."

The women who work in the welding machines, she explains, are supposed to wear protective glasses. But, she smiles, she never has and neither do most women. Nobody's eyes have ever been hurt at Loupal's, she says, but women frequently suffer "little burn marks" on their legs, arms and face.

Victor DeCesare, the owner, nods in agreement.

"The sparks can be a problem," he admits, "but it's not a dangerous job."

To minimize burns, each machine is fitted with plywood between the welding point and the worker, he explains. If the weld is applied right — and most times even if it isn't — the wood will catch the sparks, he says.

What about the smoke? "There isn't anything in those fumes. It's just heat. We don't use solder here," he says. "The metal joins the metal."

Barrels with thousands of neatly stacked bracelets waiting to be polished and painted are clustered all over this jewelry plant. There are no customers for them. So there has been no need for women to weld more.

Miss Florio — Loupal's bookkeeper, secretary, factory worker and "Girl Friday" — is only demonstrating how it is when things are busy.

DECESARE IS a congenial man who trained to be an engineer, but whose uncle brought him into the jewelry business 16 years ago and eventually turned Loupal Originals over to him.

Like Double B, however, it is a manufacturing house, not a job shop. Bangles — brightly painted metal bracelets — are made, soldered together, painted, boxed and shipped from the 40,000-square-foot plant behind the door.

In the spring, DeCesare says, he had 20 women working full time. Now, at midsummer, it is slow.

"I laid off the last of them on Friday," he says. "We had a sprayer here, he'd been with us 20 years, since we started. I had to let him go Friday. He was the last," DeCesare says.

"It wasn't easy for him, and it wasn't easy for me. I don't like to lay people off. But, well, if I kept him and the others on for another couple of months waiting this thing out and I didn't ship, I'd be out of business."

Despite the layoffs and empty factory this day, DeCesare says there are enough orders coming to pay the bills and keep the factory open until better times arrive.

His firm's net profit in 1979 was "in the neighborhood" of $100,000. He adds that he did not spend it on new cars, trips or expensive homes, as he says many other jewelry shop owners do. He was able to "shrink" his overhead fast enough to avoid any large loss when the orders slowed.

"If I get a big order in today, I can have a full staff of girls in tomorrow to get it out. It's the kind of flexibility that's going to see us through these bad times," he says.

The "flexibility" means his employees live on unemployment insurance as much as on paychecks from Loupal's. One week they work, the next week or so they collect unemployment, then there is another week of work.

DeCesare says he doesn't like using the unemployment system that way. He has always protected his "core" of workers before, never timed them or stood over them yelling for more production. And, he adds, he's always given holidays.

Pay at Loupal Originals is minimum wage or close to that level, he admits, and there are few fringe benefits. "But that's jewelry," he says.

"This is a good place to work," says Miss Florio. "I worked in two other jewelry factories before I came here, and, compared to this place, they were sweatshops."

"It's a cutthroat business," DeCesare agrees. "A very bad business for a lot of these workers."

Color Glass and Design

Near the end of a summer workday Betty Godfrey drives along the front of 50 Aleppo St. looking for Color Glass and Design.

A reporter waiting outside the loading platform by Building 2 goes with her to the back of the complex where the pavement is cracked and sprouting weeds.

Color Glass and Design is there, a small place on the first floor of the Building 1-A, with two plywood-covered doors and plywood-covered windows.

A small sign with the name of the firm is beside one door. It is dwarfed by a much larger sign above, advertising a polishing firm upstairs.

Mrs. Godfrey parks and waits to pick up her niece from her first day ff work. Seconds before her niece emerges, a gust of wind sends the large sign crashing directly in front of the door through which employees have begun to leave.

They step over the old sign as if it has always been there.

"I'm not sure this is the kind of place I want my niece working in," Mrs. Godfrey says.

Despite her misgivings, Mrs. Godfrey's niece, Nancy, continues to work at Color Glass and Design through the summer, earning minimum wage with no benefits.

She is 18, quiet and shy. She attended Rhode Island Junior College for a year, she says, but will not go back for a second year until she makes some money.

She hopes to do better at Color Glass and Design than at her last job. That job — her first in jewelry — was at R & A Manufacturing in the CIC Complex near downtown. She worked there two weeks before the plant owner locked the doors one morning and put up a sign saying he had gone out of business.

Nancy never did get paid. Job Service — the state-run placement service that had sent her to R & A Manufacturing — sent her to Color Glass and Design for a second try.

"I need a job, so I've got to stay here," she says. "It's not that bad, I guess."

The only problem, she adds, is the overpowering odor of paint and epoxy that filled Color Glass her first day. A fan in the small workroom was turned on only half the day. "Maybe tomorrow will be better," she says.

The next day is not better. Neither is the next week, nor the next month. But as the weeks pass, Nancy says she grows accustomed to the odors.

"I get a headache once in a while. Some days — when they don't turn the fan on — I get a little sick by the end of the day. But it's a good place, I guess." At least, she says, she is paid fully and on time.

DAVID TUDONE, an officer of Color Glass and Design, is suspicious when people ask questions about his plant. Although he refuses to let a reporter into the plant, he agrees to be interviewed in his small paneled office just inside the locked front door.

The odor of what smells like epoxy resins is overpowering, even in the office, and nearly gags the reporter. But Tudone dismisses it. "That isn't epoxy you smell," he says. It is, he says, polyester, a chemical used in the casting process he has formulated for a new type of plastic jewelry. Federal limits on exposure are 50 parts per million in the workplace, he says.

"I doubt there's more than three parts per million in the plant," he maintains, though he concedes that it has never been measured.

Tudone is a serious 31-year-old man who started in the jewelry business seven years ago with his father. Tudone runs the business now, he says, and is doing well with a special line of plastic jewelry he casts and paints for Avon.

He says he is secretive about his plant because the jewelry industry is filled with people who will steal others' designs to "make a quick buck."

"You can't afford to trust people in this business," he says.

Still, he eventually allows a reporter a one-minute "peek" inside his plant. It is a long, low-ceilinged manufacturing operation that appears to include three large rooms adjoining each other. An epoxy operation is in one room, boxing and packaging in a second, and the casting and mixing operation in a third.

Two wall fans, one off, are the only apparent ventilation in the plant where 30 people work. All windows are covered with plywood.

There is a heavy paint odor in the plant, but Tudone insists: "We have excellent ventilation."

THROUGH THE SUMMER, Nancy says, a few girls quit because of the odors. Another girl gets rashes and "like pimples" on her arms and face wherever epoxy touches her skin.

Nancy works there two months. She is laid off the end of August. That bothers her because she works hard and still needs money, she says. But she has no major complaints other than the occasional headaches and sick feelings when the wall fans are not running.

Four other women, interviewed separately, complain of similar conditions, each asserting that the fans in the walls are turned on only a few hours a day. Tudone, each says, is fanatical about keeping the doors locked. One maintains that there is even a special code for knocking on the doors if you are an employee and want to get inside.

THE COMPLAINTS bring a reporter back to Color Glass at the end of the summer for a final, unannounced visit. Reluctantly, Tudone agrees to give him a look inside.

A large wall fan creates some air movement in the otherwise sealed room. Four women are putting epoxy on jewelry. There is a small, unused bench with a local ventilation device, but it is not operating.

Tudone admits that the exhaust fans are not always on. He says the epoxy work produces few odors. The heavy odors come when the epoxy is mixed using resins, he says. Then the fans are on unless employees turn them off because of drafts.

Tudone allows a reporter into the front half of the plant, but continues to refuse access to the casting area where the plastic resins are mixed and cast for jewelry. He concedes that there are no exhaust fans at that end of the plant. There is local ventilation over the casting operations to take the plastic fumes out to the street, he says, but no room ventilation.

"There's a back door they can open if they wish," he says. OSHA, he adds, inspected the plant and found nothing wrong.

OSHA records reviewed by the *Journal-Bulletin* show Tudone's plant was visited by inspectors in 1979.

The records note the epoxy bench had local ventilation, which workers say is never used, and fans, which workers say are on only occasionally.

Further, the records note that inspectors looked only at the epoxy operation a worker complained about. As Tudone says, OSHA found nothing wrong.

Tasdell Polishing

The two floors above Color Glass and Design in Building 1-A of the Riverside Mills are busy places judging by the confusing collection of signs plastered around a staircase entrance.

Federal Polishing, Rhode Island Polishing, Amanda, R & R Enterprises, Mon Del Jewelry and Tasdell Polishing are all up there, the signs say.

But on any given day, most are not open, if they are in business at all.

This day, the only shop operating is Tasdell Polishing.

Tasdell Polishing is protected by two doors, one halfway up the third-floor staircase and the other at the top of the staircase.

The second door has a sign: "No Work."

Domenic Tacelli, president of Tasdell, answers the door after it is pounded on for several minutes. The sign, he explains, is to keep out "drop-ins" who are always searching for a few days' work.

Yesterday, he said, he hired one at $5 an hour to polish. But today, the man did not return. Tacelli shrugs:

"It's one of the things we have to live with. The best polishers all go to work for the bigger firms where they can get benefits and vacations and things. I'm just a small shop. I can't afford any of that. A man gets an hourly wage here and that's all. When there's work, he works. When there isn't work, he gets fired."

Tacelli is clearly a man not afraid of work. He wears old work clothes, and his hands are split and covered with the grime of one who polishes jewelry 12 hours a day.

This day he is working alone with his son at a bank of a dozen polishing wheels. Since they are working alone, they say, they have not bothered turning on the blower system designed to take away any silica and metal-fiber dust created in the polishing process.

"It's too much noise anyway," he says.

Tacelli says he's been polishing for 25 years. "I've been a cop. I've been a little of everything," he announces.

Right now, he's a full-time polisher having trouble making ends meet. "Business is bad. Been that way for two years now," he says. Today, he and his son are polishing gold rings. They get 4 cents for each ring. "If we work steady and don't take breaks" they can polish 300 an hour.

That means $12, a price that doesn't leave much room for overhead and supplies, he says. "Now, I can hire somebody for $5 an hour and still make a buck or two on the job, but it's tight. So, like I say, we don't get the best of help here. We usually do it ourselves."

Premier Metal Specialties

Before you even walk through the door, you hear it. And nowhere in four floors of the plant are you away from it. It is a deep, earth-rattling pounding of big machines that never stops till the day ends. It is the sound of metal being cut, shaped and stamped into jewelry.

The sound comes from Premier Metal Specialties, a factory where buckles and metal jewelry clasps for various types of clothing are made from rows of constantly stomping machines.

In a single operation, the jewelry is cut from ribbons of steel, shaped, fitted together and spit out into barrels. The men who tend these machines spend eight hours a day in noise levels so high it is necessary to shout into their ears to be heard.

The company, its president says, makes sure everyone is equipped each day with earplugs to muffle the sounds.

But in all but two cases, the plugs hang uselessly around the workers' necks instead of over their ears. "We can't get most of them to use them," a foreman shouts. "They say they gotta hear the machines. When something goes wrong, they say, they wanta hear it."

Premier Metal Specialties is the largest, most modern plant in the complex. Its work areas are clean, well-lighted and, workers say, managed with a minimum of harassment.

"It's not a country club, but I got no complaints," says one employee assembling buckles.

Raymond DiPetrillo, the 35-year-old president and the owner of the blue Mercedes parked outside, says he and his managers work hard to make conditions as good as possible.

"It's not that I'm such a great humanitarian. It's just good for production," he says.

THE PRODUCTION occupies three floors in an entire wing of the mill complex.

On the ground floor, in a windowless cellar-like room, steam rises from two banks of plating into which two men constantly lower and raise racks of jewelry.

There are exhaust fans in walls and hoods over several of the tanks that suck most of the fumes and acrid odor. DiPetrillo says it all meets health and safety standards, but admits that "it is not a nice place to work." One of the company's priorities is to find a new plating facility.

The pounding machines are in a wing of the second floor. The factory's degreasing tank — a large, tub like structure in which metal is dipped into trichloroethylene — is next to the entrance to the wing.

An old man works over the tanks, pulling up cleaned jewelry findings slowly so that the fumes in the tank have time to be condensed by a ribbon of cold-water coils near the top.

He fidgets with a gas mask-like device that he says he has been ordered to wear whenever he works over the tanks. But DiPetrillo candidly says the mask has proved ineffective and but for show the old man never bothers putting it on.

"He had it on today because he knew you were coming," DiPetrillo admits.

Twice, he says, the company has switched chemicals in the tank to make it safer to work with, but each time switched back because "the chemicals we were told to switch to turned out to be more harmful than the one we used before."

The factory has a tool room, a room for designers and a "quality control room" where finished jewelry is inspected by electronic machines.

Most of the 125 workers are unskilled, low-paid assemblers, electric solderers and press operators.

DIPETRILLO DOESN'T dispute the low wages and repetitive nature of much of the unskilled work. His firm does what it can to make the work attractive.

Though he says he starts unskilled help off at minimum wage, he says everybody makes more than that after a few months or less on the job. The better workers make 40 cents an hour or more over minimum wage for the lowest-skilled jobs in the factory, he says.

After 60 days a new worker gets a benefit package including paid holidays and individual Blue Cross coverage with the option to buy family memberships at group rates.

For those who stay long enough, he adds, there is a paid vacation. But labor turnover in the factory, he says, is 20 percent a year, even in the best of times.

"We have people that fall into the pattern of working as long as they need until they get enough credits to collect (unemployment)," he says of the turnover.

For many jewelry factories, he says, such an arrangement works well. But his operates on a steady supply of buckle orders and needs steady work.

"I shouldn't say this, I suppose. But it makes me mad. You have these places that advertise for jewelry workers and say they have good pay, benefits, paid vacations and holidays.

"But they bring in the people for a few months, then lay them off. I'll bet a paycheck most never see those benefits," he says.

Colonial Industries

On the other side of the mill complex, far from the sound of Premier Metal's pounding machines and a world away from the blue Mercedes outside, Richard Carvalho struggles to become a new jewelry success story.

Three months before, Carvalho, 26, formed Colonial Industries with a few thousand dollars and a contract to solder cheap costume jewelry rings for a friend.

It wasn't a big start. And now, near summer's end, it hasn't gotten much bigger.

A single workbench cluttered with Dunkin' Donuts coffee cups, illegal asbestos soldering boards, solvents, solder and cups of water to cool the finished product are all there is to the production.

Two women sit at that bench. One is 62 and frail in a worn brown sweater with holes in its sleeves, bent over setting pieces of rings together for soldering. She is Carvalho's mother.

The other is a 20-year-old woman hired at minimum wage who says she hopes to become a musician. She sits on the other side using a butane torch and lead solder to fuse the pieces together.

No, the young woman smiles, she doesn't want her name used. She's been soldering in small shops since she was 15 years old. Her girlfriend's mother taught her the job weekends and nights. "I really don't like this work. But it's work," she says.

Carvalho's mother does like the work. "I couldn't sit home and do nothing," Nina Carvalho smiles. "I'd rather be here working. Besides, it helps my son," she says.

Mrs. Carvalho has been working in jewelry shops off and on all her life. It was for extra money at first. When her husband died and her son was still in elementary school, it was to put food on the table.

At 17, Richard Carvalho went out and got a job to help buy that food. It was, like his mother's, in jewelry — a plating shop where he broke off pins on plating racks and got the racks ready for stringing again.

That job led to one as a tubber, dipping jewelry in tanks of acid to clean it off before plating. Then he was a degreaser, dipping jewelry into tanks of trichloroethylene to get grease off it. Eventually, he became a plater's helper and finally a plater.

Though he is only 26, his hands and arms are scarred and pock-marked.

"They're not burns, they're acid marks," he says. "But not all of them. Some are from cyanide."

"If you get cyanide in any cut or scrape, you're going to get a scar. There's no way it won't cause a scar. That's how I got this, and this and this one here, too," he says, pointing to more marks.

"Course, it was my fault for never wearing gloves. But most platers don't like gloves. With gloves, you can drop a rack and splash yourself too easy. It's better to be sure-handed and take the burns. They don't hurt anyway," he says.

MORE THAN the soldering bench where his mother works, Richard Carvalho is counting on making money in his old line of work — plating.

During the day he helps solder the cheap rings. Late afternoons and nights, he works to find old plating equipment and install it along the outer wall on the other side of the mill space he has secured.

"In a month or so, I'll be operating. Everything looks a little old, but it works good," he says. Carvalho has also installed a bank of fans to vent any chemicals that boil off the tanks.

To an observer, the operation looks better than a dozen well-known shops — with one exception. Carvalho's degreasing tank is an open 55-gallon drum with trichloroethylene sitting in the bottom of it.

He plans to run it "kinda cold," he says, so it doesn't generate fumes. As soon as he has enough money, he adds, he will get a proper degreaser.

"I'm not looking to get rich," he says. "I just wanta make a good living."

How I wrote the story

The story

"Behind the glitter lies a tarnished world" was the main piece on the second day of the six-day series. It was essentially written to take the reader on a journey into a part of the industry not widely seen or understood.

I don't recall the week it was completed, or even the week about six months before that when the research began. But I remember the day I drove into the old mill complex at 50 Aleppo St., looking for jewelry shops.

It was late winter, 1980, and steam and various noxious fumes seemed to ooze from every pore of the old brick buildings. There didn't seem to be any main entrance, just a series of side doors and loading platforms where the wind had piled up assorted debris.

I felt like I'd stumbled into an industrial backwater. In a way, I had.

I drove around, jotting down the names on all the signs and my initial impressions of the place. There were 16 separate jewelry shops, according to the signs. Some were handwritten above loading docks. Some had permanent "help wanted" advertisements attached.

In future months, I'd tour a half-dozen such old mills honeycombed with similar jewelry shops. But I knew from the start that I would concentrate on this first mill on Aleppo Street.

In the early stages, I didn't know what kind of story I would write about the place, or even if I would write a separate story on it. But as I worked other aspects of the jewelry series, I kept going back to this mill complex.

Sometimes, I just drove through on my way somewhere else, and watched people coming and going for a few minutes. Other times, I'd stop and chat with a worker or two. It had that kind of attraction, that kind of feel to it. I couldn't get the place out of my mind.

I think I did this four or five times over a

month or so before I got the idea that I would make a study of the place for the series. It was then late spring of 1980.

In July, August and September, I concentrated heavily on the place, visiting it more than a dozen times for lengthy interviews with workers leaving work or just hanging around looking for work. From these people, I began to collect stories of what it was like to work inside. Several times, they referred me to former workers, whom I traced down and interviewed at their homes. I also went to the homes of eight current workers, to interview their families and get a sense of what their lives were like outside the job.

At least one firm in the complex, I learned, was running an extensive homework network (sending jewelry work out for people to do in their homes, at rates that violated minimum-wage standards).

In a bit of foolishness (I usually sneer at reporters trying to play the role of cop), I staked out the place until I established what I thought was a pattern of work being shipped out to people's homes. I really didn't have much, but I confronted the owner with it anyway. Somewhat to my surprise, he agreed to lay out his entire operation for me. He even opened up his secret record books, which detailed the homework operation, and helped me set up interviews with some of his homeworkers.

(This is one of the few times in the entire series I agreed to take information for use without publicly naming the firm or owner. So, while I later used this information in the series, I could not name it in the story on the mill complex.)

That left 15 other firms in the complex. I began moving into those job shops and factories one by one.

In most cases, I got extensive tours of the shops. In all cases, I met the shop owners or managers and got at least a peek at the operations.

More interviews with workers on the job followed, and return visits to many of the shops.

By October, I was ready to begin putting it all together.

The early writing

In a way, the writing on this piece began the first day I happened onto the mill complex. After driving around the complex, I went back to the *Journal-Bulletin* office and wrote a description of what I had seen and felt.

On many of my trips out there after that, I did the same. In part, this was for note keeping. On a long-term story, with many parts being reported at once, notes get stale fast, so I try to put the stuff in writing immediately, in sort of vignette form, to preserve the tone and feel of the interview, as well as the accuracy of quotes and factual data.

If I've taped part of the interview, I make a working transcription of it, so I can see at a glance what I've got and haven't got, and so I can merge the information with observations or notes I may take.

A few words more about this technique. You can't do this enough on a series. With other stories and research running at the same time, it's essential to get notes and impressions and such things as physical descriptions down on paper (or terminal screen) as they happen and unfold.

I didn't always get it done, and it hurt. You can't expect to catch the description and detail of the moment several months after the event by flipping through a notebook.

I also learned that in the process of reporting there are moments of inspiration regarding the writing that will be lost if they are not put down at the time. In the end, the inspiration may turn out to be mush that can't be used. But sometimes, it will be the difference between a flat story and a vibrant one.

Organizing the writing

The actual drafts of the story were written, as I recall, in October and November, 1980. (I polished and updated the story several months later, when the series was closer to publication.)

I knew at this point that I wanted the story to be a journey of sorts into the mill complex and the various jewelry shops housed there. The problem was how to lead off and get the reader, and myself, going on the journey.

I reviewed my typed notes and vignettes. Fortunately, I had done a long running account of my meeting with Carl Pfanstiehl and follow-up interviews with him. The image of him sitting on that weedy stone wall with his hand bandaged, waiting to be called back to work inside, was a natural.

The only problem, from a writing point of view, was his name. Pfanstiehl is hard to get by without a pause, and it was the second word in the lead. I remember wishing he had an easier name to digest. But then, nothing perfect is real.

Hard name or not, Pfanstiehl was my man. He had to be in the lead.

From there, the organization was fairly simple. I would move from firm to firm, mixing comments of workers and employers with physical descriptions of conditions and, when possible, with records of official inspections.

The first firm would be the one Pfanstiehl worked in, which happened also to be one I had extensive notes on. After that firm, the natural selection was to move the reader to the neighboring firms in that section of the mill.

That meant the House of Borrelli would come first, Double B Industries second and Loupal Originals third.

From there I decided on simply jumping around the complex, mixing the firms according to size and type of manufacturing.

In all, I used seven firms. They fairly represented the type of jewelry work being done in the old mill, and fairly represented the conditions. I had tried to find a way to give brief descriptions of all 16 firms, and even wrote them.

But the story was unmanageable, and far too long. Also, I felt I could not mention the homework activities of that one shop where I had agreed no names would be used; to write about that shop ignoring the homework was out of the question.

The main writing

It's hard to separate the writing from the organization. Actually, the organization came about in part by trial and error. The lead stayed the same, but a lot of decisions on what would be used and what would not came about by trial and error in the writing.

I remember at one point that the story was nearly twice as long as it finally appeared, and that is pretty darn long.

Also, as the first rough drafts were begun it was clear that there remained holes in some of the reporting that had to be filled. Part of this was due to not having transcribed my notes fully enough during the earlier reporting. Part was faulty reporting. But part is a natural process in doing a long-term story.

I had, for example, an interview with a young polisher at one of the firms who said he had worked extra hard to prove himself, only to be laid off as soon as work got slow. I wanted to use the hope of this young man, but realized I hadn't verified his employment or talked to the chief polisher about his performance.

Was what he said true? Was he a good worker? I went back to the firm and found both to be true, and got a fresh look inside the place, to boot.

You never know fully what you have and don't have until you actually start to write. A second stage of reporting is, in my experience, always a must on such a project.

I made several more trips out to the mill complex for another reason, as well. I like to write with clear images and feelings for the people and events in the story; often, having good notes and replaying a tape or two bring back those images vividly. Sometimes they don't.

I remember this was particularly true with a story on homeworkers that was part of the series. Months before I wrote the story, I had spent a day with a woman in a three-decker in the city of Pawtucket. She was old, alone, surrounded by pictures of her children and a husband who had left her.

Before I could write the piece, though, I had to go back to that apartment again and sit with her. This was not for more quotes or information, or even detail — I had all that. I just wanted to get close to the source of the story again, to the feel of the story.

For the story appearing here, it was the mill complex. The last thing I did, before writing the first draft, was to go out and walk around the place.

The Class of '56: It was a very good year

By Doug Cumming
The Providence Journal, October 5, 1981

The long, bittersweet season of high school reunions is winding down.

In the spring the old graduates begin clustering, drawn like locusts by a magic number of years. They bring to country club ballrooms and places like the Venus de Milo in Swansea the booze-and-buffet airs of a testimonial. But this particular American institution is really much more than that.

A high school reunion is a sudden compression of history. The yearbook's "ideal senior" comes back as a clinical psychologist from Pittsburgh; the girl who was class vice president is a radio host playing "adult contemporary" music.

The life stories tell what became of an era, how its spirit survived or floundered through wars and presidencies, through inflation and a rising divorce rate. Social classes are not as strong in America, it seems, as the year of one's graduation from high school. That's what sets the stamp.

Not upper-middle or lower-middle, but the Class of '56.

The East Providence High School Class of '56 gathered Saturday night at the Venus de Milo for its 25-year reunion, its silver anniversary. (The season for reunions usually peaks around June, graduation time, but reunions for high school classes seem to be continuing well past the summer this year.)

A RED BANNER hangs behind the small jazz combo, proclaiming EAST PROVIDENCE SENIOR HIGH SCHOOL. Many of the name tags, with their pictures from the 1956 *Crimson,* have come unstuck from lapels and dresses. So classmates frequently greet each other through a fog of memory, a dream-recognition of a long-lost brother without a full name. "John," says one man, over and over, frantically shaking hands with another. "John. John.... Big John."

Many look prosperous. Teresia Ostrach — Terry Hamel in high school — has come up from New York, where she is an executive of Dunhill Temporary Systems. She is aiming a Polaroid flash camera at a friend, then recognizes another face.

"How are you ... uh, Charlie?" she asks a man in a red blazer who holds a shot glass of bourbon.

"Bob," he answers, "Bob Cooper. You're probably thinking of Charlie Reilly. We look alike."

She remembers them both. Robert G. Cooper had been sports editor of *The Townie,* the school newspaper. He had enlisted after graduation, spent a few years in Italy, went to college, married, had three children and became assistant to the president of ITT-Grinnell. His look-alike, Charles T. Reilly, is the former chairman of the Democratic State Committee and an insurance company executive.

IT WAS a fine time to be a teenager, 1956. Eisenhower was president and Ronald Reagan was your host on "Death Valley." You could go to the Alhambra Ballroom at Crescent Park, or the Friday Nite Teenage Dance at Rhodes-on-the-Pawtuxet, where admission was "50 cents plus proper dress and proper behavior." Bill Haley was in "Rock Around the Clock" at your local cinema.

You could buy a '56 Hillman convertible for $1,465, advertised with an older use of words: "Hey Look! The Gay Look.... We're living in a happy era — and the '56 Hillman is completely in harmony with the times — luscious, luxurious, alive!"

Almost everybody at the reunion remembered the era that way: happy, happy, happy. John L. Palazzi, manager of a trucking firm, leaned against the bar and talked about how much more you appreciated what you got back then. Guidelines were clearer. Happiness more accessible. "I'm making more money now than I ever have in my life, but I'm not getting any further ahead."

Indeed, the East Providence Class of '56 seems possessed with a collective urge to return to itself, not only in the reunions every five years, but also in marriage. Palazzi married a classmate. Some have divorced classmates and remarried other classmates.

There have been heartbreaks, failures and deaths. Nine deaths out of a class of 358: from cancer, suicide, alcoholism, car accident, heart attack.

In part, it is a trick of memory that makes the good old days seem so good. It is the ancient fable of Paradise Lost, of innocence betrayed. Nowhere is this wistful sense stronger than in the late hours of a high school reunion.

"It was like 'Happy Days.' That's exactly what it was," said Jacqueline Bryant. "The class was like a family."

Mrs. Bryant, who lives three blocks from where she grew up in East Providence, was almost made to repeat her senior year because allergies had kept her home a total of 89 days. "It didn't bother me; I would've enjoyed doing it again."

THE 150 CLASSMATES came back from as far away as California, Florida and Texas. Peter Whitford, a compact, soft-spoken businessman, flew in from Houston, Tex., but not in his own jet this time ("It's not the greatest place in the world to live, no, but it's a living.") He is wearing a suit, a starched white shirt and a tightly knotted tie.

Joseph Conti, who still lives in Seekonk, Mass., sidles up and shakes Whitford's hand. Conti removes a toothpick from his mouth to explain that he works for Leviton, an electrical manufacturing plant in Warwick. This is the first reunion Conti has been able to attend. He remembers Whitford ("steady, always a solid person") from the year they were both on the state wrestling team, and the wrestling team won the state championship.

"What do you do for extracurricular activities?" Conti asked. "Like, to keep yourself in shape?"

"Oh, for about 20 years, I've played racquetball," Whitford said.

"Really," Conti said. "You must be pretty good."

"I THINK WE were lucky to have been raised in the 1950s, because we were taught the traditional values." Joan Crocker Pfeiffer, the class vice president, is reading her speech into a microphone at the front of the room.

"And yet we were young enough at the time, open-minded enough, not set in our ways, to respond to the changes that happened in the '60s and the early '70s. And we were able to hold on to the best of both worlds."

Ten years ago, she was divorced, lonely and living in New Jersey. An invitation came to her, out of the blue, to attend the class's 15-year reunion. Why not? she thought.

At the reunion, Joan Crocker saw an old classmate, Peter W. Pfeiffer Jr., who was also divorced. The two had not known each other very well in high school. Shortly after that reunion in 1971, she married him and came back home.

"Oh, there are a few extra pounds here and there," she is saying, "a wrinkle or two, or three or four maybe, a little gray hair, maybe not as much hair, but we're still young."

How I wrote the story

My story on the 25th reunion of East Providence High began as an assignment from Al Johnson, *Journal* city editor. He suggested in a note that we might pull a good feature out of one of the reunions that had been appearing for months, as brief advances, in our zone pages. He attached a recent Boston *Globe* article as evidence. It wove historical flashbacks in italics *(Nasser seized the Suez Canal. Chet Huntley teamed up with David Brinkley. Don Larsen pitched a perfect game...)* into a roving-reporter account of a 25th-year party for Waltham High. Al also attached the latest advances on reunions. Five were impending; he had circled the 1941 class of Mount Pleasant High School.

1941 didn't pan out. I called the organizer

(these poking-around pre-story phone calls can be awkward, but are important) and learned that the class was small and had held reunions every five years. Chances of good, revealing material seemed slim. So I made another call, and found what seemed to be a better opportunity at the East Providence 25th.

The challenge of the story, I knew from the start, would be to tap the inner meaning, music and pathos of the thing. I expected a fairly dull event, and it exceeded my expectations. So: How do I get at the hidden poetry?

Background, for starters. I went to the Providence Public Library and spun through microfilm of May, 1956, *Journal*s. This is an experience no reporter should miss; if not for a story, then simply for the way the Zeitgeist lingers, sometimes ridiculously, in old news and ads — especially the ads. I also reread a John Updike short story called "The Egg Race," because I remembered that it had an excellent high school reunion scene in it — a 25th year, in fact.

Now here's the problem. How do I bring the part of me that responds to Updike and to the civilized melancholy of Cheever (the other writer who came to mind) in writing a Providence *Journal* feature? I had some real feelings about that reunion, about the place of a class in history, and about my own place and memory. I couldn't enter the scene as a subjective member of the reunion class (as Updike does in his third-person protagonist, or as *Journal* reporter Doug Allan could have done in reality for this party). Yet I didn't want to be an objective reporter — couldn't be: An objective reporter would have shrugged and left. I was some wistful angel-ghost looking down on the whole phenomenon of high school reunions, brimming with emotion, but lacking a reason to be there.

I did all I could to excavate material to support the emotion. I used a tape recorder at the party, stayed late, eavesdropped all over the place. The next day, I went to the organizer's house for more detail, and to pore over yearbooks. This is what they call tertiary recovery in the oil industry. But there simply wasn't much there.

I wrote the story on Sunday, two days after the event, for Monday's *Journal*.

I started by transcribing my tape and notes, separating this material into a rough sequence of scenes. When I began writing, I set the scene with the red banner at the end of room. I knew my ending would be with Joan Crocker Pfeiffer's speech, because it seemed to give meaning to the event, and also to express her character.

But beginning with the red banner wasn't satisfying. So I added an introductory sentence about reunions — something about the bittersweet feeling, I think. I expanded on this. I wrote slowly, polishing as I went, as if writing poetry.

I found myself speaking for myself, actually discoursing upon the meaning of what happened. This pattern of focus is the opposite of most journalism. I started big and abstract, and then focused on a scene; I did the same thing in miniature for each scene in the story ("It was a fine time to be a teenager," "In part, it is a trick of memory that makes the good old days seem so good"). This is a pattern used well by Cheever. He talks about a type of town, party, marriage, whatever; lets fly a few disembodied details; and then slides decorously into focus. It seems to violate all the rules of good reporting: Leave yourself out; show, don't tell. But somehow, in this story, if I didn't tell, the event would have had a lot less to show.

Incident in Ward 4

By Bruce DeSilva
The Providence Sunday Journal, December 20, 1981

CRANSTON — 11 p.m. Monday Nov. 16.
Tom Terracciano, registered nurse, reported for the graveyard shift on Ward 4 of the Mathias Building at the state General Hospital. Except for muffled footsteps, the ward was silent. Thirty-nine chronically ill men and women — suffering from stroke, injury and old age — slept in steel hospital beds in rooms arranged along both sides of a hallway lighted by fluorescent tubes.

Terracciano, the only nurse on duty in Ward 4 between 11 and 7, usually began his shift by looking in on all of his patients.

But not this time.

The building supervisor was off, so Terraccciano took charge. He checked each ward to see who had reported for work. He found an overtime replacement for a worker who had called in sick. He sat in the nurses' office on Ward 4 and filled out payroll sheets.

About 1 a. m., as Terracciano remembers it, he finished those administrative duties and began checking on his patients. Two hours had passed since the start of the third shift.

Albert Farrands, 76, lay on his bed under extra blankets. His breathing was shallow.

Terracciano peeled the blankets away and saw fluid oozing from gauze pads draped over the old man's skinny legs. He could not arouse the patient.

He took the man's blood pressure. It was 60/40, dangerously low.

The patient was in shock.

ALBERT FARRANDS, who once ran a hotel in East Greenwich, had been a patient at the state hospital since his stroke more than three years ago. He suffered from a seizure disorder and from several conditions of old age including arteriosclerosis.

He could not speak and was confined to bed and a wheelchair.

Several hospital employees who knew him said he always had a blank look on his face. They said his expression hadn't changed in years.

That's how Farrands looked to all of the workers except Anthony Barkett, a 41-year-old hulk who was hired as an attendant last May. Where others saw nothing, Barkett looked closer and detected an occasional quiver about the mouth and light in the eyes.

"He always appreciated what you did for him," Barkett said. "He smiled."

One of the things Farrands liked best, Barkett said, was to be washed while sitting in the Century Tub, a rectangular porcelain tank filled with swirling warm water.

Hospital officials said most patients get washed in these tubs once or twice a week, but Barkett bathed all of his patients more often. He bathed Farrands in the Century Tub almost every day that he worked in the ward.

About 8:30 p.m. on Nov. 16, 2½ hours before Terracciano started work, Barkett pushed Farrands' wheelchair across the black and tan tiles of the Ward 4 bathroom to the Century Tub.

Barkett, working a double shift, was into his 14th hour on duty. He had just given two other patients baths. Farrands was to be the last bath of the day.

The attendant turned the mixing valve and stuck his hand under the water that gushed into the tub though the green hose. It felt comfortably warm. In a few minutes, when the tub was full, the needle on the tub's round temperature gauge read about 95.

Barkett dipped his hand in just to be sure. Then he put the wheel chair next to a white vinyl seat, slid Farrands into it, strapped him in and pushed a button. A hydraulic lift raised the vinyl seat and its passenger over the lip of the tub and deposited him in the water in a sitting position. The water came up to his chest. The attendant flipped the aerator switch and the water began swirling.

Barkett squirted some soap into the tank and yanked on thin rubber gloves. The gloves barely reached the big attendant's wrists.

The mute little man sat still, a peaceful look on his face, as Barkett gently rubbed him with a white washcloth. At times, Barkett was up to his elbows in the water.

Barkett estimates that the bath took five to eight minutes. Guesses from hospital officials range as high as 12.

When the bath was done, Barkett pushed the button on the hydraulic lift again and Farrands rose dripping from the tub.

Barkett began toweling him, then suddenly stopped.

The little man's legs were red. Wisps of white skin were peeling from his ankles.

Farrands had been burned.

Barkett looked in puzzlement at his own unburned arms and hollered for the licensed practical nurse.

FROM THE MOMENT of the accident, Albert Farrands was fighting for his life, in the opinion of several physicians interviewed about the case.

About 20 percent of the patient's body had second-degree burns — burns that destroyed two of the three layers of skin — Farrands' medical record shows.

His feet, the backs of his legs, the front of his legs below the knees, and his buttocks all had second-degree burns, said a Rhode Island Hospital doctor, one of several physicians who eventually became involved in the case.

The doctor, who asked not to be named, said that injuries such as Farrands suffered would be serious, but probably not fatal, to an otherwise healthy 76-year-old man. But Farrands was far from healthy. With the best of care, he had no better than a 50 percent chance of survival, the doctor said.

Dr. Donald S. Gann, chief of surgery at Rhode Island Hospital, never saw the patient but said that a burn of the extent described was life-threatening to an already seriously ill elderly man.

Dr. William Q. Sturner, chief state medical examiner, after examining the patient's medical records and autopsy results, concurred that the injury was life-threatening.

Proof of that, he said, is that the burns ultimately killed Albert Farrands.

IN RESPONSE to Barkett's call for help, Jeannette J. Joyal strode into the bathroom. The licensed practical nurse stared at the patient and yelled for the registered nurse in charge, Irene Riley.

Mrs. Riley appeared in seconds, looked at the patient's legs, walked briskly from the bathroom to the nurses station a few yards away and telephoned the doctor on call.

Barkett wheeled Farrands into his room and slid him from the wheelchair to his bed.

Mrs. Riley appeared and began applying vaseline-coated sterile gauze to the patient's legs. It was a popular treatment for burns when she was in nursing school 40 years ago.

The doctor was there in minutes.

He looked at the patient's legs and pronounced that he had second-degree burns. The nurse should continue with the treatment she had begun, he said. Then he left.

Mrs. Riley and Nurse Joyal finished wrapping Farrands' legs in Vaseline-coated guaze. They gave him some Tylenol for pain and put extra blankets over him.

It was 9 p.m.

Mrs. Riley made the following entry in her nurse's notes:

"Attendant put patient in whirlpool and apparently the H2O was too hot although the attendant said that the water was set between 90-95. When patient taken out of the tub, the skin was peeling — Dr. Albala notified and saw pt. and stated pt. had second degree burns — sterile vaseline gauze applied to legs, but he was burned from the waist down. Irene Riley."

Mrs. Riley confirmed the accuracy of her notes and said no other treatment was prescribed before she left for the day at 11.

In fact, Vaseline gauze and Tylenol were all the patient was to receive for at least the first five hours after the accident.

The charge nurse refused to comment further on the case and nurse Joyal declined to comment at all. They, and almost everyone else at the hospital connected with the case, were warned by hospital administrators that talking about it could violate the state's patient privacy law.

ABOUT 11, Terracciano and five attendants arrived to man the 39-patient ward for the third shift.

Before leaving for the day, Mrs. Riley told Terracciano about the accident. The patient was sleeping and stable, she said. She had been checking his blood pressure periodically through the evening, although she neglected to record that in her notes.

Terracciano got the impression that Farrands' injury wasn't serious, so he turned to his temporary building supervisor chores.

THEN CAME 1 A.M., when he finally pulled back Farrands' covers.

Several telephone calls were made from Ward 4 in the next half-hour, Farrands' medical record shows. The first two were to Farrands' relatives. The third, at 1:30, was placed to the physician on call.

Although Ward 4 is part of the sprawling state medical hospital, it operates as a nursing home. Acutely ill patients are not admitted to this ward, and patients who become acutely ill while there often are transferred to other parts of the hospital.

The physician on call issued an order over the telephone. Farrands was to be moved to Ward 6 of the Louis Pasteur Building, the state hospital's intensive-care area.

Farrands' medical record contains the following entry:

"Dr. Albala was called (at) 1:30 a.m. and notified of pts condition. Authorized verbal order for transferral to LP6 — T. Terracciano, RN."

Terracciano and his attendants slid Farrands into a gurney and wheeled him through a connecting corridor to LP6.

It was about 2 a.m., more than five hours after the accident.

A PATIENT with burns like those Farrands suffered faces two serious threats, according to Dr. Gann, the Rhode Island Hospital chief of surgery.

The first is infection. Bacteria can invade the body through areas no longer protected by three layers of skin.

The second is dehydration. Fluids begin leaking into the damaged areas because of a variety of complicated biological mechanisms. Blood volume declines. The heart beats faster and blood vessels constrict to try to keep blood pressure up. This works for a while. Then blood pressure collapses.

In an old man with several diseases, both of these risks are multiplied and either can kill him, Dr. Gann said.

To prevent infection, an anti-bacterial ointment should be applied, Dr. Gann said. There is controversy about how soon this needs to be done, with some physicians maintaining it is not needed for hours. At Rhode Island Hospital, it is usually done immediately.

Vaseline, Dr. Gann said, provides no protection from infection.

To prevent dehydration, the patient needs fluids. Usually, a saline solution is administered intravenously, Dr. Gann said.

The chief of surgery listened to a description of the patient and the extent of his burns as described in the medical records. It is almost inevitable, he said, that such a patient will go into shock if fluids are not administered promptly.

One of the Rhode Island Hospital physicians who was later to participate in Farrands' care concurred. Farrands needed fluid desperately after the accident, he said. It was important to start the treatment within the first two hours and it would have been better to start it immediately, he said.

When Terracciano pulled back the covers at 1 a.m., what he saw was an old man who had been robbed of his body fluids by his burns, Dr. Gann, Dr. Sturner and the Rhode Island Hospital physician all agreed.

Dr. Maurice Albala refused to answer a reporter's questions about the case. He referred inquiries to the hospital's legal department. The department issued a statement saying specifics of the patient's case could not be discussed.

Dr. Johannes Virks, chief of medical services at the hospital, issued the following statement:

"I have carefully reviewed the patient's treatment record. The review of the evidence in the case record and the information provided to me by physicians who were involved in the treatment of this patient has revealed that medical management of the case was appropriate and competent."

FARRANDS spent the early morning hours in LP6. Then he was taken by ambulance to the Rhode Island Hospital Emergency Department, where he was logged in at 9:42 a.m.

It is uncertain what was done for Farrands at LP6. Medical records for this period could not be obtained. Workers in the ward declined to talk.

But there is evidence that care on the ward was good.

When Farrands arrived at Rhode Island Hospital, his blood pressure was up. It was not good, but it was much better than it had been at 1 a.m.

He had rallied from the early morning crisis.

Furthermore, Farrands had a full bladder. A catheter was inserted to help him empty it. Dehydrated patients usually don't have full bladders.

The improved blood pressure and the full bladder suggests that the patient had been give intravenous fluids on LP6, medical authorities said.

In the Rhode Island Hospital emergency room, dead skin was stripped from Farrands' burned legs and buttocks. He was washed with an anti-bacterial cleaner. An anti-bacterial ointment was spread on his burns. An intravenous needle was inserted and a saline solution was dripped into one of his veins.

About four hours later, Farrands was sent back to General Hospital with instructions for the staff to continue the ointment and fluid treatments. The treatments are not complicated, one Rhode Island Hospital doctor said. Although they are vital to the patient, they do not require sophisticated medical facilities.

WHILE FARRANDS was on his way to Rhode Island Hospital on the Tuesday morning of Nov. 17, General Hospital administrators were learning about the accident.

An internal investigation was begun.

Anthony Landi, the hospital's "risk management officer," gathered incident reports from those who were in the ward at the time of the accident.

Landi found that the round temperature gauge on the tub consistently read 10 degrees colder than the water in the tank. (As of last Wednesday, it still did, although the tank has not been used since the accident.)

However, Landi said, workers in the ward knew about the gauge. They automatically added 10 degrees to whatever it read.

A mercury and glass thermometer mounted on a piece of wood was supposed to be hanging in the tub so that attendants could double-check the temperature, Landi said, but on the day of the accident the thermometer was missing.

Barkett said that in the seven months that he worked in the ward he never saw a thermometer on the tub. After the accident, one appeared there.

A field representative of the Century Tub's manufacturer was called to the hospital. He went over the machine and proclaimed it in good working order.

However, he replaced a small part in a safety valve. The valve is engineered to stop water from running into the tub the second the flow reaches 110 degrees Fahrenheit.

There was nothing wrong with the valve, the representative said, but the company is replacing that particular part with a longer-lasting component.

Hospital officials kept the old part.

Landi and other hospital officials were puzzled. Was anything wrong with the tub? Why didn't the water seem hot to the attendant?

They had no answers.

They still don't.

Two things can affect the severity of burns, doctors say. One is the temperature and the other is the length of time a person is exposed to that temperature. Therefore, it is possible, but not proved, that someone taking their arms in and out of a bath would not be burned, while someone who was sitting in it for a period of time would be.

The state police are trying to find answers. They are still questioning hospital workers, and last week they impounded the part taken from the valve.

FARRANDS went back to Rhode Island Hospital on Nov. 25 after gangrene developed on his toes. Emergency room doctors decided that the condition was superficial, affecting only the skin and nails. They sent him back to the General Hospital.

Two days later, Albert Farrands was dead.

He got infected. His resistance was low. He went quickly.

It was Nov. 27, the day after Thanksgiving.

The state medical examiner's office later concluded that the infection resulted from the burns.

ON THE MORNING of Nov. 28, Farrands' body lay on an autopsy table in the General Hospital morgue. Incisions were being made. Organs were being weighed.

A big man stood watching the pathologist work.

Anthony Barkett had to know what had killed that little man. He didn't believe the water was hot enough to do it.

He still doesn't.

How I wrote the story

Albert Farrands, a 76-year-old patient at the state-run hospital for the chronically ill, was dead — boiled to death by a whirlpool bath that was supposed to soothe his muscles.

Hospital officials kept the incident quiet; and when it finally leaked out, nearly a month later, they made contradictory statements.

Assignment: How and why did Albert Farrands die?

Deadline: Five days away.

A Rhode Island law, passed in 1978, makes it a criminal offense to break the confidentiality of a patient's medical records. But in a case like this, a lot of copies float around. The state police, the medical examiner, the attorney general's department, medical and clerical workers at the hospital and the hospital's lawyers are all potential sources.

Within two hours of getting the assignment, I had Farrands's record.

The record showed that Farrands was very sick before the accident. It noted that date and time of the accident. It showed that he lingered for several days after it. It described the seriousness of the burns — second-degree over 20 percent of his body. And it showed the treatment afterwards: nothing but Vaseline and Tylenol for at least the first five hours. And at the end of those five hours, Farrands was near death.

The story immediately took a turn. Not only the accident itself but also the treatment Farrands received afterwards had to be researched.

The records gave me the names of the three nurses who had been in charge of Farrands on three different shifts, as well as the name of the doctor who prescribed the treatment for Farrands after the accident.

Over the past 10 years, I have done dozens of stories about the state medical center. I started calling old sources. Who worked on the ward where Farrands had been treated? My sources didn't know, but promised to find out.

Within hours, they were calling back with names of attendants and nurses. They also had other news. The administration had forbidden anyone to talk about the case, threatening firing and criminal prosecution. And the word around the hospital was that Tony Barkett, the attendant who had put Farrands in the water, was to blame for the death. He had had gloves on and couldn't test the water and he had left the patient alone in the tub, they said.

The rumors about Barkett proved to be wrong.

The next day, Tuesday, I asked for the guided tour. Hospital administrators showed me the ward where Farrands had been a patient, the bathroom where he had been washed and the whirlpool that had killed him. I took in the atmosphere of the place: nurses' heels clicking on the black-and-tan tile floors, fluorescent lights running down the middle of hallways. I also found out everything I could about how the whirlpool worked, how the temperature of the water was regulated.

For the next several days, I worked almost around the clock — knocking on doors of nurses and attendants in working-class neighborhoods; making 3 a.m. calls to nurses on the overnight shift.

Most hung up the receiver or slammed the door. A few of them talked to me on the second or third attempt. No one talked without persuasion.

Here's an example of how I worked one of these sources:

The voice on the telephone gave me an instant picture. This nurse was efficient, stuck to the rules, put up with no nonsense, and had no use for reporters.

Reporter: I understand you were working the night Mr. Farrands had his accident.

Nurse: You know perfectly well I can't talk to you about that.

Reporter: I have copies of your nurse's notes from that night, and I'd like to ask you about them.

Nurse: Where did you get those? You're not supposed to have them.

Reporter: Well, I was just wondering if your notes are accurate.

Nurse: Of course they're accurate.

Reporter: Are you sure that Mr. Farrands didn't get any treatment that you failed to record?

Nurse: Most certainly not. My notes are absolutely complete.

And then she hung up.

She had given me a vital piece of information: She had confirmed what the records showed — that for hours after his accident, Farrands had gotten nothing but Tylenol and Vaseline.

So what? Maybe that's the treatment you are supposed to give to 76-year-old men with these kinds of burns. I called the experts.

One of the experts I chose had examined Farrands many hours after the accident and had ordered a change in his treatment. The other two experts listened as I described Farrands from his medical records.

Doctors don't often criticize other doctors, so it was surprising that all three were willing to say Farrands's original treatment was inadequate. I gained confidence that I was on solid ground. Two of the experts were not willing to let me use their names; the other, one of Rhode Island's most prominent surgeons, went on the record.

By Thursday afternoon, I had a lot of detail about what had happened to Albert Farrands from the moment he was put into the bath until the moment of his death.

But three pieces were missing.

First, who was Farrands? What had he done in life? What was he like? I tried repeatedly to interview members of his family. They refused to talk, and my attempts made one of them weep and beg me to go away.

Second, why had the state doctor prescribed such apparently inadequate treatment? He refused again and again to talk to me.

Third, what light could be shed on the accident itself by Tony Barkett, the attendant who had put Farrands in the whirlpool? Tony wanted no part of newspapers.

On Friday, writing day, I made another round of calls to Farrands's family, the state doctor and Barkett.

I was troubled that the physician not only wouldn't answer questions but also refused to listen to what they were. Finally, I called the public-relations man for the hospital, dictated a long list of questions for the doctor and asked that they be passed on to him. I tape-recorded this call, for my protection. The doctor was given the questions and chose not to respond.

By 2 p.m. Friday, I started to write.

The telephone rang. It was Barkett. He'd decided to talk, he said. Would I meet him at Mr. Donut in Cranston?

Barkett showed up 20 minutes late, and we talked for over an hour.

He was a simple man, honest and straightforward, with an affection for Farrands and a burden of guilt. He gave me some of the story's best moments.

The story was written between 6 p.m. Friday night and 3 a.m. Saturday morning. I chain-smoked cigars and swilled mud from the coffee machine to stay awake.

As I began, I had to decide what kind of story I wanted to write.

There are always options. The firing of nuns from teaching jobs at a parochial school can lead to a story about conflicting ideas on religious education, about politics in the Church, or about a parish rent by controversy — to name just a few possibilities.

Usually, I know what my story is about when I write the first paragraph. It was not like that with the story about Albert Farrands. I banged out two leads. One was a news lead that said a man had died at the state medical hospital after receiving inadequate treatment. The other was a description of Barkett putting the old man into the tub.

Did I want to write a story about how a doctor had made a mistake, or did I want to explain how and why an old man had died?

Several colleagues argued strongly, both before the story was written and after it was published, that I should have written a hard-news story with an accusatory tone. I had more than enough to write such a story. But this was a case of a single mistake by a single, probably overworked physician. Turning the full wrath of the Providence *Journal* on him seemed ridiculously out of proportion — like nuking a shoplifter.

Besides, there was too much more in the Farrands story that intrigued me: the characters, the ironies, the sights and sounds of the hospital, and most of all, the dramatic moments, such as when Barkett showed up at the patient's autopsy.

My story, I decided, was about how and why Farrands died. He died because he was in the wrong hospital. The immediate cause was an accident, but this hospital was the kind of place where accidents happen. It was a state-run hospital where equipment didn't work, thermometers disappeared, large wards were staffed by a single nurse, doctors responded to emergencies by issuing orders over the telephone, attendants worked exhausting double and triple shifts, and there were so many critically ill people that none of them got enough attention. It was also a place were people like Tony Barkett tried and cared.

For my lead, I selected a scene that showed graphically what kind of hospital this was. A nurse comes on duty, finds he is alone, and has to carry out administrative duties while an old man lies dying unnoticed in a nearby bed.

After that scene, I flashed back to the accident in the tub, and told the story chronologically the rest of the way through, breaking into the narrative where necessary to explain medical matters, such as the severity of the burns and the inadequacy (according to experts) of the prescribed treatment.

I ended with Barkett at the autopsy for two reasons. Chronologically, it was the logical end of the story. More important, it reinforced the irony that the man who cared the most about Farrands had a hand in his death — that the man who tried the hardest couldn't overcome faulty equipment, missing thermometers and the other shortcomings of the hospital.

VonBulow sentenced to 30 years

By Gayle Gertler
The Providence Journal-Bulletin, May 8, 1982

NEWPORT — As spectators gasped and moaned, Claus vonBulow was sentenced yesterday to 30 years in prison for trying twice to kill his wife. He then was released on bail pending the outcome of his appeal.

His $500,000 bail was increased to $1 million, effective next week.

VonBulow sat stoically as he was sentenced to 10 years in the Adult Correctional Institutions on the first count of attempted murder, and 20 years on the second. A few feet away, his daughter, Cosima, 15, clasped both hands under her chin, but betrayed no more emotion than her father.

It was the first time Cosima, the daughter of Martha and Claus vonBulow, had entered the courtroom since her father went on trial in January, accused by his two step-children of trying to kill their mother by injecting her with insulin on Dec. 27, 1979, and Dec. 21, 1980.

Superior Court Judge Thomas H. Needham said he "had planned all through the night" to hold vonBulow without bail. But he said he decided at the last minute that his "own personal doubts" that vonBulow will remain in the country could not justify refusing to set bail.

INSTEAD, NEEDHAM increased vonBulow's bail, effective on Friday. He also gave vonBulow until Friday to provide the attorney general's office with a list of assets totaling $1 million.

VonBulow's lawyers have contended that he is a millionaire in his own right, but Asst. Atty. Gen. Stephen Famiglietti has labeled their statements a "misrepresentation."

Once the list is provided, Needham said, vonBulow must put up $100,000 in cash. The Danish-born financier has been free on 10 percent surety of his $500,000 bail since he was denied a new trial early in April. He must provide the state with another $50,000 to remain free.

Needham also told vonBulow he cannot sell any of the assets he lists. But he agreed that vonBulow may leave Rhode Island to compile the list. That means that vonBulow, if he mails the list to the attorney general, need not return to Rhode Island, unless his appeal fails.

Defense lawyer John F. Sheehan filed a notice of appeal yesterday. The appeal process is expected to take up to two years.

SPECTATORS WERE LINED up outside the Newport County Courthouse an hour before vonBulow was scheduled to appear. A few shouts of "Good luck, Mr. vonBulow" greeted him as he arrived, but the crowd saved its noisiest demonstration for after the sentencing.

By then, several hundred spectators and photographers were poised to witness what is expected to be vonBulow's last leave-taking of the Newport County Courthouse. They waited patiently behind the yellow plastic tapes strung by police, then broke into applause and cheers as vonBulow strode out the side door of the courthouse.

VonBulow and defense lawyer Herald Price Fahringer smiled at the people who hung from lampposts, stood on stone fence pillars and waved wildly from the steps of the building across the street. Still smiling, they got into the yellow taxi waiting at the curb.

A new round of cheers followed the cab as it drove away.

FAHRINGER HAD ARGUED to Needham that vonBulow should get a suspended sentence on the first count, which he said was not as serious as the second count because

Mrs. vonBulow recovered. He asked that vonBulow be put into a work-release program on the second count.

The only function of prisons is to protect society from "the incorrigible offender (who) must be uprooted and isolated from the rest of us. That's the major premise of putting people into cages," Fahringer said.

"There's almost the reaction, 'Well, we've got to put him in jail,' " Fahringer said. "But does this man need rehabilitation? He doesn't. Is he a threat to the community? He isn't."

The only basis for jailing vonBulow would be to have his sentence serve as a deterrent to others about to commit the same crime, Fahringer said. But he added that studies have shown that potential punishment does not deter crime.

VonBulow, he said, is not a habitual offender, but a man who had "an unblemished record throughout his life. This is the only mark that exists on it." Fahringer said vonBulow is also a man who contributes to his community.

As evidence, Fahringer pointed to letters written by John Winslow, president of the Preservation Society of Newport County, and Mrs. John Nicholas Brown, a leader of Newport society, who testified for the defense. The letters attest to vonBulow's character and are part of the pre-sentence report given to Needham earlier this week.

Fahringer dropped his voice and raised both hands in front of him, palms up. He said that if Needham wanted to take community feeling into account, he need only look at the crowds that cheered vonBulow even after the guilty verdict. He said he had never seen such a response in 25 years of practicing criminal law.

BUT PROSECUTOR FAMIGLIETTI told Needham that vonBulow should go to prison for 40 years, the maximum allowed. He said he saw "nothing mitigating" about either count of attempted murder, even though Mrs. vonBulow recovered in 1979.

VonBulow, Famiglietti said, was greedy, intelligent and cunning, and his crimes were not committed "in the heat of passion." Instead, Famiglietti said, both attempted murders were carefully planned against an "unwitting, trusting and a completely vulnerable victim."

One attempt would be bad enough, Famiglietti said, but vonBulow tried twice. That, Famiglietti said, "is heinous, the state feels it is merciless."

Famiglietti said he would recommend more than 20 years on the second count if the law allowed it. In 99 percent of cases, he said, 20 years is enough for attempted murder, but he said that for the second count, 20 years is inadequate.

He agreed that vonBulow is not dangerous, but argued that if vonBulow were not sentenced to prison, "and the word got out . . . that a man could murder his wife or vice versa with impunity, that kind of attitude would be a danger to the community."

VonBulow did not look at Famiglietti throughout the prosecutor's brief speech. He stared insted at the wall over Needham's head, his hands folded in his lap, occasionally turning his head for a quick glance at his daughter.

MISS VONBULOW, tall and thin with short blonde hair and blue eyes, sat with crossed legs and clasped hands. She sat motionless, except for an occasional effort to keep the collar of her pink shirt upright.

Her presence in the courtroom left Famiglietti "somewhat perplexed," he said, because great care was taken to shield her from publicity during the trial. Famiglietti accused defense lawyers of a "blatant attempt to evoke compassion and sympathy" for vonBulow.

That brought defense lawyer John F. Sheehan to his feet. Miss vonBulow was in the courtroom because her doctors felt it would be therapeutic "for her to show the world she was behind her father," Sheehan said.

Needham said the pre-sentence report shows Miss vonBulow to be "an immature lady, though bright, who's trying to cope the best way she can." Then he offered vonBulow, who did not testify during the trial, a chance to speak.

VonBulow stood at the defense table, ramrod straight, head high. He clasped his hands behind him.

"Thank you, your honor, I'll not avail myself of that," he said in a deep, steady voice, and sat down.

JUDGE NEEDHAM, with little preamble, sentenced vonBulow to 10 years on the first count, then paused a second as gasps rose from the packed courtroom. VonBulow lifted his head higher, but showed no emotion.

A lengthier sentence was justified on the second count, Needham said. Fahringer frowned as Needham, holding the yellow, closely-typed pages of the pre-sentence report, said that vonBulow has not visited his wife since Jan. 30.

In an interview with Barbara Walters on ABC-TV's "20-20" program in April, vonBulow said he visits his wife frequently and talks to her about Cosima. He said he has been told she cannot hear him, but that sometimes the intimacy between two people can "transcend aspects of medical science."

In 1981, Needham said, vonBulow visited his wife an average of twice a month.

He said he rejected Fahringer's suggestion of a work-release sentence because the program excludes capital offenses, and because vonBulow "stands convicted by a jury of his peers of having tried, but failed, to commit murder... (Granting work-release) would be something of a reward for having failed to kill her."

Needham noted that "some have said" it would have been better for Mrs. vonBulow to die, rather than live "in a vegetable state." He agreed with Famiglietti that "perhaps the maximum is not sufficient," and then imposed a 20-year sentence on the second count.

VonBulow made a prism of his fingers in front of him.

JUDGE NEEDHAM at first ordered vonBulow to report to the ACI next Friday at noon, but agreed to release him on bail pending appeal after Fahringer argued that it is "unbelievable" to think vonBulow would flee with his daughter and keep her in hiding.

Fahringer also said that flight would cost vonBulow $200,000 in income from a trust fund established by his wife; from the long-running Broadway play "Deathtrap," in which vonBulow invested, and executor's fees for his wife's estate.

"I do not have the great assurance and great faith that you express as his counsel," Needham told Fahringer. Then he increased bail to $1 million.

"The trial of this defendant is over," Needham said. "The trial of the trial justice is about to begin," he added, referring to the state Supreme Court's review of his legal rulings in the case when it considers vonBulow's appeal.

How I wrote the story

As always with the Claus vonBulow trial, the reporting was the least of it. Every element of a good story was there for the viewing. All you had to do was sit in the alternate jury box and scribble frantically as great quotes flew by, trying to capture (in a handwriting that would be legible later) the interchanges between the lawyers and Judge Needham while keeping one eye on vonBulow and the other on the gallery.

Throughout the trial, the challenge was to get the story done before the last drop of adrenaline disappeared and before the deadline began to press. It seemed as if the sentencing would be an improvement over the trial itself in that department, because how many sentencings begin at 9:30 a.m. and end at 4:30 p.m.?

Unfortunately, the sentencing was scheduled for 2 p.m. The lawyers made speeches; the judge made a speech. The bail setup was so complicated even the lawyers were confused. So when Needham left the bench after 4 p.m., it was necessary to watch vonBulow leave the courthouse — crowd reaction was a major part of the story — and then to race around looking for someone to explain exactly what vonBulow had to do to remain free.

It was 6 p.m. before the writing job began, which actually was later than during the trial, when reporters would race for terminals as soon as Needham's black robes disappeared behind his chamber door.

After two months of daily trial coverage, the elements of a vonBulow story had defined themselves pretty clearly. So I went to the sentencing looking for several specific things: who was in the courtroom and who wasn't; whether vonBulow's demonstrative supporters had absorbed the guilty vote and abandoned their hero; the usual hard-news explanation of the legal maneuverings; the reactions to the sentencing.

One thing about vonBulow stories was clear from the beginning: It was never necessary to search for interesting things to write about, because nothing that involved vonBulow was ever unemotional or dull. Even things that had the potential to induce sleep — such as the days of medical testimony during the trial — turned out to be fascinating.

The sentencing was no exception. The usual personalities were present, and I was pretty sure they'd provide the usual bag of quotable quotes and surprises.

Surprise one: vonBulow's daughter, Cosima, who'd been kept out of sight ever since vonBulow was indicted. The sentencing was her first appearance, and every reporter in the room was riveted when she walked in. Luckily, she sat a few feet away from me. It was easy to watch her, and I did, feeling like a voyeur the whole time.

She was a smaller version of vonBulow — outwardly calm, composed, with the kind of posture that gets A's in gym classes. The interplay between her and her father was almost nil.

Clearly, her presence distinguished the sentencing story from the daily trial stories, and was a major thread in the opening paragraphs. The prosecutor, Stephen Famiglietti, made it easy to bring Cosima into the story again later, by mentioning her as he argued for maximum sentences for vonBulow.

The other thing I decided to put up high was Judge Needham's statement that he had at first planned to hold vonBulow without bail, but had changed his mind. It brought up the possibility that vonBulow would skip the country without my having to say it myself.

After the first five grafs, the story, as always, wrote itself. After an explanation of the bail terms and a description of spectator reaction outside the courthouse, the narrative becomes chronological. I'd grown used to recapping the highlights of the lawyers' arguments; their mannerisms were well known, and, besides, it's easy to write about a lawyer like Fahringer, who argued that vonBulow's record would be unblemished if not for the small exception of two attempted murders.

The story was filed shortly after 8 p.m.

Our stolen cars

By Ira Chinoy and Ward Pimley
The Providence Sunday Journal, May 16, 1982

Carol Cianci answered the doorbell.

She found two men standing in the cold March air.

One was Cpl. John O'Neil, head of the state police auto-theft squad. The other was Ronald Potter, an investigator for the National Auto Theft Bureau.

"Do you mind if we look at this Oldsmobile?" O'Neil asked, pointing to the two-year-old Cutlass, dark blue with a white top, parked in the driveway of the Ciancis' house at 9 Brenda Drive in Johnston.

Mrs. Cianci was stunned. "It *can't* be stolen," she thought.

The Cutlass belonged to Carolyn, her 16-year-old daughter. The teenager had worked after school at a jewelry shop and saved earnings from baby-sitting jobs to come up with the down payment. Her father, Raymond, a self-employed plasterer, had paid for repairs, tires and sales tax. A loan covered the rest.

Mrs. Cianci gave O'Neil and Potter the go-ahead. Seasoned hunters looking for something out of place, they went to work. They examined a small strip of letters and numbers riveted to the dashboard. They looked at another tag on the door post. They looked under the hood. They crawled beneath the car and poked around with a flashlight and mirror. They used a chemical degreaser and sandpaper to cut through layers of grime on the metal frame.

At last they found a spot where some code numbers had been ground off — the likely mark of a thief trying to conceal the car's true identity.

O'Neil asked if he could take the Cutlass to state police headquarters for further examination.

"This can't be happening," Mrs. Cianci said.

"It happens all the time," O'Neil replied.

That was Friday, March 23, 1979. O'Neil returned on Monday. He told the Ciancis the Cutlass was a stolen car and handed them the license plates. That's all they got back, except for a few trinkets Carolyn had hanging from the mirror.

"She cried for weeks," Mrs. Cianci recalls.

POLICE SAY that hundreds, perhaps thousands of unsuspecting Rhode Islanders like the Ciancis are driving stolen cars. Others are driving autos repaired with parts that were stripped or cut from stolen cars in clandestine "chop shops."

Rhode Island has had the second highest car-theft rate in the country for most of the last 15 years — a rate now nearly double the national average. During that time, Massachusetts has ranked number one. That meant 62,000 cars stolen in 1979 — about one in every 60.

Increased attention to the problem in Massachusetts has been credited for a decreasing car-theft rate there — down 16 percent in the last two years to fewer than 53,000.

But it's a different story in Rhode Island, where car thefts increased 13 percent in the same two-year period. The toll last year was 8,200 cars, worth $22 million.

About one car in every 70 will be reported stolen this year in Rhode Island.

In the 1950s, car theft was largely the work of joy-riding teenagers. About 90 percent of the stolen cars then were recovered.

Now, with more professionals at work, nearly half the cars stolen are never recovered, and many that are found are stripped of salable parts.

The toll last year in Rhode Island of cars that were never recovered — whether sold *again or cut up for parts — exceeded $10 million.*

THE CIANCIS LEARNED that their Allstate insurance policy, typical of those written by companies selling in Rhode Island, would not cover a loss like theirs: a stolen car confiscated by authorities.

So the Ciancis sued Regency Auto Sales, Inc. the Johnston dealership that sold them the car. But that suit was just a technicality: Regency had gone out of business.

The family also sued Western Surety Co., the company that had bonded Regency for $5,000.

The Cutlass had sold for $4,600. The Ciancis had invested more than $3,500 cash: the down payment, the first few monthly loan payments, repairs, tires and sales tax. They still had $2,500 to pay on the car loan.

More than two years after Carolyn's car was taken away, Western Surety settled for the 1978 sales price, $4,600.

Louis F. Robbio of Providence, the Ciancis' lawyer, got one-third, $1,533.

Nationwide Consumer Services Inc., their loan company, got its $2,500.

The Ciancis got the rest: $566 and change.

THE CIANCIS LOST $3,000 when the police took away their car. Thousands of others lose sizable sums each year when their cars are stolen and their insurance policies fail to cover full replacement.

But everyone who buys car insurance in Rhode Island and Massachusetts is a loser, too. Motorists in Providence are likely to pay three or four times more for auto-theft coverage than drivers in much larger cities, like Pittsburgh and Milwaukee. Boston motorists pay even more.

RAY CIANCI gets angry as he compares his misfortune with the way John DeCristofaro Jr., vice president of Regency Auto Sales, made out.

DeCristofaro sold the stolen Cutlass to the Ciancis.

He did not challenge the three charges of receiving stolen goods worth more than $500: the Ciancis' car, another car and a pickup truck. For his no-contest plea, he received a deferred sentence and had to pay $150 to the state's crime-victim fund.

"That's justice in this state," says Ray Cianci. "And you know what he's doing for a living? He's selling cars again."

THE FACT that DeCristofaro was caught was unusual; his sentence wasn't.

An FBI report, based on 1980 figures, shows that car theft has the lowest arrest rate — 14 percent — among seven major crimes. One professional thief, now serving a prison sentence in Massachusetts, boasts that he stole 5,000 vehicles and was arrested only 15 times.

Yet, a Massachusetts study, based on auto-theft cases from 1975 through 1978, found that only one in four of those convicted went to jail. Half the convicts drew suspended sentences. The rest got probation.

THE EVENTS that would cost the Ciancis thousands of dollars started in a rainstorm in Raynham, Mass., on the night of Nov. 17, 1977.

Ronald R. Piava, 39, of Middleborough, Mass., was driving along Orchard Street when he pulled out to pass another car and skidded on the wet pavement.

He would tell police later that as he tried to stop the skid, his foot slipped off the brake pedal and hit the accelerator. His car — a 1977 Oldsmobile Cutlass — slammed head-on into a utility pole, knocking Piava unconscious.

Police described the damage to the car's front end, the windshield and the dashboard in one word — "complete."

Piava's insurance company declared the car a total loss, paid off his claim and took title to the car. The company sent the wreck to the Braintree Dealers' Service Center, a salvage pool, to be auctioned.

Regency Auto Sales of Johnston bought the car for $1,299, seven weeks after the accident. With the car went the Massachusetts title — the document that describes the car by its make, model and the all-important vehicle identification number.

THE FREE FLOW of car titles, even for autos that are beyond repair, has enabled criminals to turn car theft into a flourishing business in Rhode Island and Massachusetts. A thief can use the title from a cheaply purchased wreck to legitimize a stolen car and sell it for a profit of thousands of dollars.

Rhode Island has a law that should take titles out of circulation when an insurance company decides not to repair a heavily damaged car and pays off the owner. Under the law, the Registry of Motor Vehicles is supposed to issue a salvage certificate for such cars. *The insurance industry ignores the law and so does the Registry.*

Massachusetts has no such law.

IN MARCH, 1978, someone — it isn't clear who — walked into the Registry of Motor Vehicles and exchanged the Massachusetts title to Piava's Cutlass for a Rhode Island title in the name of Regency Auto Sales. The title application carried the names of DeCristofaro and also of Blaise Marfeo of Johnston, Regency's president and a convicted bookmaker.

To make that kind of exchange, a car owner must submit the out-of-state title and a document called a TR5. The TR5 shows that a Registry inspector or a police officer checked to see that the vehicle identification number on the title matches the number on the car.

The TR5 submitted with the title to Piava's car indicated that a police officer from "Pawt." had checked the car. It bore a scribbled signature and badge number.

Lt. Charles Dolan, head of the Pawtucket police special squad, says there is no one in the department whose name or badge number is even close to the scribble on the TR5.

IT'S AS EASY today as it was in 1978 to slip a doctored TR5 form through the Registry.

"Do we check every police officer's name?... No. It would be ridiculous if we did," says Salvatore Butera Jr., head of the Registry's title section.

IT'S APRIL, 1978. Bruce E. Clark, 26, a traveling salesman from Chelsea, Mass., arrives at the South Shore Plaza in Braintree, Mass., at about 2 p.m. and parks his car. He has business to tend to.

Clark returned to the lot after dark and walked to the spot where his car was parked. He couldn't see it.

Maybe it's one aisle over, he thought.

Maybe two.

After a few minutes, he stopped.

His 1977 Oldsmobile Cutlass, dark blue with a white roof, was gone.

A THIEF WITH an order for a make, model, year and color usually can find what he wants at a mall, hospital, airport, restaurant or hotel — wherever cars are plentiful and the selection varied.

Of the 931 cars reported stolen in Warwick in 1981, 530 — more than half — were reported stolen from the large lots surrounding the Midland and Warwick Malls. There are 8,500 parking spots at the two malls. More than 30,000 cars park there every day.

IT'S EARLY SEPTEMBER, 1978. Ray Cianci is on his way home when a 1977 Oldsmobile Cutlass catches his eye. It is dark blue with a white roof, sports dealer plates and a "For Sale" sign, and is parked in front of Montagno's Mobil gas station at the busy intersection of Greenville Avenue and George Waterman Road in Johnston.

The car looked just right for Cianci's daughter, Carolyn, so he stopped to ask about it. He took the car for a drive, and then Carolyn tried it out. They liked it.

But Ray Cianci was cautious. Someone he knew had ended up with a stolen car. Cianci wrote down the vehicle identification number from the title and asked a relative in a police department to check the computer of the National Crime Information Center (NCIC). The answer: No car with that vehicle identification number had ever been reported stolen.

The Ciancis bought the car.

MORE THAN A MILLION cars are stolen every year in the United States. Police report the vehicle identification numbers of all stolen cars to the NCIC computer network. Police, in turn, use the computer network to check the numbers of suspicious cars. Some state motor vehicle registries check with NCIC on routine title applications.

That's why a smart thief changes the vehicle identification number of a stolen car before he sells it. He can get a "safe" identification-number tag and title from a wreck.

IN LATE 1978, an employee at the Registry of Motor Vehicles noticed something curious on a TR5 form: the signature of a "Capt. Managia" of the Cranston Police Department. There is a Captain Manocchia, but no Captain Managia.

A check of other TR5 forms submitted at the same time turned up two others with similar signatures.

The forms had come into the Registry from David Folcarelli, 28, of Cranston, who authorities said had been doing business with Regency Auto Sales. The name of the dealership was on at least one of the forms.

Edward McKenna, chief of the Registry's enforcement section, called in the state police.

Corporal O'Neil, who was assigned to the case, drove out to 60 Dyerville Ave., the address Regency gave when it received its state license to operate as a used car business.

O'Neil found two construction companies and a real estate developer at that address, but no auto dealership.

When he inquired inside the office shared by the three businesses, O'Neil was told that Regency Auto Sales used 60 Dyerville Ave. as a mailing address. When he asked how he could find Regency's owners, someone from the office made a phone call and John DeCristofaro arrived within minutes.

O'Neil asked about the cars that went with the curious TR5 forms. DeCristofaro took him to the gas station at the corner of Greenville Avenue and George Waterman Road. Two of the cars were there, and DeCristofaro said he could get the third. All three turned out to be stolen cars with altered vehicle identification numbers. So did the sporty black Pontiac Trans Am that DeCristofaro had been driving that day, O'Neil recalls.

DeCristofaro had bills of sale showing that he had bought the cars at wholesale rates from Folcarelli, according to O'Neil.

Folcarelli was indicted on four counts of receiving stolen goods and 13 related counts of obtaining money under false pretenses, forgery and submitting false documents to the Registry. He served about 10 months at the Adult Correctional Institutions before being paroled.

(Folcarelli and three other men in the car sales business also were charged in another scheme involving four stolen cars with altered numbers. Each pleaded no contest. They received suspended three-year sentences and were ordered to contribute to a state fund for crime victims. The levy for each suspect was $30 to $90 per car.)

Corporal O'Neil wondered whether Regency Auto Sales had been the channel for other stolen car sales, so he searched microfilmed documents at the Registry.

In early March, 1979, O'Neil got the records of a car that Regency had sold to the Ciancis. The prior Massachusetts title indicated that the car had passed from Ronald Piava, the original owner, to an insurance company and then to a salvage yard.

O'Neil called Piava and learned about the accident in Raynham and the heavy damage.

That's when O'Neil decided to inspect Carolyn Cianci's Cutlass, and he enlisted the help of Ronald Potter, the investigator from the National Auto Theft Bureau. Checking the Cianci car, they found a vehicle identification number that differed from the one on the title.

A check with the National Crime Information Center computer confirmed that the Cutlass was not Piava's rebuilt wreck, as the vehicle identification number on the dashboard and title indicated. It was the car stolen from Bruce Clark in Braintree.

The Ciancis were victims of a "salvage switch."

THE SALVAGE SWITCH is the most common method of marketing stolen cars.

Is it easy to get your hands on a title from a wreck? Yes, say car dealers who buy damaged autos at insurance salvage auctions. One Tiverton salvage-yard operator says he has more than 1,000 titles from wrecks that he has sold for parts or sent to the shredder. He says he won't do anything unsavory with the titles. Others will.

The two-man state police auto-theft squad uncovered about 100 salvage switches last year in Rhode Island. "And if we've turned up hundreds," says Corporal O'Neil, "there must be hundreds more. Thousands."

EPILOGUE:

• Carolyn Cianci's dark blue and white 1977 Cutlass was returned eventually to salesman Bruce Clark's insurance company. Last year Clark got another call. His memory is a bit foggy, but he thinks it was from the FBI, and that the car had been stolen again and surfaced in Canada, with phony documents.

• John DeCristofaro, the man who sold the 1977 Cutlass to the Ciancis, was reached recently at Deluxe Auto Sales, Putnam Avenue, Johnston. He says he doesn't sell cars anymore, but works occasionally picking up and delivering cars for Deluxe and Executive Auto Sales Annex, the dealership across the street.

• Carolyn Cianci now drives a maroon 1981 Cutlass. "She saved her money for a couple more years. This time she bought a new one," her father says.

RAY CIANCI, on a break from his plastering business, sits in the kitchen of his Johnston home and strikes the table with a clenched fist, shaking his head.

"How do you protect yourself?" he asks.

"Next time I need a car, I'm going to steal one," Cianci says with a harsh laugh. "I would've got probation and I wouldn't be out five thousand dollars."

How we wrote the story

The Ciancis' story — the frustrations of a Johnston family that unwittingly bought a stolen car — was intended to be an alternative to the traditional first-day story that culminates a months-long project.

We did not want to lead with the typical umbrella piece that bullets major findings to be explored in subsequent stories later in the week. In this case, that approach could be dry (insurance-company practices, Registry incompetence, salvage sales, etc.), could leave the reader feeling he was going over old ground later in the week, and could give the subjects of the stories a chance to rebut our summaries before the supporting details had been printed.

Also, we wanted to personalize the series. Most of us, in our stints as bureau police reporters, rarely pick up stolen-car reports. But we wanted to show that car theft isn't just people losing material goods they can replace, with the insurance companies picking up the tag. It's individuals and families who suffer plenty of frustration and financial loss; prosperous insurance companies and comfortable bureaucrats who create conditions that are ripe for car theft to flourish; and the rest of us, who subsidize the insurance companies and the thieves with inflated premiums.

So, with Carol Young as guiding light, we proceeded to take one very telling narrative — the Ciancis' story — and intersperse it with our general findings.

At first, the findings were not designed to correspond directly to points in the narrative. But as the Ciancis' story was traced back, it became clear that nearly every specific point we wanted to make in the series — and not just the big picture of people as victims — had a correlation in the narrative.

In some instances, looking for correlations even led to greater depth in the single tale: the discovery, for example, that the stolen car sold to the Ciancis had been given a Rhode Island title earlier, when someone simply scrawled a phony policeman's "signature" on an inspection form. That fact had not been mentioned in any of the police records in the case, but surfaced when our findings about weaknesses at the Registry led to questions about how this particular stolen car had slipped through.

An obstacle was to avoid losing the readers with technical details while informing them about the lucrative and nearly risk-free "salvage switch" scam (the use of titles from wrecked cars to disguise stolen ones). We decided simply to let the scam evolve through the narrative, rather than define and explain it directly.

We chose the Cianci case as the lead after checking out several others referred to us by state and local police.

Ray Cianci came on very strong from the start, as if after three frustrating years without a sympathetic ear, he had suddenly been uncorked. He made the initial reporting easy by producing documents from his purchase of the car and from his settlement with the car dealer's bonding company. He was also receptive to repeat interviews, as were the state police officers and National Auto Theft Bureau investigator involved in the case.

Finding the other players in the story involved tracking down names from court records, like the former owner of the stolen car, Bruce Clark. He was no longer living in Chelsea, as he had been then, but calling all the Clarks with Chelsea addresses eventually yielded relatives who got word to Bruce to call us.

A title search provided the name of Ronald Piava, the original owner of the wrecked car that had been used in a salvage switch to disguise the identity of Clark's car. The recollections of state police that Piava's car had been totaled in an accident in Raynham, together with the date on which his insurance company took title to the car, provided enough information to track down the police report on that accident. Repeated attempts to locate Piava were unsuccessful.

John DeCristofaro, the dealer who had sold the stolen car to the Ciancis, had gone out of business as "Regency Auto Sales," but he had a car with dealer's plates in front of his house. A check with the dealers-license commission gave the name of the dealership that owned those plates, and a call to the dealership led to information that DeCristofaro was working at the dealership across the street.

Blaise Marfeo, the convicted bookmaker who had been president of Regency Auto Sales, was listed in the phone book. An individual we are not at liberty to identify provided information that Marfeo could be found doing business, as it were, at Quality Auto Body. A check with the secretary of state showed that Marfeo was, in fact, an officer of that business, but a check with the dealers commission and the auto-body commission showed that they had never been notified formally of his role as a principal.

Several reporters — Bruce Butterfield, Chip Scanlan and Phil Kukielski in particular — provided helpful comments along the way.

Carol Young wanted nothing less than perfection. Her insistence on writing and rewriting was responsible for making the story a readable piece. Tom Heslin was the copy editor and a fresh voice to help fine-tune the story.

A death in the family

By Jeanne Edwards
The Providence Sunday Journal, May 30, 1982

WEST GREENWICH — The call from the nurse came about 10:20 p.m., just as Robert Caldwell and his wife, Irene, were going to bed.

Did they have a son named Robert C. Caldwell? Yes. Come to Kent County Memorial Hospital immediately. It's an emergency.

This was the night of July 3, 1981, a night the Caldwells will never forget. This was the night their teenage son, an honor student who was fascinated by computers, was killed.

Robert "Craig" Caldwell would have been 18 years old today.

Last July 3, a masked man walked into the Warwick gas station where Craig Caldwell had recently started working. He shot Caldwell in the back of the neck and ran off with $366. A state medical examiner ruled that Caldwell died of a gunshot wound to the neck with perforations of the skull and brain.

FROM THEIR HOME in rural West Greenwich, Robert and Irene Caldwell drove to the hospital in Warwick as fast as they could. The doctor took them to a side room.

"Our first question was, 'Is there any hope?'" Mrs. Caldwell recalled. "And he said, 'Absolutely none,' so I said, 'Take me to my son.'"

The doctor told Mrs. Caldwell, "I don't think you should," and then looked at her husband. He told the doctor that his wife was a nurse. "She can handle it," Robert Caldwell said. "I can't. Let her go."

A nurse took Irene Caldwell to see her dying son.

CRAIG CALDWELL was a lanky teenager with glasses who lived in jeans and cords.

He graduated with honors from North Kingstown High School at 16 and was on the dean's list at the University of Rhode Island. He wanted to graduate from URI in three years and then get a master's degree in computer science. He was well on his way. With advanced placement exams taken in high school and a heavy course load at URI, by the end of his freshman year he had accumulated almost half the credits needed for graduation.

Craig arranged his school schedule so that he could spend two days a week with his mother, who had been home nursing an injured leg. They would sit in the family room for hours, talking about all kinds of things.

"JUST TWO WEEKS before he was shot, he sat in that chair and we got to talking about death and dying," Mrs. Caldwell remembered.

"He said, 'Mom, if something drastic ever happens to me, don't let them keep me alive on machines.'" Mrs. Caldwell said she told her son that she would "pass the message on to your sister because I'll probably be dead and gone long before that."

Craig told his mother that it wouldn't be "that long" before his death.

"He had incredible insight," Mrs. Caldwell said. "We found a poem he had written two weeks before that gives you the creeps." The poem is about enjoying life before it quickly passes away.

WHILE GOOD GRADES came easily, Craig had some personal conflicts with teachers, his father said. "He was one of those, that if the teacher wasn't teaching what he thought was right, he'd rebel against them to a certain extent," Caldwell said.

Craig was a noncomformist about such things as dressing up. But his politics were ultraconservative, said his father.

His parents believe that Craig's passion for speaking out and his intense dislike for thieves may have contributed to his getting shot. "He probably told (the robber), 'Why the heck don't you go out and get a job and work for a living like I have to?' and turned around to walk from the guy and that's when he shot him," his father speculated.

The Caldwells believe their suspicions were confirmed by the testimony of James "Jay" Powers, the 23-year-old convicted on May 20 of murdering Craig. Powers said that his friend, Peter J. D'Ambra, robbed and shot Craig. He said D'Ambra told him that he shot the attendant when he "tried to be a hero."

Powers is to be sentenced next month.

The Caldwells take some consolation in the conviction. "I realize that nothing will bring Craig back. But at least the murderer was found," Mrs. Caldwell said.

THE CALDWELLS raised four children in their home on Route 102. There is Christine Southworth, 27, a teacher in Exeter, Karen Ann, 24, who is working on her doctorate in chemistry at the University of Wyoming, and Stephen, 20, a pre-med student at Purdue University.

The family moved from Warwick to West Greenwich 13 years ago, in part because they were impressed by the Exeter-West Greenwich school system's program for gifted students.

Mrs. Southworth said she and Craig were extremely close. Because of the nine-year difference in their ages, she was like a second mother to her lively, precocious brother. They used to talk a lot, she said. Sometimes she looked to him for support when she was unable to communicate with anyone else.

Like Craig, Mrs. Southworth's husband, Gary, had a knack for computers. They would spend hours in Craig's bedroom, dabbling with a computer lent to Craig by a friend who went away to college.

CRAIG READ BOOKS, all kinds of books. On a wall of shelves in the family room, his books are placed alphabetically by authors. They cover mythology, science fiction and history. He loved war games, especially Dungeons and Dragons. He and his buddies started a war game club and held classes in North Kingstown.

One reason he started working at the E-Mart gas station at 1836 Warwick Ave., Warwick, was to pay for attending a Dungeons and Dragons convention in New Jersey last summer.

Craig agreed to work for Robert Potter, a family friend, although he hated the smell of gasoline. He had been working at the E-Mart less than a month when he was shot.

Despite his high IQ, Craig would sometimes act much younger than his age, his family said. "At one point he was 40 years old and sometimes he was 3," Mrs. Southworth said.

There were days when he'd have temper tantrums, such as when he'd get a Christmas gift that was no surprise. But he was also blessed with a sense of humor that made him fun to be with, family members said.

CRAIG WAS THE ONLY child still at home for the two years before his death. He would vacuum the house, do the dishes, shop for groceries and split two or three cords of wood a year.

Now a housekeeper does most of the household chores, leaving the cooking for Mrs. Caldwell, who still can't break the habit of cooking enough for three.

Coping with Craig's death is difficult, she said. But she is consoled by a poem that reminds her God gave her Craig for 17 years.

ON THE NIGHT Craig's life ended, Mrs. Caldwell walked into the treatment room at Kent County Hospital.

She saw her son lying on a table, blood running out of his ears. He was hooked up to a respirator.

She pushed his hair back from his forehead and talked to him, knowing he couldn't hear. She told Craig she didn't know why anyone would want to harm him. She said she was going to miss him terribly.

Then she remembered the promise she had made to her son just two weeks before. And she ordered the respirator shut off.

How I wrote the story

The murder of Craig Caldwell was an incident that deserved and got a lot of coverage. Even before the trial started, editors were talking about some kind of feature after the jury's verdict.

What the feature would be was uncertain. Several suggestions were floating around. At one point, it seemed that a story about the travel of the gun would be it. (The gun used to kill Craig passed through several hands before it got to James Powers, the man convicted of the shooting.)

I thought we'd had enough stories about how Powers got the gun. It seemed that what was needed was more information about who Craig Caldwell was and how his family was coping with his death.

I made a nervous phone call to Craig's mother, not knowing how she would react. Fortunately, she was decent about the whole thing and agreed to an interview, as long as the story did not give the impression that her son was a saint.

Her stipulation made the story more interesting, but harder to write. It was difficult, at times, to get into the faults of a 17-year-old near-genius whose promising life had ended so brutally.

I wondered, for example, whether readers would lose sympathy for Craig after reading what his father thought he may have said to his assailant.

I decided to put it in the story anyway, since it helped to show the kind of person Craig was. In any case, I rationalized, his father didn't hesitate to talk about it.

The first interview was with Craig's parents in their West Greenwich home. Another evening, I talked to his sister, Christine Southworth. Their recollections about Craig were the same. He was a nice kid, really smart. But sometimes he could be impossible to live with.

In writing the piece, I tried to get a good balance between who Craig was and the effect his death had on the family. There were times when I considered paraphrasing some of the quotes to make the story flow better. But I wanted the family to express their feelings in their own words, since it was their story.

The lead came right away, although a phone-call lead is not one of my favorites. I decided to go with it because one of the things I often thought about while listening to testimony in the trial was how and where the parents had found out about their son's death. I thought readers who had been following the stories may have wondered about that, too.

Initially, the description of Mrs. Caldwell ordering the respirator shut off was nearer the top of the story. Mark Silverman suggested it would be more effective at the end. And it was.

As an orator Pastore is a Rolls amid the Cadillacs

By M. Charles Bakst
The Providence Sunday Journal, June 20, 1982

The little Rhode Islander, who stands no higher than a two-pound keg of mail-it-home salt water taffy, was in the grand tradition of convention orators...

His sonorous organ-like voice, now mellifluous and pleading, now cutting with a fine edge of sarcasm, now deep with a doomsday emphasis on the dark days ahead, seemed to out-pipe the convention hall pipe organ, which local boosters claim to be the largest in the world.

— Associated Press account of John O. Pastore's keynote address to the 1964 Democratic National Convention in Atlantic City.

Last Sunday at the state Democratic Party kick-off dinner at Rocky Point Park, I heard virtually every top Democrat in Rhode Island speak. People like Governor Garrrahy, Sen. Claiborne Pell, Rep. Fernand J. St Germain and former Atty. Gen. Julius C. Michaelson.

All of them obviously are pros; they know how to talk. But it is no denigration of them to say that if they are Cadillacs, John O. Pastore is a Rolls Royce.

Now *there* is a man who can speak.

And that is just what the 75-year-old former governor and former senator did. He was the keynoter of this $25 affair. It was, compared to his famous keynote address to the 1964 Democratic National Convention, really only a cameo appearance. The Atlantic City speech was delivered before a live audience of thousands and was carried on national television to millions. It ran for 36 minutes and was interrupted by applause at least 36 times.

AT ROCKY POINT, Pastore addressed maybe 300 people. His speech at the end of an evening of speeches ran for seven minutes and was interrupted twice.

But even at that it was fine, because a good politician knows when his audience has had enough, and seven minutes was sufficient for Pastore to demonstrate he remains the champ. Even veterans like Garrahy sit in wonder when Pastore speaks. What does he have that they don't? How does he pull it off?

"I figured it out," one of the politicos told me. "It's the cadence. It's the cadence and the gestures." It *is* that — and more.

1964 WAS the year of Lyndon Johnson and Barry Goldwater.

"When it was announced in the paper and appeared in the New York *Times* that I was selected to make the keynote address," Pastore told me recently, "I received a letter from Barry Goldwater. He said, 'I won't agree with any damned word you say, but I'm going to love the way you say it!' "

Listen to a recording of Pastore's 1964 speech:

It has ridicule and humor.

He zeroes in on the bitterness and confusion of Goldwater's Republican Convention in San Francisco. He refers to Mark Hatfield, the GOP keynoter.

"As for the Republican keynoter," Pastore booms, his voice rising, "I must say tonight that he tried real hard. But he just didn't quite make it. (Laughter and cheers). He wrote his speech for Rockefeller! He made his speech for Scranton! And (now Pastore rushes to the climax) he ends up with Goldwater and now he won't buy it! (Applause)."

Now he is utterly contemptuous:

"Ooonhh, and how eager they were to drag the Bay of Pigs into the Cow Palace. (The crowd responds, "Yeh! Yeh!") Pastore booms again: "Why didn't they tell the American people of the real Cuban crisis of October nineteen-hundred-and-sixty-two, when the world stood still and all of us held our breath, and there stood John Kennedy, 10 feet tall! (Long cheers). 10 feet tall! But determined, courageous and strong, and for the first time — for the first time — we saw Nikita Khrushchev pick up his marbles and go home. (Stormy applause)."

Now Pastore sneers, "Now I hear that Barry Goldwater doesn't think we're the mightiest nation in the world," and he says, off-handedly, "Well, I can understand that. He's a candidate. But I say to Barry Goldwater — when Nikita Khrushchev looked down the barrel of that Kennedy cannon, he knew differently! (Wild applause)."

ST GERMAIN, who was a delegate, tells me that there was "absolute electricity" in the air. He says, "The Rhode Island delegation had the front row. He led the crowd just like a conductor of a symphony orchestra. Total silence when he lowered his voice to about a whisper. But when he reached the crescendo, the applause was there."

What may be the best remembered passage of the speech was a reference to the extremism controversy that gripped the Republicans that summer. It seems so long ago now, but you recall the John Birch Scoiety and the charges about Dwight D. Eishenhower.

Here is the recording again, and here is Pastore thundering:

"And when these fanatics — when these fanatics dare to call a President of the United States — a Republican at that — a conscious (pause) agent (pause) of the Communist conspiracy, then I say, shame! shame! on all your houses! (Again, stormy applause)."

For all the noise, it was the silence that Michaelson, who seeks to reclaim Pastore's seat for the Democrats, recalls. Michaelson was an alternate delegate and his most vivid memory is of a portion of the speech where "you could hear a pin drop."

Extraordinary. National convention delegates usually do anything but actually think about what a speaker is saying. But Pastore remembers it too and the recording bears him out. The retired senator recalls, "I knew that the people were listening, because that was the solid part of my speech, where no applause would be appropriate. When I got to the part where I said, 'If an all-out atomic war ever comes, every home, every kitchen, every cradle, could well become a cemetery,' you *could* hear a pin drop."

On the recording, there is no applause at all there, nor when he went on to the next memorable line, "The sanity of America is the security of the world."

You may be hearing a lot about Pastore's 1964 sentiments on nuclear holocaust because Michaelson, preparing for a speech he intends to give on the subject, recently obtained a copy of Pastore's address and re-read it. In fact, in his own speech at Rocky Point, Michaelson alluded to it and he noted that it was delivered 18 years ago. "Now the weapons are greater and more destructive," he said.

EVERYONE HAS a particular memory of Pastore, who assumed the governorship in 1945, who was elected to the Senate in 1950, and who retired in 1976.

State Rep. Victoria Santopietro Lederberg, the Democratic candidate for Secretary of State, sported a blue-and-white Pastore donkey button Sunday night. It was from back when he was governor. She was a child living on Shafter Street in Silver Lake. Pastore lived nearby on Elmdale Avenue. "His mother lived on one floor and he on the other," Mrs. Lederberg told me. "We knew the governor lived on the next block. His car would go by. We would stand on the sidewalk and salute the black limousine."

Sometimes, she said, the kids would go over to the Pastore house and approach his mother. "We would ring the doorbell. We would say, 'Mrs. Pastore, do you have any pins for us?' And she would give us one of these."

When it was Mrs. Lederberg's turn to speak Sunday night, she mentioned the button and said what an honor it was to be on the same program with Pastore.

Pastore's speech often was an angry denunciation of what is happening in the United States. But at one point he turned into a proud uncle. He praised the Democratic candidates. "We know Joe Garrahy," he declared. "We know Julius Michaelson." And then, softly, sweetly, "And we know that lovely little girl, Victoria, who said such wonderful things. I knew her family going way, way, way back."

SUNDAY NIGHT'S affair was on the subdued side. The crowd was small. There may have been 400 there at the beginning of the macaroni and chicken dinner, but by the time the various candidates had spoken, the audience had dwindled. Toastmaster Marvin

Holland introduced Pastore at 10:12 p.m. The band played "Happy Days Are Here Again."

I was curious myself about how Pastore would do — or, more specifically, what exactly it is that he does. As I said, the speech was short, but it was long enough for him to display a variety of emotions — a sampler, if you will, of what it might have been like to go back across the years and see him in Atlantic City.

Ironically, the 1964 speech bragged of 42 months of a continuous climb in the economy. Perhaps that was on Pastore's mind when he eased into the heart of his remarks Sunday night. He pointed with the index finger of his right hand, and he spoke as the Voice of Experience:

"Now in my lifetime, I've made hundreds of speeches. And I don't know how many times I have boasted of the fact that we were the most industrialized nation in the world" — he was in a kind of sing song — "and indeed the richest nation in the world — and that we possess 40 percent of the *wealth* of the world.

"Well, things have changed. And when I look and see what's been happening to us through the policies in Washington over the last year and a half, I'm a little *ashamed* to be making that claim any more.

"Only a few weeks ago — and Mayor Walsh was there — I was invited to address a group of shut-ins, and the party was held here at the Pilgrim Lutheran Church" — he enunciated each syllable — "on Warwick Avenue. And there were these lovely people" — there was a sweeping gesture with his hand — "about 150 of them, most of them in wheelchairs, others were completely blind so that they had to be guided around the room to their seats, and I said to myself" — he was almost whispering now — "How can anybody hurt these people? How can anybody deny them anything?"

And he made a fist and he roared:

"Where is the glory and the wealth of America?"

And he screamed:

"Are we beginning to forget our own people?"

The right hand pointed and chopped through the air, and he declared:

"We have spent *33 billion dollars*" — pause — "in order to rehabilitate the economy of Europe.

"We have given 8 billion dollars to Turkey alone. We have spent 23 billion" — he broke the word into two distinct syllables for emphasis — "dollars in Food for Peace."

Then he opened his palms in disbelief. His voice became softer, but high-pitched, and he said increduously:

"And now we're saying a child in school cannot have a glass of milk because we can't afford it."

Now he boomed:

"We're saying that you can't have a hot lunch for the elderly because we can't afford it."

The hands took turns now chopping the air, and he continued: "We're beginning to say that we can't put a roof over the heads of the elderly because we can't afford it."

Now he lowered his voice and confided:

"Well, of course we can afford it."

And then he suddenly grew louder again, and he said:

"The point in America today is the primary challenge: put the 10 and a half million (unemployed) back to work and you will resolve your deficit and you will resolve your Social Security!"

And the crowd applauded and whistled.

Then he turned to the Reagan administration's reducing unemployment programs.

"It's absolutely inconsistent," he cried, and he added, softly, "All we're saying here tonight is let's have a little compassion. Let's bring back a little heart in the structure of American government. We're not poor. We need some redirection." He gathered steam now, and he spoke more quickly, and he bellowed, with *both* hands chopping the air, "And that redirection will come the day the Senate of the United States is under Democratic control!"

The crowd loved it.

He said that speeches do not win elections. What is required, he said, is a get-out-the-vote effort. "You need the votes," he said "and you've got to realize that the vote of an elderly person or a poor person counts as much" — he thumped the lectern — "as the vote (thump) of a rich person (thump). That (thump) is (thump) America (thump)."

From anyone else, it might have sounded corny. From Pastore, it sounded eloquent.

But it was in keeping with the man. The 1964 keynote address is remembered for the shame! shame! quote. It also is remembered for a huge double-page picture of the senator that appeared in *Life* magazine. But before the headlines and the publicity, a passage was tucked away that was not in the text of the adddress at all.

When Pastore, after receiving a standing ovation, began his speech, he told the delegates: "This is not in my script, but indeed it is in my heart. I would be a strange person indeed if I did not acknowledge this marvelous and wondrous manifestation of good will. This is something that can happen in America alone. I am a first generation native American of immigrant parents who came to this great land at the turn of the century. My state has already honored me with the two highest positions in the gift of our people to bestow...

"And if that were not enough, my party has seen fit to grant me the privilege to speak to you tonight as your keynoter. My cup tonight runneth over and the best way that I can express it is to say: God bless America!"

From Pastore, it sounded like a command the Almighty would dare not disobey.

How I wrote the story

Re: The June 20 "Rhode Island Politics" column about former U.S. Sen. John O. Pastore.

Believe me, I ran into a lot of surprises. Some of them frustrating. Some of them fortuitous.

When I heard that Pastore would be delivering the keynote speech at the June 13 Democratic State Committee kick-off dinner at Rocky Point, I immediately thought of his 1964 keynote address in Atlantic City. It also occurred to me that I really had never, in person, heard Pastore deliver a good old-fashioned political speech. In my early years as a political reporter, I almost never ran into him, and in later years it was usually a matter of just exchanging pleasantries at fund-raisers.

I had heard the 1964 speech on television, but remembered virtually nothing of it except for the cry "Shame, shame on all your houses."

So what I wanted to do was go to hear Pastore and a real stemwinder of a speech, and see what it is he does (or did), and play it off against the 1964 performance.

A week or two in advance of the 13th, I started to do a little research. I could not locate either an audiotape or a videotape of the 1964 speech. The Rhode Island Historical Society does have a kinescope of it, but it is of poor quality and the equipment for viewing it proved to be impossible.

I did have our library make blowups of various stories and pages from *Journal-Bulletin* microfilm.

This gave me a familiarity with the speech text and with the scene. It also yielded the Associated Press story from which I chose two paragraphs as the lead-in to the column. That material was colorful, and it gave a quick idea of the range of the man's speaking style. In essence, the message I was trying to communicate right away was "Here's a guy from Rhode Island who was something special on a national stage."

One decision I made in advance of the 13th was not to approach Pastore ahead of time. I do not know if this was such a smart idea, but my thinking originally was that this project might not come off. Suppose, I thought, that Pastore bombed that night, or that no one was listening. I did not want to get a 75-year-old man excited about the thought that he was going to be the focus of a major story and then have it turn out that there was no story.

As things developed, I modified my thinking. Here's what happened. On June 10, Governor Garrahy announced for reelection at the Biltmore. Pastore was there, and was called upon to say a few words. After the festivities, I happened to notice Julie Michaelson, the Senate candidate, and went over to chat with him. The conversation turned to Pastore. Michaelson told me he had just obtained a copy of the 1964 address for a speech he would be giving later in the month on nuclear war. He also told me he had been in Atlantic City. I asked him about the reception Pastore received. He told me about how you could hear a pin drop, which stuck in my mind.

The next night was the night of the Democratic State Convention, again at the Biltmore. Michaelson had a hospitality suite, and I stopped in. He told me Senator Pastore was there and wanted to see me. Michaelson had told him of our conversation. Pastore wanted to mention something the New York *Times* had said about his speech. So there I was with him and — despite my original intention not to talk to him ahead of time —

we had a chat.

He told me about the Barry Goldwater note. And when I told him that Michaelson had told me you could hear a pin drop, he said, yes, that was true, and he quoted verbatim from the relevant part of the speech. So I knew right there that those were two things that would be in the column. The Goldwater anecdote proved to be a good introduction to the section about the 1964 speech itself, at a time of great debate about extremism, etc.

Pastore also mentioned that he had a phonograph record of the speech. I did not immediately ask to borrow it, but I kept the thought in my head, just in case. At this point, I did not know to what extent the column would emphasize the 1964 speech and to what extent it would emphasize his 1982 remarks.

At the state-committee dinner, I ran into Vicky Lederberg and noted her old Pastore button, and she told me the story about how she used to live near him, and, again, I knew I'd use it.

But the most fateful conversation I had was with Congressman St Germain. During a lull in the dinner, I took a seat next to him, and we chatted about 1964. He had been a delegate. He said Pastore played the crowd like a conductor leading the orchestra. That may not be a novel simile, but it turned out to be the key: That is what Pastore did, and that is what he still does, and when I sat down to write, I tried to capture that and document it.

St Germain told me that he too had a record of the 1964 speech. (Although I did not know it at the time, Senator Pell had had a number of copies run off.) St Germain said that he had it in his Woonsocket home and that if I called him late that night or early the next morning he would bring it in to Providence.

"That's good constituent service," I said.

"Have I ever let you down?" he replied.

Pastore spoke for seven minutes. I had figured he'd go on for half an hour or so, and, frankly, I was stunned when he finished so quickly. And I wondered whether I really would be able to pull this off.

But the next morning, because of the record from St Germain and because I had made a tape of the Rocky Point remarks, everything began to fall into place. And I realized that although the Rocky Point speech was not in the same league as the 1964 speech, it was reminiscent — because of the range of emotions. It was, as I wrote, a cameo, or a sampler.

As I say, I wanted to document exactly what it is that Pastore does when he speaks. That is where the record proved to be invaluable — where it had it all over the printed text. From the record (I made a tape of the record and could start and stop it at will), I could describe his moods and moves, and the crowd response. The italics and punctuation, etc., helped do that.

There still was one drawback. The record did not, obviously, capture what Pastore looked like — what gestures he used. There was nothing I could do about that in regard to 1964, but at least I could do something in regard to the portion of the column about 1982. At Rocky Point I took notes, and later was able to match the gestures with his words.

By the way, it was not until I listened carefully to the tape from Rocky Point that I realized he had been thumping the lectern when he said, "That is America."

In the writing, when I got to this point in the column, I remembered again my conversation with St Germain. We had talked about how Pastore can get away with saying things that would sound corny coming from someone else. St Germain had told me, in fact, that although he himself thrills to the sight of the Capitol dome lit up at night, he rarely talks about it, except to youth groups, because it sounds so corny. He was right. From St Germain, it did sound corny.

So that's why I wrote, "From anyone else, it might have sounded corny. From Pastore, it sounded eloquent."

The line "That is America" and the thought of corniness reminded me of the part of his 1964 speech about coming from an immigrant family. So I played back that section. He really laid it on thick when he said, "God bless America." I thought, "How is he saying that? What makes it so different when he says it than when I might say it?" And that's when I realized it: He made it sound like a command to God Himself. So that was the natural end of the piece.

So I wrote the column and submitted it. And I knew I must be on the right track because a couple of the more veteran guys here read it and told me that years ago they used to cover Pastore and think, while listening, what terrific stuff this was, and then, when they went back to the office to write about it, they had trouble figuring out what, if anything, the senator had actually said. The Pastore style had triumphed.

Senate returns to square one

By Thomas E. Walsh
The Evening Bulletin, July 9, 1982

The humming fan fought for attention with Lt. Gov. Thomas R. DiLuglio's gavel; but its blades did not stir the stifling, sticky atmosphere as a humorless state Senate returned to the State House yesterday to try to put a new shine on its tarnished image.

Nobody particularly wanted to be there.

Sen. John W. Lyle Jr., a Lincoln Republican who had missed much of the Senate's work earlier this year as he recovered from injuries he suffered in a car crash, acknowledged the good wishes of his colleagues.

"I'd like to say it's good to be back, but I'm not sure," said Lyle. "I think I'd rather be at the beach."

The state Supreme Court had made it official just one day earlier. The Senate's reapportionment plan was, indeed, an unconstitutional political gerrymander, and the Senate would have to redo it — and quickly, if the regular Senate elections are to be held.

Senate Democratic leader Rocco A. Quattrocchi said the court order would be carried out.

"Everything will be done in the open; all considerations will be in the open," Quattrocchi promised the Senate as he submitted a resolution to set up a special Senate commission that is to oversee the second round of redistricting.

GIVEN THE COURTROOM revelations two months ago about how districts got carved up among politicians in backroom conclaves, Quattrocchi's words sounded right.

But his avowed good intentions did not lighten the heavy atmosphere, nor did they signal that yesterday's Senate session was anything other than politics as usual at the State House. Even the Senate's tiny band of six Republicans were squabbling among themselves.

GOP leader Lila M. Sapinsley complained that the seven-member panel proposed by Quattrocchi was just a vehicle to give Democrats control as usual. Why, even the other Republican on the panel besides herself — Sen. John A. Romano of East Greenwich — had voted with the Democrats for the original plan and could probably be counted on to be with the Democrats again.

"He would not be my choice to serve on this commission," Mrs. Sapinsley said of Romano.

Mrs. Sapinsley had informed Romano of her displeasure with his selection just as the Senate was called to order.

"I was so shook, I forgot to press the button for the roll call," Romano said later.

His voice cracking, Romano told the Senate he resented Mrs. Sapinsley's remarks. He also told his colleagues that if it was all the same to them, he'd just as soon not serve on the panel. "That would be fine with me," Romano said. "If my time is being considered wasted up here, take my name off. You would do me a great favor."

The Democratic leaders were not about to replace Romano, any more than they were about to put Sen. Richard A. Licht, D-Providence, on the panel.

IT WAS LICHT — whose East Side district was combined with Mrs. Sapinsley's district under the reapportionment plan that was struck down — who had challenged the plan, as had the state Republican Party.

Several Democrats, mostly those mavericks who often buck Quattrocchi and his leadership team, told the Senate that Licht — first among Democratic Senate mavericks — should be on the panel because he now has considerable knowledge about redistricting.

The idea was simply ignored by the leadership.

Licht, meanwhile, sat in his front-row seat near the corner of the chamber, chin resting on right hand, and listened. He had been greeted warmly by his colleagues, he said. Many congratulated him on winning his case in court. And, he said, nobody blamed him for this special session on a hot summer day that made political rhetoric seem more biting, more threatening, than it does in the winter.

"This was not done by me," he said. "It was done by the Senate leadership."

There has been considerable speculation about what Licht would say at yesterday's session, and how he would say it.

When his turn came, he started by telling the Senate how he has been "most intimately involved" with this reapportionment business over the last few months, how he had read hundreds of pages of legal briefs in the case.

"WE NOW FACE a herculean task," Licht said. "This is no time for intraparty squabbles about how it should be done." He added, "This is not the time for business as usual, nor for recriminations."

But the burr in his side that had been there since his district had been done away with was still rubbing him raw, it seemed.

Licht took out after Quattrocchi. He said the majority leader had the wrong attitude about the second try at redistricting. He cited a remark by Quattrocchi the previous day that the majority leader would go along with the court but still disagreed with Superior Court Judge James C. Bulman's decision, upheld by the Supreme Court, that the redistricting plan was no good.

"I stand by my statement," Quattrocchi replied. "I think Bulman was wrong. He's not infallible."

The give and take between Republicans and Democrats over the merits of the new commission was, as usual, chippy. The GOP said this whole business had been "our own form of Watergate here." The Democrats bristled at that.

Sen. William C. O'Neill, D-Narragansett, glared at Mrs. Sapinsley as he labeled GOP remarks an "orchestrated pontification." O'Neill said Republicans were not without their own political failings. "You've got a few skeletons in the closet, too, Sweetie," O'Neill declared.

"Darling, I don't react well to innuendo," Mrs. Sapinsley replied. "If I had any skeletons in my closet, I would be happy to bring them out."

The Democrat-controlled commission won easy approval on a party-line vote. Mrs. Sapinsley, who had had her own legislation drawn up for a different commission, didn't push hard for it.

"It would be an exercise in futility," she conceded.

With that, the Senate adjourned and the commission went upstairs to get organized.

Under a timetable announced by Quattrocchi, tentative new redistricting proposals are supposed to be ready next Wednesday and are to be made available for public inspection at the State House next Thursday and Friday. The House and Senate are to meet July 20 to ratify some new plan, as well as a condensed pre-election schedule that will get ballots finished in time for the Sept. 14 primary.

How I wrote the story

The story about the state Senate trudging back to work on July 9 to consider a new redistricting plan was one of those pieces that almost wrote itself.

The assignment was to do a story on the first day of the special Senate session for the next day's *Bulletin.* John Kiffney was doing the first-day story for the *Journal,* and I wanted to present something besides the rhetoric and the straight-news political arguing that he would be reporting in his story.

I was struck immediately by the atmosphere. It was a hot, muggy day. The State House is at its absolute worst on these days, because the ornate House and Senate chambers have neither open windows nor air conditioning. If people are not in a snit before they get there, a day like this at the State House will put everyone in a foul mood in no time.

Thus the lead with the fan failing to stir the sticky air. It occurred to me that the collective mental state of the Senate was much the same as the air — and if the fan could not stir the air, nothing that would be said by the politicians could refresh their minds, either.

I didn't want to be there. The politicians didn't want to be there. And when Senator Lyle, who had missed much of the regular Senate session because of an injury, told the Senate he didn't want to be there, it was perfect.

What happened next was consistent with the theme that was developing in my mind for this story. Rocco Quattrocchi said everything would be done in the open.

Now everyone knows this is not true. What happens in the open at the State House is almost always carefully orchestrated in some back room. This would be no different. So Quattrocchi's statement did nothing to lighten the miserable atmosphere, because everyone knew it was bull.

It was politics as usual — stifling, hard-handed politics — at the State House. All I had to do was write it that way. There was no lack of good examples on this day.

There were some interesting asides, other than the obvious, to help make the case. The Republicans had just won this big court victory on redistricting, forcing the Senate back to the drawing board. One would think the tiny GOP Senate contingent would be euphoric. Not so. Even these people were fighting among themselves over which Republicans should be on the new Senate redistricting committee. The public and private lamentations by the GOP, I thought, provided a nice example of how miserable everyone seemed to be this day.

Senator Licht was an obvious choice for special treatment in this piece. It was his suit that, along with the court challenge brought by the GOP, had forced the special session. I wondered about him before the session started. How would his colleagues react to him? Would they resent him? And would he use the Senate as a platform to say "I told you so?" In the story, I tried to answer those questions.

I wanted to end the story with a sampling of the nasty rhetoric that marked this nasty day at the State House. The snide exchanges between Senator O'Neill and Lila Sapinsley seemed perfect.

Darigan has learned to relax

By Bob Wyss
The Evening Bulletin, July 26, 1982

PROVIDENCE — They stood together on the stage: the tall, square-jawed, handsome Irish politician with just the touch of gray in his wavy black hair, and the thick-set Italo-American with the thick horn-rimmed glasses.

Frank Darigan and Tony Bucci waved through the din and smoke at the crowd of 500 that jammed the hall. Then Bucci took Darigan's hand, raised it with his and vowed that together they were going to win the mayoral race.

The applause and cheering rose. The excitement was electric.

The scene, which occurred recently at the Bowling Green Tavern, is still talked about with wonder by local politicians. Two months ago such a scene was impossible to imagine.

Bucci, the Democratic city chairman, had told associates for months that the party's next candidate had to be an Italo-American. Darigan knew that when he entered the race, but then he didn't expect any favors from Bucci. Politicians in both parties have said that Bucci worked for Darigan's arch foe, GOP incumbent Vincent A. Cianci Jr., in the mayoral race four years ago.

So even political insiders were shocked when Darigan won the endorsement in June. And now, here was Bucci, openly vowing to go all the way with Darigan.

Talk to most Democratic politicians and they will tell you that Darigan won the endorsement over tremendous odds because he led in everyone's political polls.

"In the late spring, four or five of the polls commissioned by candidates and the party all showed him way out in front of everybody else," confirmed House Speaker Matthew J. Smith, Darigan's close friend since childhood. "It sent a clear signal all the way down in the line."

Darigan agrees, but he also thinks that a series of speeches, personal appearances and TV and radio spots that came out in a one-week period shortly before the Democratic City Committee met to issue the endorsement also helped.

"All of these activities in a blitzing fashion did exactly what they were designed to do, which was to focus public opinion on me," Darigan said. "It had to impress people who had a vote for the endorsement on the city committee."

BY THE TIME the Democrats met on a Saturday night in June at the Marriott Inn, Darigan's rivals for the endorsement had dropped out. He won by a landslide.

Now he is embarked on his third campaign for mayor, the second as the party's endorsed candidate. And the question that must be asked is this: Has Frank Darigan changed in the last four years? Is he different from the candidate who lost to Buddy Cianci in 1978?

Darigan sits behind the desk of his Elmwood Avenue law office and ponders the question. The air conditioner blasts as he sits, cool in a white, short-sleeved shirt with a smooth, narrow blue tie.

The office, part of a converted tenement, is small. Law books share space with framed editorial cartoons depicting previous political campaigns and with a sketch of John F. Kennedy.

"I think I am substantially the same person, but my attitudes about some things are a little different," he replied. "I think that with the maturing process you become a little more relaxed.

"When I ran in 1978, I was an angry person. I was angry because of what the mayor had done to the City of Providence.

And I came across as a stiff, angry, unsmiling, unyielding person."

OTHERS AGREE that Darigan, 39, has become smoother and more polished with groups and individuals.

"The difference between Frank Darigan now and four years ago is that now he will sit down and compromise with people," said an old political hand. "And I'm not talking about making deals, but about compromises, because politics is the art of compromise. That's what I see is different."

What hasn't changed is that burning desire to be mayor, the one that he nurtured as a boy growing up in the one-time Irish political hotbed of the city's south side. Priests were his first heroes, but by the time he was 15 he knew he wanted to be a politician, and his dream was to be mayor.

It seems that ever since then Frank Darigan has been running for something.

At 17 he was elected president of the Catholic Youth Organization council in the Diocese of Providence and two years later he was president of the national CYO, which has seven million members. At Providence College, where he majored in political science, he was president of his junior and senior classes.

Then in 1970 he won election to the City Council from Elmwood's Ninth Ward.

BUT THE DREAM crashed in 1974 when he lost a bitter four-way primary fight for mayor to incumbent Joe Doorley. The primary shattered the Democratic Party, and although Darigan tried to pick up the pieces over the next four years as the party's city chairman, his failure was obvious in the 1978 election when Democrats like Bucci failed to support his endorsed candidacy.

That second overwhelming defeat could have ended the dream. But close friends like Matt Smith say that within weeks of the election Darigan was talking about coming back.

Darigan and his wife, Hope, moved their four children out of their modest house on Warrington Street to a more spacious Victorian cottage on Lenox Avenue in the same Elmwood neighborhood.

He and his wife plunged into the affairs of several organizations in the neighborhood, which formerly had been almost all Irish but today has a growing sprinkling of Hispanic, black, Portuguese and Hmong families. He also moved his law office from downtown to Elmwood Avenue.

IN 1979 he was elected to the Home Rule Charter Commission, which wrote the city's new constitution, which takes effect in January. As a result, Darigan knows more about the new charter than any other candidate. But when he ran for the commission, it was a political gamble because no one knew if the charter movement would succeed.

It was not until the city's financial crisis in early 1981 that a Darigan comeback looked possible. A number of the fears Darigan had voiced about the Republican mayor's freewheeling and free-spending ways were perceived by many as coming true.

"I had people who came up to me and said, 'You know, I supported Mayor Cianci, but I don't trust him anymore. I think he's misled us and you were right,'" Darigan said.

Finally it came down to a holiday party last December for 500 friends and supporters at the Edgewood Yacht Club. There were no political banners or trappings in the hall that night. But the message had gone out that Darigan wanted to run again, and now he wanted to know what his friends thought of the idea.

By the end of the night, virtually no one had told him he was making a mistake. The message, he said later, "gave me great encouragement."

The dream of being mayor was alive again.

How I wrote the story

I knew the major task in writing a campaign profile of Frank Darigan was to make it fresh. That was a challenge because I have been covering the man for five years and he has been in the public eye, off and on, for the last twelve years. But as I thought about it I realized that the key was to concentrate on what has happened to him in the last four years, since his crushing defeat to Cianci.

The reporting

The clips produced the basic biographical information.

I received a great deal of help when I started calling various political sources and people who have known Darigan for years. Several told me about the scene at the Bowling Green Tavern, and the moment I heard about it I knew that was my lead. It was the perfect symbol for the story, because the two had been such archenemies four years ago.

However, my sources were less helpful in explaining why Darigan had received the endorsement. Ever since he had received it, on June 10, I had been asking people why he had won it. Repeatedly they told me the polls showed Darigan stronger than anyone. I was not happy with the answer, because no one could document that point.

The primary interview was conducted in one hour in Darigan's office. I was able to accomplish a great deal in this one-hour taped session, because I have been covering Darigan for so long. That familiarity allowed me to ask specific questions in specific areas. He was direct in his answers, and there was not a great deal of wandering off the subject, as can sometimes happen. Virtually all of the questions concentrated on the point from election night, 1978, through the currrent campaign and his future plans.

Unlike other political profiles that have been appearing in the newspaper, this one did not follow Darigan on the campaign trail. I did not see that as a primary ingredient in this story, and I was afraid it would only interfere with the story line I wanted to follow.

The writing

When I was looking for details for the lead, I asked my sources to tell me exactly what Darigan and Bucci had said at the Bowling Green. They gave me varying quotes. I was disappointed as I realized I could give only a description of the scene, and not report exactly what had been said. In retrospect, that probably strengthened the lead. With quotes, I would have had to eliminate some of the description or lengthen the lead. Neither of these alternatives would have been desirable, especially the latter, because the reader would have had to wait too long to find out why this scene was important.

The next section of the story concentrates on how Darigan won the endorsement. I still find it the most disappointing area, because I cannot be certain what the answer is.

Then a change of pace. We get to the heart of the story with the question of whether this is a different Frank Darigan from four years ago. I tried to highlight the question by describing Darigan and his office. The whole sequence worked, because Darigan came back with the strongest statement of the entire interview.

From here the story became easy. I simply tried to pack as many biographical details into the story as I could in a very short space. I was aided by an excellent profile Bill Collins had done four years ago, and by my own extensive knowledge of Darigan.

There were several possible endings. I chose the December party because it was an obviously strong conclusion. The problem is it left out many details about Darigan's campaign this summer, and the fact that he is really gearing up for Cianci, rather than his primary opponents. The other problem is that my ending was lopped off in the City edition of both the *Journal* and the *Bulletin*. It ran only on a back page of a few *Bulletin* editions.

The interns

The first crisis comes quickly as lives replace the textbooks

Residency, for new doctors, is the on-the-job training that follows medical school. Its first year, commonly called internship, is medicine's boot camp where young men and women are transformed from students into doctors. Real patients replace their textbooks. To find out what that first year is like, Journal-Bulletin *staff writer Irene Wielawski spent 14 months reporting and writing the story of three interns. This is the second of six parts.*

By Irene Wielawski
The Providence Journal and *The Evening Bulletin*, August 22, 1983

PROVIDENCE — The telephone's ring, the blare of the hospital public address system and an insistent electronic pinging from the beeper at her waist jerked Dr. Alessandra Kazura to her feet.

She had been stealing sleep on a cot in the residents' lounge at Roger Williams Hospital. It was early on the Sunday of a 36-hour weekend shift and now what Sandi had dreaded most was happening.

The phone, the beeper and the intercom were all screaming the same message to her: Code Blue. A patient near death was coming to the hospital.

The patient would be a child, Sandi knew, as she raced down one and a half flights of stairs and a hallway to the emergency room. That's why they were calling her. She was the only pediatrician on duty.

She beat the rescue squad, but in a minute they hurried through the emergency room doors with a small bundle.

She had never handled a code before. It was her first weekend at the hospital, the first time in her three months as a doctor that she was without experienced pediatricians to back her up.

THE BUNDLE was a six-month-old baby.
"It came in blue, unresponsive, no heartbeat, no nothing," Sandi said. She never noticed if it was a boy or girl.

The baby's veins were collapsed. There would be problems getting an intravenous line in. It was grayish looking and the skin was cold to the touch, indications that the baby hadn't been breathing for some time.

Sandi yelled to a woman at the emergency room desk to call Women & Infants Hospital — just across the back parking lot — for more pediatricians. The woman tried, but reported that she couldn't get through on the telephone.

"Try again!" Sandi shouted.

She turned to the baby, trying to guess its weight and figure what size endotracheal tube to put down its throat. The tube would be connected to a respirator to make the baby breathe.

She chose a tube, and then whipped out her calculator to begin figuring drug doses, again based on an estimate of the baby's weight. She was nervous about doing it this way. It was too rough. She hadn't handled enough babies to be good at estimating weight. But there was no time to get a scale.

The resuscitation room was crowded by now with technicians, respiratory specialists, nurses, and doctors who, while not pediatricians, were more experienced than Sandi in running codes. But they looked to her for direction because the patient was a baby and she was the only pediatrician.

"I was overwhelmed, thinking I was going to have to intubate and figure out the drug doses and read the EKG," she said.

A senior medical resident offered to insert the endotracheal tube. She said yes. There were crises enough to go around. She concentrated on how to get the drugs in.

None of the technicians had been able to thread an intravenous line through the baby's constricted veins.

Sandi pushed through the crowd, began working on the baby's other side. She tried for a vein in the leg, then the wrist, then the arm — poking, probing with the needle, trying to keep her hand steady.

IT SEEMED to take forever, but Sandi would learn later that only 8 minutes elapsed since the baby reached the emergency room.

"I just got into the vein, but there were so many people in the room. I kept getting bumped and I was afraid we were going to lose the only access we had," she said. "That was the biggest thing on my mind — not losing that vein."

She was only dimly aware that the pediatricians from Women & Infants had arrived. She focused on the needle piercing the baby's arm. The drugs were starting to flow. She looked up briefly but everything outside the circle of people around the baby was a blur.

"About this time I began to realize how badly off the baby really was. Also I was getting more bits and pieces of the history," she said. "The rescue squad essentially had found the baby dead."

They had been working for what seemed to Sandi like a half-hour when the medical resident ordered an end to the effort. The signs of life — breathing, a heartbeat — would not be sparked.

"I was blown out," Sandi said. "Someone had to go tell the mother and on my way out the door, I just broke down. I started crying. One of the nurses and a resident who came over from Women & Infants said to me, 'Look, she's been waiting for 20 minutes. She can wait two more. You go over there in the corner and cry it out.'"

Sandi struggled to control the tears. Her stomach heaved. She thought she might throw up. She remembers being scared stiff, now that it was all over.

"This fear I think I'd been having all along — I suddenly was aware of it. I kept thinking, 'What if I'd been able to get into that vein sooner?'"

She wiped her eyes, breathed deeply and got up from the chair in the corner to take her first steps toward the waiting room.

The baby could not have been saved, Sandi was sure now. But that was little comfort. She hadn't felt qualified to be the pediatric expert. What if there was a chance and she'd blown it?

She kept walking, searching frantically for words to use on the mother, fighting down the fear that she would say the wrong thing.

Later she would remember almost nothing — the woman's appearance, her reaction, how long they conversed or what she finally said. Did they sit down together? Was there anyone else in the room? Did Sandi offer her comfort or just the bad news?

DR. LOUIS COLE, a classmate of Sandi's at Brown medical school, was grappling in his own way with the switch from insular classrooms to the realities of a hospital.

He had drawn the Rhode Island Hospital emergency room as his first assignment of a five-year residency in orthopedic surgery. A couple of "M.A.S.H." reruns would have prepared him better for the feeling of the place.

You never knew what would come through the door, or when. You could expect to be busy on Friday and Saturday nights, and then without warning there would come a crazy Wednesday. There were theories about the full moon, weekends, holiday time, but inside you knew that anything could happen, any day, any time.

On this July night, besides the crazy woman who swallowed knives, there was a conventioneer from Kansas who'd broken three ribs in a fall and a man who was certain he'd caught gonorrhea from his male lover. There was also a 7-year-old boy with a deep, silver-dollar-sized scrape in his heel whose parents spoke only Spanish.

Then about 10:30 p.m., George sauntered in.

He arrived with two East Providence policemen at his sides. His hands hung oddly from wrists wrapped in bloody gauze.

George talked non-stop, cocktail-party smooth. The policemen were baffled. Less than an hour before, he had attempted suicide in his jail cell.

"He was picked up for driving without a license. We were just holding him overnight," one policeman murmured to Lou. How he got the razor was anybody's guess. George only smirked when asked.

Lou began stitching the wrists.

"A Mercedes for you, Doc?" There was sarcasm in George's voice. He launched into a lecture about orthopedic surgeons and their fat wallets.

Lou kept his voice even, took it as a joke. It seemed the best way to keep George from moving his wrists.

"Hey doc," George said. "I can see you married, maybe at 35. Three women on the side, one in each state. Dating any pretty nurses, yet?"

The policemen decided to go find a soda machine.

As soon as they were out of sight, George jerked his head up and fixed Lou with eyes suddenly gone wide and hollow.

"Lou, Lou — is there any way you can keep me here? Keep me away from those cops? They're gonna be mad at me, cutting myself like this. I don't want to go back there."

Lou answered with his all-purpose calm voice. Now, now, you're going to be fine George. We're going to fix you up in no time.

George turned toward the wall. He stayed sullen until the policemen returned, and then he became his old cocky self. He waved merrily as the cops led him back to their squad car.

Lou figured him for a streetwise attention grabber. He rated the suicide attempt "a 5 1/2 on a scale of 10" in a conversation with some other residents.

It was about 3 a.m. when George and the policemen returned. The weary officers hoped to get some doctor to commit George to the Institute for Mental Health.

"He tried to chew through the bandages," one of the policemen explained. "He tried to rip out the stitches with his teeth."

DR. MILTON GAVLICK JR. had few doubts about his ability to handle whatever came in the door at Rhode Island Hospital. He was smart, he had done well in medical school, scored highly on tests, and in his spare time was happy to while away the hours reading medical journals.

He measured himself often against peers — whether in medical school or at the hospital — and always came up with the same equation: "If they can do it, I can do it."

He couldn't wait.

On his first day at the hospital, June 23, 1982, he was a portrait of impatience, squirming in his auditorium seat as welcoming speeches for the hospital's 63 new residents droned on.

To Milt, the preliminaries seemed endless. He had spent all those years in school. Now he had to wait one more day — a day of speeches, registration forms, I.D. pictures and other collegiate stuff — before plunging, finally, into the real life of a doctor.

Impatience turned to anger when Milt learned his rotation assignment for his first month at the hospital.

The rotation system is designed to expose residents to different facets of their specialties. Milt was starting a residency in internal medicine, which deals with disease, curable and chronic. Depending on their illness, patients are housed in different parts of the hospital and even different hospitals around Providence.

Milt pounded his fist into his thigh and swore as he stared at the assignment list posted on the auditorium wall. "I'm so mad," he hissed as other residents milled around him. "I can't believe this. No weekends! No nights on call!"

He had drawn the renal consult service. It was a nine-to-five, Monday through Friday sort of job in the hospital's clinic for kidney dialysis patients. It also involved seeing patients on the wards who were having problems regulating their body fluids.

Someone called Milt's attention to the brilliant sun outside, to the fact that with such a soft schedule he would be one of the lucky ones to see the beach this summer.

"You don't understand," he murmured, and walked out of the auditorium.

A MONTH LATER his mood was much better.

"Renal's been good," he said, laughing at the memory of his initial chagrin. "I've really learned a lot about fluid levels and electrolytes. It hasn't been bad at all."

One of his first patients this day was a 62-year-old woman who had been hospitalized a month before with kidney failure.

Milt had helped care for her then and now she was delighted to find he would be seeing her on this followup visit.

"He's got such beautiful shirts," the patient confided to another woman in the examining room. "I particularly like the orchid one." Turning to Milt, she crooned: "You're a peach."

Milt put a stethoscope to her belly and listened intently. She narrowed her eyes and watched his face. Would the news be good or bad?

"Hey," Milt announced, pulling the stethoscope from his ears. "You're doing great. In a couple of minutes we'll have your tests back from the lab and see how they are."

The woman chuckled and turned to her confidante at the end of the bed. "Isn't he something? He rescued me from the dead, yes he did. ..."

ON AUGUST 1, Milt joined the doctors he had envied in June — those with night and weekend duty.

He was moved from a consult service to the floor, which means he had responsibility for the complete care of patients assigned to him, not just a single part or function of their bodies.

The schedule for residents on the medicine floors required them to work every fourth night, in addition to their daytime duties.

August 1 was a Sunday.

"It's the worst possible day to start," Milt said. "It's a weekend so you're covering for the other residents. You're picking up a list of your own patients that you're responsible for — I think I got 13 — and you're admitting new patients."

Milt started work at 9 a.m. Sunday. "I didn't close my eyes till 7 o'clock the next night. It was a rough day, but I made it through. I think I performed okay. When I went home Monday night, I was real tired and I thought, well, it's going to be rough."

The next two days went by in a whirl, and before Milt knew it he was starting another 36-hour stretch. By the end of the first week, he was exhausted. His body ached, his mind was dazed, he felt drained.

The nightmares started in the second week. He couldn't sleep no matter how tired he was. He couldn't relax. He couldn't get the hospital out of his mind.

"What was going through my head was the care I hadn't given, all the things I should have done but couldn't get to because of all the other stuff I had to do," Milt said.

"Things that bothered me were like there were patients who were real nice people and deserved good care but if they weren't a real sickie, you saw them for two seconds a day and that was it.

"An attending (a private physician) would call and say why didn't so and so get that test, and you'd say, 'Well, I don't know. To tell you the truth, I haven't gotten to him yet ...' I found myself saying that a lot."

Milt searched for a role model among the second- and third-year residents, who obviously had survived their internship and might offer some clues to coping with its stress.

But all around him, he said he found bitterness and anger.

"A patient would be coming up to the floor, and they'd say, 'Oh God, another hit.' That's the word for an admission. They'd say, 'That's my tenth goddamn hit on the unit.'"

There were other words, too, for the sick. A "gomer" was a chronically ill old person. The acronym stood for, 'Get Out Of My Emergency Room.' Referring to patients by their illnesses — 'the gallbladder in room 202' — was another in-house shorthand.

One of the patients assigned to Milt was an old man, dying of cancer. He had been in the hospital a long time, undergoing extensive and often painful treatment even though the cancer was incurable. Milt wondered about that. Why didn't they just tell the old guy's family to take him home and let him die in peace?

Milt often saw the man's children. They would take turns sitting with him. It was a nice family, Milt thought. And he could sense that they were anxious to talk to somebody about their father.

"But I couldn't spend the time with them," Milt said. Guilt and a feeling of worthlessness were added to his nightly struggles for sleep.

How I wrote the story

Being stuck on rewrite is a great stimulator of story ideas that will allow one brief escapes from the grind. I think it was during a week of daily weather stories in the sodden spring of 1982 that I came up with the scheme to follow some medical-school graduates into their initiation year as doctors.

I had done a similar story two years before on police rookies, attending the Providence police academy with them and later following them up after they'd been a year on the street. The changes — in their ideals, their perspectives on life and career, their motivations — were profound: something we all experience after we have left school for the real world.

I tried to represent the police story in such a way that the reader would relate to the three characters as human beings. This was a device to get behind the stereotypes of cops as either swashbuckling heroes or pigs, mind sets that I felt the reader had to leave behind or else miss the subtleties of the rookies' transformation.

That was a trial-and-error story for me. I was on maternity leave at the time (I wrote it on a free-lance basis for the *Sunday Journal Magazine*), I was working alone, and I was flailing in the dark as far as organization, voice and other writing considerations were concerned.

This is what I learned and incorporated in the interns project:

• The business about getting behind the stereotype was key here also, because doctors are another very much misunderstood group — either hated for their Mercedeses and Wednesday golf games and 5-minutes-$100-please consultations, or worshipped as all-knowing miracle workers.

• Everybody is unique and reacts differently to stresses. Therefore, to choose only one character and try to make him or her a prototype of the internship or police experience is artificial, and inevitably shallow. I had gone with three subjects in the police story and did the same in the interns series, deciding to stick with what I knew worked.

• In order to show the uniqueness of characters, you have to interview them to death, so that you have enough detail to let them portray themselves through their own actions and words. That makes the story harder to dismiss, especially for people who have an interest in attacking its credibility. With the cops, I had both interviewed them during off-duty hours and ridden around with them on patrol in the middle of the night.

Early on in the interns research, I realized the interns had amazing stories to tell — that I might not have believed had I not heard them from the interns backwards, forward and inside out.

That realization made me determined to keep myself as far in the background as possible, an operating philosophy that extended to the prose and organization of the series. I didn't want the interns' stories to be loaded or qualified or defused by constant juxtaposition with the opinions of their superiors, medical-school muckymucks or national experts in medical education and training.

This belief, which was supported by Joel Rawson, led to the sidebars. These were independent of the main stories in that they did not attempt to answer point by point, but were loosely related by theme. They provided the context for the interns' stories, and a forum for those responsible for the training system to respond.

Every interview with the interns — and I must have met with each of them at least six times off-duty during the year — lasted three or more hours. I also spent shifts with them at the hospital, which gave me a lot of observable detail (there was little time for conversation or asking questions during those times, because they were so busy).

I didn't know these people before beginning the story. I asked the PR person at the Brown medical school to choose three graduating seniors for me, all slated for internships at Rhode Island Hospital. This was for logistical simplicity.

The only criteria I set on the selection of these people was that they be fairly self-confident and articulate, and represent the three main training disciplines: surgery, medicine and pediatrics. I knew it would be an intrusive story, and I didn't want subjects who were shy about talking about their feelings or nervous about a reporter trailing them during what I and they knew would be a very stressful period.

When I did introductory interviews with the three, I told them that I would try to wring every detail of their experiences and thoughts and frustrations, and that being in the spotlight could be unpleasant, and that some of their colleagues would undoubtedly be critical of their participation in the project. Then I told them to think it over and feel free to reconsider going through with it. I did this because I knew that I and the newspaper would be investing a great deal of time, that the project had to have a certain duration to succeed, and I didn't want anyone dropping out half way through. One of the three almost begged off at this point but then decided to stick with it.

I also told them that I would attempt to verify much of what they told me through third-party interviews, so they had to be scrupulously accurate. I didn't want them to exaggerate; I knew much of the story would depend on their veracity. If they knew at the outset that I'd be checking on their versions, I figured, it might encourage their accuracy the first time around — and I wanted what they themselves experienced, not hearsay.

In the verification period of the research, I interviewed many people who never appeared in the series.

The big crisis for me was not the reporting but the writing. I kept filling more and more notebooks with great stuff, and growing more and more panicked about how to write it. My first draft was a three-part series, each installment of which featured the complete story of a single intern. It was a repetitious, formulaic sort of thing, but it was safe — logical in its time-line organization, and each story, each day, stood on its own. I didn't know what else to do and so followed the standard journalistic rules for series. I was in despair, because I knew I was selling the material short by my boring presentation.

I picked at the thing until April 18, when I went into labor, four days past my due date. Andrew Edward was born in the afternoon of April 19. I was furious that I had to go back to work to finish the series; I wished I'd never started it. I had a nightmarish time in Women & Infants Hospital, because I knew too much. I wished I'd gone into horticulture or some other nice thing, instead of nasty journalism.

Also, I knew in my gut Joel was going to make me rewrite the whole series when I went back. I tried to convince myself, during the eight weeks I was home recovering, that the series needed only fine-tuning. I failed.

Joel Rawson finally read the whole thing when I returned in early June. "Hmmmm, let's do it this way," he said, and in about a half-hour of fiddling came up with an outline for the episodic, narrative style that became the published version. I sat back and watched a genius at work.

Rewriting was agony. I would have killed for a nice, straightforward weather story. The big risk was the dependence of each story upon the one that went before. It was not a series that could be picked up in the middle, and I initially was very nervous about going along with Joel the rule breaker on that one.

But it worked, I think. One doctor at Rhode Island Hospital called me during the week the series ran to say he couldn't get his morning work done, because his staff wouldn't budge until they'd read the latest installment. Another person called me on the night before the last part ran and asked if I'd please tell her whether "that nice young Dr. Gavlick" gets into another training program; she said the suspense was killing her. I was amazed.

Though I often felt I was all alone on this one — and indeed I was for much of the research period — the result was a great team effort. Joel Rawson had that essential overview that a reporter inevitably loses on a long project. He can also spot a superfluous word in what you'd swear is the tightest of phrases; his line editing was expert.

Bob Thayer took his usual stunning photographs and Teddy Sherwood produced a terrific layout. Copy editors and other people in the back shop, whose names we never know, also did a great job, I thought.

Because so much depended on the interns' coming across as flesh-and-blood types who could evoke emotions in a wide range of readers, I tested the story at various stages on friends in the newsroom, my baby sitter, a nurse friend from Rhode Island Hospital, my mother, my husband, my 2-year-old. All made valuable comments. All, that is, except Emily, aged 2, who said some very unconstructive things when I offered it instead of "Winnie the Pooh" as a bedtime story.

Crissie's last chance:

She gambled that trip to edge of death could save her life

Part one of a three-part series

By Marialisa Calta
The Providence Sunday Journal, November 13, 1983

SEATTLE — The woman lies on a narrow stretcher in a windowless basement room, covered by a sheet. A red beam from an overhead laser marks an X on her stomach, dead center.

She is bald from past cancer treatments: brutal chemicals forced into her veins and radiation aimed at her head. Her face shows no emotion; her hands roam over the sheet.

A loud whoosh escapes from two pot-bellied orange casings that stand sentry at opposite sides of the stretcher.

Deep inside the casings, an air-driven piston has pulled a tungsten rod. At the end of each rod, twice wrapped in stainless steel, is a thimble-sized piece of cobalt. The cobalt is raised to a hole in the lead casing until it is exposed.

Gamma rays now bombard an area six feet by three feet, centering on the red X.

Over the next four hours, the woman will receive twice the lethal dose of radiation — equal to 50,000 chest X-rays, or to standing a half-mile from the atomic bomb when it hit Hiroshima.

The treatment is part of a gamble to save her life.

A technician's voice crackles over the intercom: "The process has started."

The technician watches the patient on the video monitor for a few moments, then turns to the Joseph Heller novel on her lap.

The patient wriggles restlessly, moving her legs in circles. She looks at the camera and says: "Marialisa. You can start reading now."

In the control room, I speak into the microphone.

"The Secret of the Lost Tunnel. Chapter One: Double Warning. The telephone in the Hardy home gave a long, urgent ring, as the clock struck four. Blond-haired Joe bounded into the hall and lifted the receiver ..."

"FIRST OF ALL, call me Crissie," wrote Cristalyn Marie Cagle.

It was 1969, August. A clerk in the Georgetown University housing office in Washington, D.C., had decided that we were to be freshmen roommates.

She was from Mobile, Ala., and her letter revealed a Sagittarius, who hated math and Latin, and who LOVED Joe Namath and the score from the musical "Hair."

The girl I met a month later was tall and blonde, and a natural pack rat. For weeks, her stuff kept arriving: boxes of costume jewelry, grade-school memorabilia, and an enormous second-hand muskrat coat for her first winter "up north." She didn't walk, she sashayed, and she talked just like she wrote, all capitals and italics.

We were both from strict Roman Catholic families, and a little rebellious. We joined campus protests, but still felt a little uneasy when finals were canceled because of unrest over the Vietnam War.

From the start, there was a special bond; we were among the first 50 women admitted to Georgetown's liberal arts college and among 12 picked for an intensive humanities program. "Female eggheads," the student newspaper called us.

We all lived together on one floor, an experiment the college hoped would have us discussing 19th-century German philosophy while frying our hair with electric rollers.

It didn't quite work that way. Instead, we spent hours dreaming up diversions to entertain our friends. We dressed as gypsies, and roamed the dorm passing out homemade fortunes. We staged the death scene from "Heart of Darkness," and vignettes from "Lives of the Saints." She made me stay up all night playing Beatles records backwards to find out if Paul was really dead.

College was more than pranks. We struggled with the issues raised by student protests, we were dissatisfied with our classes, and we were troubled — in a vague way — about our futures.

When we got sick that winter, Crissie festooned the room in black crepe, declared us quarantined, and devised a pulley system for the Big Macs and sausage pizza sent up by friends.

She drew up a last will and testament and left me her costume jewelry, and all the junk under her bed.

"CHAPTER FIVE: Dangerous Journey. Joe dashed into the yard, and peered over the fence, but no one was in sight. . . .

Thirty-six minutes into the radiation, Crissie signals that she wants it stopped. The side effects have started; Crissie has diarrhea and has to use the commode. A nurse goes in to help.

This is one of 10 times that the radiation will be stopped, as nurses give Crissie medication — anti-vomiting drugs and sedatives — and hold a pan for her while she throws up.

Crissie is at the Fred Hutchinson Cancer Research Center in Seattle, because she has leukemia, cancer of the white blood cells. She is having a bone marrow transplant.

A few days before, Crissie had been given a huge dose of a drug that kills leukemic cells. Now, the gamma rays are killing her bone marrow, where the cancer cells are produced. In a few hours, she will receive new marrow, intravenously, from a donor.

Without marrow, she would die within four weeks. The hospital will keep her alive until the new marrow starts working.

She will be here 100 days; about 30 days in the hospital and 70 in an outpatient apartment nearby.

Today is June 2, Day 0.

The nurse rushes into the control room through the swinging doors that separate it from the radiation.

The whooshing sound signals the radiation has begun again.

Crissie thrashes on the stretcher. She feels nervous and hemmed in. She knows the radiation will leave her sterile.

If the gamma rays are killing her bone marrow, she wonders, what are they doing to the rest of her body, to her heart and liver and kidneys? Research on the subject is reassuring, but research can be wrong.

Her mind is wandering. She asks for a repeat of a passage from the Hardy Boys.

The day before, she had decided that the children's detective book would be the perfect distraction during the radiation. She had found it in her hospital room, two floors above the radiation bunker. The name "Terry" is written, in a childish scrawl, on the front page.

I wonder if Terry is alive.

WE KEPT IN TOUCH after college.

Crissie moved around, finally settling near the University of California at Berkeley, where she enrolled in a Ph.D. program in botany.

In January, 1980, on her way to study in Costa Rica, she invited me to join her in Mexico.

The trip rejuvenated the friendship. We lazed on hot white beaches, laughing at each other's jokes. We drove miles into the jungles of the Yucatan, talking about our work, men, being single.

She knew little about my job, but listened attentively as, camped under a palm tree, I worried aloud over my future as a reporter. Night hours, problems with co-workers, questions about the ethics of journalism — she helped me sort out my feelings.

In November, 1981, an ebullient Crissie came East to be maid of honor at a friend's wedding. A devoted runner, she looked trim and terrific in a hot-pink, gauze-and-satin outfit which brought her more compliments that day than any other in her life. The morning after the wedding, when the other guests were recuperating, she ran five miles; she was in training for a half-marathon. We parted with plans to see each other soon.

Two months later, the telephone was ringing as I walked into my apartment after a weekend trip.

Friends had been trying to reach me for days to tell me the news: Crissie's in the hospital, she might die. Doctors discovered she had leukemia after a bruise she got skiing failed to heal.

I called Crissie. She answered on the second ring.

She was ready for my call. Single and living alone, with most of her family back in Mobile, she'd been comforting frantic callers all week. "Don't worry, it'll get easier," she said. "The first day is the worst."

The doctors went to work.

The drugs they gave Crissie made her vomit, gave her headaches and made her hair fall out. They carried warnings like: "May cause severe reactions including sudden death."

After four weeks of treatment, doctors could find no symptoms of leukemia in her body. She was in remission.

But because the possibility of relapse was great, the treatments continued. Family members flew out often to visit.

Her brain was irradiated, to try to keep the cancer from invading her central nervous system.

The treatments made her so nervous she couldn't sit still. She and her mother would play cards for a few minutes, then Crissie would leap from the table to pace. Sometimes, in the middle of the night, mother and daughter would throw coats over their nightclothes and wander the streets of Berkeley.

During the next few months, she was in and out of the hospital with infections. She continued to audit classes.

She met my midnight flight at Oakland Airport in May, 1982. She looked slightly bloated and pale — her eyebrows had fallen out and her face lacked definition. A scarf covered her bald head.

I was relieved that she didn't look worse.

We went hiking one day, but mostly we sat around her small apartment and ate and watched television. She was listless and uncommunicative, running a temperature and afraid to leave the house. She slipped into a depression that would last several months.

In July, she went home for a visit with family and friends. Back in Berkeley, she volunteered with a group that works with cancer patients. Suddenly, there was something to do. Her spirits rose.

In January this year, the leukemia came back. Crissie called, crying.

She was convinced that she would go into remission again, but she knew that her future held only more of the same: remission, relapse, remission, relapse until, finally, there would be no more remission, only death.

A bone marrow transplant seemed to be her only hope of breaking the cycle.

Even though MediCal — the California state medical insurance plan — would not pay for a transplant outside the state, she decided that her best chances for survival would be at the Hutchinson research center, which pioneered the procedure.

The cost: $100,000. Her father, a real estate developer, paid the bill.

"CHAPTER THIRTEEN: The Snare. Joe's hand was barely six inches from the rifle when he pulled it back. "This may be a trap!" Frank warned. . . .

One hour of radiation to go.

The phone in the control room rings. It is Nina Harris, Crissie's sister.

She had stepped off the plane in Seattle 18 days ago, a housewife from Mobile with a wallet full of pictures of her husband and her children.

She had a shag of fluffy blonde hair and five suitcases stuffed with clothes, romance novels, an iron and even spray starch. I told Nina that spray starch is sold in Seattle. "That's what Daddy said," she told me in her honeyed Alabama voice. She arched one eyebrow, winked and laughed. "I didn't believe him."

Her eight weeks in Seattle will be the longest that Nina has been separated from her family. Except for delivering her children, she had never been in the hospital before.

She is seven years older than Crissie, separated by age, lifestyle and 2,000 miles. She never thought she'd be called upon to save her sister's life.

Bone marrow transplants require a matching of genetic markers, called antigens, between patient and donor — a discovery made in the late 1960s.

Identical twins have identical antigens and, in the early history of transplants, only patients with identical twin donors survived. But in the general population, the chances are one in 10,000 for a match.

Among siblings, the chances for a match are one in four. Nina's marrow matched.

While Crissie's radiation was starting, doctors at Swedish Hospital across the street began removing marrow from Nina. They stuck a long needle through Nina's skin into the pelvic bone — once, twice, up to 300 times. Each time the needle was removed, blood and bits of marrow came with it. They collected about a liter.

The operation will leave her sore for about two weeks, but the greatest risk for Nina, as it is for all donors, was the anesthetic. But besides her marrow, Nina's contribution will be her time. She will stay in Seattle to give Crissie blood when she needs it.

"I can't imagine saying no, not even to a stranger," Nina said.

When Nina told Crissie of her decision, Crissie cried.

Now, Nina is on the phone to the control room, asking how Crissie is doing. Nina says she feels woozy and numb. She sends her love.

I relay the message to Crissie, who smiles and nods.

LEAVING BERKELEY for Seattle, Crissie had to pack all of her belongings and put them into storage. It was eerie not knowing if she would see her things again. She kept thinking about her mother opening the boxes if she died, and she wanted everything to be neat and orderly.

A champion list-maker, she made lists for everything — lists of things for storage, lists of things for Seattle, lists of people to say goodby to, lists of telephone calls to make.

Control became a big issue — what item went in what box, what got stored where, what was taken with us in the U-Haul carrier.

"I can't control my disease," she said often. "I have to take control of what I can."

Another college friend flew out to help with the packing, and learned — after a few tug-of-wars — to let Crissie have control. We had to swallow our opinions and sometimes our anger, and let Crissie run the show.

The three of us left Berkeley on May 11, driving Crissie's silver Honda up the coast of California and Oregon, taking turns at the wheel.

"With my life expectancy," Crissie said, "it's amazing that you guys let me drive."

Crissie-the-Botanist identified the flora: yellow scotch broom, white and purple lupines, digger and ponderosa pine. A large blue bush had Crissie hanging out the car window — it's ceanothus, she said — and she'd never seen it in bloom before.

We rarely talked of our destination. But our second day on the road, as we woke from sleep in a cheap motel, Crissie's baby-bald head peeking out from the blue chenille bedspread was a jolting reminder.

Her family met us in Seattle, where the attending physician spoke of the scores of complications that could kill Crissie: she could die of infection, she could die of marrow graft complications — and she could relapse and die of leukemia.

The marrow transplant kills the cancer in about 50 percent of the patients who survive the first 30-day period. But there is a good chance, the doctor said, that Crissie's leukemia would return.

The "ultimate statistic," he said, is that there is a 30 percent chance that she will be cured.

"I mean by 'cure' that you'll be alive in 3 or 5 or 10 years, without leukemia."

The room was very quiet. Crissie felt she had been prepared, but she was stunned by the doctor's chilling litany. One thought dominated: Risky as the transplant would be, without it, she would die.

She signed the admission papers.

"CHAPTER FIFTEEN: A Suspect Disappears."

Crissie's head hurts, so the radiation is stopped.

A nurse hangs a bag of medication on an intravenous pump next to the stretcher. She attaches the bag to Crissie's Hickman catheter, a tube that runs from just below her collarbone through veins to her heart. It is used to feed her drugs and to draw blood.

Crissie's teeth are on edge. She can't believe the number of delays; each minute seems like an eternity. The 185.6 minutes of radiation needed to kill her marrow has grown, with all the stops and starts, to more than 210 minutes. She wants to scream at the nurse to hurry up and get the radiation started.

When she vomits again, she holds the pan herself. She says over the intercom that she does not want the radiation stopped.

She asks how many minutes of radiation are left. Twenty-one.

She closes her eyes.

SLEEP ELUDED Mary Ellen Cagle on the morning of June 2.

She awakened at 5 a.m. to say a Rosary for her daughter, who would face the radiation room in four hours.

We were both staying at the outpatient apartment, about a half mile from the hospital.

Mrs. Cagle is 69 years old, small and round and sweet. She made the coffee that morning as she did every morning and fussed over a breakfast that neither of us could eat. We kept bumping into each other.

She and Crissie had told Crissie's father, Bill, that he need not fly out to Seattle for the radiation day, so he is back at work in Mobile. Mrs. Cagle wishes he were here now.

At 8:10 a.m., we arrived at the hospital. Crissie was asleep.

Down the hall, an empty room gaped at us. The mattress where, the night before, a man with a swollen belly had struggled for each breath on a respirator, was stripped of sheets.

Mrs. Cagle's eyes widened, and her grip on my arm tightened. "He's gone," she said. Her voice was thick.

Crissie woke at 9 a.m. We sat quietly in the semi-dark room, making small talk about the weather and listening to the approaching murmur of the small herd of doctors and nurses on morning rounds. In minutes they loomed in Crissie's doorway, blocking the light from the hall.

They wished her luck.

Crissie walked to the elevator, pushing her intravenous pump while a nurse and the radiation technician steered the stretcher in front of her. At the elevator, another patient's father wished Crissie good luck.

Two floors down to the basement, past the candy machine, and through the door with the international triangle warning for radiation.

TEN SECONDS of radiation left.

The nurse, the radiation technician and I recite the final countdown, cheering. At zero, the whoosh is heard — the cobalt sources returning to their protective housings for the last time.

Crissie waves at the camera, smiling, but nonetheless looking like a drowning person going down for the last time.

How I wrote the story

I faced three main problems in writing "Crissie's Last Chance."

One was keeping track of an enormous amount of technical material about leukemia and bone-marrow transplants.

The second problem was organizing the story.

The third problem was keeping some distance from the material, given my emotional involvement with Crissie.

Michael Young, my project editor, gave me a great tip on keeping track of the material. After each reporting day in Seattle, I wrote a complete story — as if I were covering the transplant on a daily basis. I tried to write just as I would for publication, complete with "color" and all that jazz.

This procedure has two benefits. First, as I wrote the stories, I was able to find holes in my reporting and patch the holes the next day. Second, when I got back to the newsroom, I had a bunch of separate stories to refer to: one on the radiation day, one on each post-radiation day, one on "what is leukemia," etc. That way, I didn't have to refer too often to my illegible notes and to the tapes that I made for backup.

I kept copies of letters I wrote during that period, in lieu of keeping a diary, which is also probably a good idea.

Once I got back, it seemed obvious to Michael Young and to me that we had to lead the whole series with Crissie on the radiation table. It was the most dramatic moment, and we wanted to start with strong stuff.

We also decided, after much debate, that each day had to lead with Crissie. I had wanted to lead the second and third days with baby Paula, another cancer patient, and with the description of the family kitchen, a lounge for patients and their families — two strong passages, I thought. But Michael and Joel Rawson, the metropolitan managing editor, insisted that the series was about Crissie, and each day had to begin with Crissie. They were right.

Once we made the decision to begin with the radiation, the material seemed to divide naturally into two additional parts: Crissie suffering in the hospital, and Crissie recovering in the outpatient apartment.

The internal organization was harder, and each day of the series was put together differently. The first day started in the present and went into the past. The flashbacks were telescoped to bring the reader from the point 14 years ago when Crissie and I met in college to the morning of the radiation day. This was Michael's idea, and I think it worked well.

The first day began solemnly, and then lightened up (I think) when I started reading "The Hardy Boys." We used this pattern in the second and third days, as well, to give it a tone that reflects (I hope) Crissie's sense of humor.

The second day was straight chronology, with breaks for descriptions about the other patients on the ward (Lisa, baby Paula), who died. We decided to save all the survivors for the third day, so we could end on a fairly positive note. The third day was a mess, right up until the end. We had no "action" for the lead and finally Michael thought of starting with a straight description, moving Crissie through the rooms. Again, I think it worked.

As I wrote, I found myself asking myself two questions: "What was it *really* like?" and, its corollary, "Who cares?" I asked myself those two questions with almost every sentence, and it helped me to delete a lot of the purplish prose that I originally spewed into the computer. I think that I have always asked myself those two questions whenever I've written anything — but this time I became conscious of asking them. This happened accidentally, after mulling a piece of advice from a colleague, Roger House: "You have to interview yourself," he said. "Be ruthless."

The trick was being personal but not *too* personal. Sometimes, I failed to ask "Who cares?" and Michael had to step in and ask. For example, he convinced me that no reader would care that I was upset and frightened when Crissie was being irradiated. Reporter Irene Wielawski also helped by tactfully telling me that some of my apostrophizing was beside the point.

I became almost totally dependent on Michael's judgment. I was so close to the material that I was unable to do some of the self-editing that usually helps me write. I was very touchy about the whole thing, and we had some terrible fights, but Michael hung in there and *made* me write.

People complain that these "How I Wrote the Story" pieces wind up sounding like Academy Award acceptances ("I'd like to thank my parents, my first-grade teacher..."), but I would argue that the process of writing that we are all so interested in is almost always a collaborative effort. And, being nice folks, we want those who helped us to share the recognition.

So, here's my list of people who helped, aside from those already mentioned: Kristen Kelch (on loan from *Newsday*; she helped me hammer out the part about college days and interviewed me about it until I got the tone right); reporters Scanlan and Jones; editor Reid; photographer Anestis Diakopoulos and artist George Sylvia (I never realized how much research the graphics people put into these things); and photo editor Chip Maury, for coaching me in person and over the phone (a neat trick) about my photographs. Apologies to anyone I forgot.

Crissie and her family, of course, helped enormously — by trusting me with their pain, and by never once trying to write the piece for me.

Joel was responsible for fine-tuning the whole thing, developing the tension in certain parts of the story (Paula's death, for example) and giving me the confidence to attempt such an undertaking in the first place.

P.S. Crissie's back in Berkeley and doing well. She liked the story.

(Editor's note. The bone-marrow transplant described in Marialisa Calta's series didn't work, and eventually Crissie relapsed. She died on Feb. 4, 1985, one month after marking the third anniversary of her diagnosis. Her ashes were scattered on San Francisco Bay. In a story about her friend's death, Calta described a memorial service at which Crissie's words, written a year earlier about her illness, were read:

"The purpose of my having cancer: For other people, a chance to share, to learn, to grow through me; to know, through me, about their own life, sickness and death.")

How I edited the story

Michael R. Young,
assistant metropolitan managing editor

The Crissie series, by Marialisa Calta, was an extremely personal story. A reporter's friend is sick with cancer. The brutal details of illness, the intimate moments of friendship, are bared for public perusal.

No matter how hardened the reporter, details like these don't just flow into a story. My relationship with the reporter became essential to getting the series into print. It had to be a series built on trust. Crissie had to trust Maria, Maria had to trust me. I had to trust my instincts, and my boss.

In the spring of 1983, Maria approached me about the story. I was regional news editor in the Warwick office and she was a top reporter. She had been doing solid work, everything from well-written news features to hard-bitten stories on polluted clams. We got along well; we thought alike. Our relationship was based on cooperation, trust and similar news judgment.

That day in my office, she laid out Crissie's plight and proposed going to Seattle to stay with her friend during the ordeal.

I said sure, on one condition: I get to edit the stories.

We started making plans. We talked. It was during those discussions that my role began.

A good editor should do more than dot i's and cross t's; in fact, should do more than rewrite copy. A good editor communicates with the writer, helping her to plan the project, to focus the story, to organize the material. This process should start when the idea first germinates, and continue through to the last rewrite of the last paragraph of the last story.

I spent nearly three months on the project full time, almost all of it helping Maria focus the material and polish the writing. Only five days were devoted to the mechanical tasks normally associated with an editor's job: editing, headline writing, cutline writing, supervising paste-up, meeting with promotion people.

I helped Maria draft a proposal, outlining cost of transportation and lodging, and other expenses, and the time she would need. Since there would be two critical times — one when Crissie received the bone-marrow transplant and one six months later when she was discharged from the hospital — we decided to do it in two trips.

The newspaper wants good writing, and it is willing to make the investment in time and money. But it helps to find some ways to save money.

Maria stayed with relatives in Seattle, so the newspaper had to pay only transportation and minimal daily costs. I helped by pledging not to whine for another reporter while Maria was off-staff. The remaining reporters in the office closed ranks and picked up her assignments during her absence.

We had a few ideas on the story's theme, but it all boiled down to taking risks. Crissie was taking a risk with this experimental procedure. Maria was taking a risk trying to cover the story. In fact, some of her fellow reporters warned her not to do it, that it would be too difficult, too emotional. But we planned to go out on a limb, like Crissie, as a way to communicate the tension.

First, we would do the entire series in first person. First person is a no-no in the macho, hard-news world of journalism. I think it's frowned upon because it's so easy to do badly, to come across as phony or sappy. You can hide behind attribution and third person, but when you write in your own voice, you really stick your neck out.

Second, in an effort to find a new angle on the oft-told "cancer story," we planned to focus not on the disease, but on the friendship of two women who had fumbled together through those formative college years.

And finally, we wanted to do the ultimate writing job. We planned to experiment with technique, to layer different styles in the same story, to showcase Maria's strong literary talents.

Thus fully prepared, Maria submitted the proposal to Joel Rawson, the newspaper's metropolitan managing editor and resident writing guru. He liked it right away. I knew Joel would bite, because he's taught me most of my editing methods, including proper preparation.

We didn't try to structure the story before Maria left. We talked over the basic theme, the medical information she would need, the pictures, etc. The only advice I gave her was to set aside about an hour at the end of each day to write a "story" about the day. This accomplished three goals:

1. It eliminated Maria's having to plow through piles of notes when she sat down to write the final story. This was especially important in this series, because there would be long periods of time when she would not be actively involved in the story.

2. At the end of the day, you tend to focus on those events that had the biggest impact. Thus, the important stuff rises to the top.

3. When Maria returned from Seattle, she had a pile of daily stories that helped me get involved early. Instead of having to wait for her to write the final series, I could review her daily stories and get an early idea of what she had.

When she returned from Seattle, we spent three or four days just talking about the story and what had happened. This was the traditional debriefing that any city editor would do with a reporter — ask questions, get the reporter to run through the material. But in a series this complex, it obviously took a lot longer and became much more involved.

Basically, I was trying to focus her material into definable stories. How would the stuff break down into daily stories, both by subject matter and by quantity of material? Where were the weak points — did she need to do more reporting? What kinds of writing styles could we use?

Reporters occasionally tell you great stuff during debriefing that never appears in the paper. I was listening for (and jotting down) good anecdotal material that Maria discussed but might forget to write as the project wore on.

We decided the material warranted a three-day series that would follow a time line: Day one would cover the radiation treatment; day two, the early stages of recovery; and day three, the release and a look ahead.

We chose the chronological approach to the overall project because that would enable us to be more experimental with the individual stories. It's like painting your walls white so that you can hang artwork with vivid colors.

We divided the photos, graphics and sidebars among the days. Maria started writing, and I left her alone until she could produced a rough draft.

From the early stages of writing, it was obvious this would be a tough one. She had great information, lovely writing, good ideas; but when it came to getting "up close and personal," Maria was having a problem. She knew she needed to get herself more involved in the story, but the trauma, the pain, the horror of it all made it difficult to write.

When the emotions became too intense, Maria tried to back away from the personal account and write a medical story. She said she was afraid of embarrassing herself, the paper, her friend. I had to be her safety net, to convince her I wouldn't allow a bad series to be published.

My only recourse was to pull it out of her. It meant we had to go through the story line by line and I had to, on occasion, almost interview her: "How did you feel here?" "Did Crissie cry when that happened?" "What was the look on her mother's face?"

Sometimes it got bitter. I was forcing Maria to relive events that she was subconsciously trying to bury. We had strong disagreements over some of the stuff. Occasionally I would give in: "You're right. This is too personal and doesn't serve the reader, doesn't advance the story. It's too maudlin."

There has been a lot of emphasis on editors' being more sensitive to the needs of writers. But editors — and writers — shouldn't lose sight of the need for honesty, even if it seems brutal. An editor afraid to offend a writer runs the risk of making the writer feel the story isn't worth improving.

At times I would lose my confidence. Maria would win me over with her emotional argument, even though I knew the material was necessary. I would then turn to Joel, who, like the trainer for a punch-drunk boxer, would throw a little water in my face, pat me on the butt and send me back into the ring. He became my backstop.

Once we agreed on the content, the writing became fun.

For day one, we settled on a complex layering of writing styles. We started with Crissie on the radiation table, the most dramatic event of her hospital stay. Since it was the first day, we had to introduce the characters; we decided to telescope back to when Crissie and Maria first met, in college. We then ran two simultaneous time lines —

Crissie and Maria's relationship, and Crissie in the hospital — until we brought the reader back to the radiation room.

Further complicating day one, we chose the "Hardy Boys" segments, to keep the whole thing in the present tense as the two past-tense time lines proceeded.

Our intent with the "Hardy Boys" references was twofold: We wanted to introduce some of the gallows humor that characterized the relationship between Maria and Crissie. And we wanted to get that surrealistic dream effect you occasionally see in movies, in which heavy breathing is superimposed over the dream; it keeps you in the present while the dream takes you to another plane. We wanted readers to remember that Crissie's body was getting bombarded, even as we carried them back through the fun-loving college years.

As we went through various generations of day one, I hit on a new method of fine-tuning the editing. Editors are always trying to look at a story from yet another perspective to see if they can improve it, and I noticed that I was able to "see" more of the story when it was set in print.

So I started setting Maria's early drafts in print, about 36 picas wide, approximately the width of a hardcover book. I would then hang the long strip of wide type on the wall, and we would sit back and stare at it, making changes in the columns. The method has since become routine on projects here at the *Journal-Bulletin.*

Day two roughed out fairly easily. The writing technique wasn't nearly as intricate as for day one, but we liked the straightforward style and thought it would be a big relief from the layered methods of the first day. Also, we planned to introduce the inside of the hospital, and some of the other patients. In retrospect it was the weakest story of the three, but I can't think of any better way to have done it.

Writing day three was tough — we didn't have a lead. We knew where we wanted to go, we had the ending, but we didn't know how to get into it. This day caused the most acrimony, because Maria had run out of strong material and couldn't figure out a way of getting in.

The solution: more reporting. We decided to begin inside the apartment. Maria had little material, so she ended up calling Crissie, her family, hospital members, to flesh it out. Since we had already settled on the mountain imagery for the end, the rest of the story flowed.

The humor Maria sprinkled throughout the series spilled over into our relationship. Since we were pulling and tugging on each other's psyche so much, we needed the relief. While we were in the final two months of preparing the series, the paper was giving saturation coverage to a young boy's liver transplant. Every day, the paper would do a little update on the child under the logo "Mikey's Condition." Maria cut the logo out and pasted it on a piece of paper. At the end of each day, she would write down my "condition": crabby, unreasonable, agreeable.

I still have the paper. The last entry is Oct. 26. The next day, two weeks before the project was due to run, my wife was rushed to the hospital, where she gave birth to our daughter, seven weeks premature.

The next three weeks were touch and go, for both the baby and the project. I would work on the project during the day, then stay with the baby during the evening. In a way, my two "lives" coexisted well. Working on the series enabled me to stop worrying about the baby. And vice versa.

And perhaps because of all the tension, this period ended up being the most creative of my life. Maria and I would spend literally two hours polishing one paragraph. When we disagreed, she would go to one VDT and I to another. We would rewrite, then return to argue. It kept getting better.

The series was published Nov. 13. My baby left the hospital five days later. Both have withstood the test of time.

Rosa Parks visits and recalls her ride into history

By Brian C. Jones
The Providence Journal-Bulletin, June 30, 1984

I did board the bus, and I found a seat in the section just back of where the white passengers would stop and we would begin. And there was only one seat available, because the back of the bus was filled up....

And when on the stop, the third stop after I had boarded the bus, a few white people came on the bus, and when they had taken their seats, there was one man - a white man - standing.

The driver noticed he was standing, and he asked the two of us to move and let him have — he described it as a "front seat." He said: "Let me have those front seats.... The first time he spoke, none of us moved immediately.

That's how Rosa L. Parks began her story yesterday.

The story of how one woman's gentle anger almost 29 years ago began the movement that banished legal segregation from the United States.

Actually, the story was told twice.

One telling was by fourth- and fifth-grade pupils from Providence's Gilbert Stuart School, who performed a play about Mrs. Parks' refusal to give up her seat to a white man while she was riding on a Montgomery, Ala., bus.

The play shows how after she was arrested, blacks in Montgomery began a year-long boycott of the city's bus system, led by the late Rev. Martin Luther King Jr. The boycott's success sparked further civil rights protests.

MRS. PARKS, 71, sat in the third pew at Pond Street Baptist Church in South Providence, and watched Varee Richardson, 10, reenact the part of Parks and Christopher Robinson, 12, play King.

The church, three-quarters filled with children, including youngsters from the vacation Bible schools of the Ebenezer and the Olney Street Baptist Churches, rang with civil rights anthems and moving words.

With the patient look of all parents and grandmothers at school plays, Mrs. Parks watched as the children dragged a large piece of cardboard, shaped like a bus, across the front of the church.

"Rosa Parks' feet hurt. Her job as a seamstress in a Montgomery, Ala., department store kept her on the run. All that day of Dec. 1, 1955, she had pinned up hems, raised waistlines...." the play begins.

Mrs. Parks broke out in a big smile at one point, as the children's reenactment of the boycott showed it beginning to take its toll on the thousands of people supporting it.

The children held up signs telling how the participants were fired from their jobs. But then Christopher ran around snatching the signs and throwing them on the floor. Mrs. Parks just had to smile.

BUT AFTERWARD, she was truly weary. Now somewhat frail, she complained that television lights hurt her eyes, and people helped her up the church steps.

She still found the strength to retell her story for reporters, as she sat uncomfortably at the end of a long, empty table in the church study, under the glare of TV lights.

And (the driver) said: "Will y'all make it light on yourselves and let me have those seats?" I don't know who stood first, the man who was on the seat with me, or the two women across the aisle.

But when the man stood up, I just moved and let him pass and stayed where I was. And then the women, they also moved. And when they moved and left me sitting down, the driver asked me if I was going to stand up.

I told him, no, I wasn't.

He said: "If you don't stand up, I'm going to call the police and have you arrested."

And I said: "Well, you may do that."

And I stayed where I was until he left the bus and came back in a few minutes.... Several people left the bus at that time. Some people asked for a transfer — he gave everybody a transfer who wanted one — and (they) simply got off without saying anything.

Cheryl Fisher was 4 years old when Rosa Parks' simple "no" made history. For the past six years, as a teacher at Gilbert Stuart School, she has made Mrs. Parks part of the curriculum.

"I try in every class of mine (to teach) that if you believe strongly in something, then you have to fight for it. And it doesn't mean that you have to be out there and be physical," Miss Fisher says.

DURING Black History month, Miss Fisher focuses on a "famous black American," and this past year, she picked Mrs. Parks, reworking a written story into a play, which her students performed at other schools.

When Miss Fisher learned that Mrs. Parks, now an aide to Rep. John Conyers Jr., D-Mich, was coming to Providence this week for a series of programs focusing on civil rights, she was thrilled.

Miss Fisher tells her pupils that because of Mrs. Parks, white and black children can now go to the same school, sit next to each other, eat with each other in the cafeteria. Some of the children are incredulous when she tells them laws once kept black and whites separate.

When it came time to do the play, the pupil picked to act the part of the bus driver — a child of Southeast Asian parents — refused, because the script called for him to use the word "nigger."

Miss Fisher changed the script to read "Negro." But she said she still had trouble casting the play when she explained that white students couldn't play parts written for blacks, and vice-versa.

"I finally did the audition and I said: 'Okay, I need so-and-so, a black person.' I had so many hands go up in the air: 'I'm not really white, Miss Fisher, I'm not all white.' I mean, all of a sudden no one wanted to be white."

"And I thought that was terrific. And I said that this is what Mrs. Parks is all about, this is what she wanted, that she is so glad that we are sitting here doing this right now, and if it wasn't for her, we wouldn't be able to."

And the policemen came on the bus.... They wanted to know what the problem was, the trouble. The driver said, well, he needed that seat, those seats, and (said): "The other three stood and that one didn't." He just said: "That one." He didn't say that what.

So one of the policeman approached me and asked me if the driver had asked me to stand up. I said yes.

And he said: "Why didn't you stand up?"

I told him I didn't think I should have to stand up.

And he said: "Why do you push us around?" . . . I quote the policeman exactly. He said: "I don't know, but the law is the law, and you are under arrest."

And the moment he told me I was under arrest, I stood up. One picked up my purse, one picked up my shopping bag, and we left the bus together.

How I wrote the story

Some stories turn out OK because you have more than enough time to do them, because the people you are covering are willing to be covered, because things break in your favor, and because the event is so inherently interesting that what you write is almost guaranteed to be inherently interesting.

Stories, in other words, like the Rosa Parks story.

Mrs. Parks was the black department-store seamstress in Montgomery, Ala., who sparked the civil-rights movement when she refused to give up her seat on a bus to a white man. After police arrested her, the Rev. Martin Luther King Jr. organized a successful boycott of the city bus system. The rest is history.

Mrs. Parks came to Providence for several days last month — it's never been entirely clear to me why — had a section of a South Providence roadway named for her, and attended some functions in her honor.

My story fell in the middle of these events, when Mrs. Parks was to appear at a South Providence church for a program involving young people. The assigning editor, Carol Young, envisioned it as a contrast of generations: Talk to some of the teenagers for their impressions of Mrs. Parks and her accomplishments.

I tried. The day before, I called up a church Bible school that was sending some students to the program, and arranged for the teacher to pick one student and keep him or her on hand after the program so journalistic brain surgery could be performed.

The "student" turned out to be one of the Bible-school teachers, and she didn't have a lot to say, other than that she thought Mrs. Parks was pretty nice, and how come more people hadn't shown up, anyway?

I thought of another angle. The main event here was a play by Providence schoolchildren about the Rosa Parks incident. Why not interview the little thing who played Mrs. Parks? "I think she is a very nice lady" was the substance of the interview.

Well, you say, what about just describing the program itself? And I answer with another question: Have you ever been to a school play?

There was, moreover, something distinctly disturbing about this program. Mrs. Parks, as the child had said, did seem like a "very nice" lady, but she's 71 years old now, and an old 71 years. She had to be helped up the church steps, it was a hot day, and I didn't think it was exactly considerate to force her to sit through a dumb school play. Frankly, I had the impression that the organizers were essentially hauling this poor historical symbol from place to place, the way St. Joseph's Day celebrants drag a statue of the saint around Federal Hill annually. But it wasn't disturbing enough to write an unpleasant story about.

Finally, two things developed. During the program, the teacher whose students had put on the play made a big deal about how she revered Rosa Parks, so I interviewed her. And she told me some really great things about her students' reaction to putting on the play — during the school year a lot of compelling things like how one kid, a Hmong, outright refused to say the word "nigger," which appeared in the script.

Further, I noticed the TV folks were set up in the church offices to do interviews with Mrs. Parks afterwards. Now, an interview with Mrs. Parks was the last thing I had planned. Bert Wade had done one already for that day's paper, and I figured we had had our shot. And having seen her carted up the church steps, I wasn't about to be known as The Reporter Who Killed Rosa Parks.

But since TV was already poised, I asked Debbie Horne, a Channel 12 reporter who used to work here, if I could just sort of watch while she finished off Rosa Parks. And she was really nice and said OK, although I thought Debbie's camerawoman was going to murder her as a result.

Anyway, to move this thing along, Debbie Horne didn't successfully make the transition from newspaper to television because she doesn't know how to ask questions. She asked Mrs. Parks straight out about the 1955 incident, a question that probably never gets asked anymore, because everyone is supposed to know the answer and because everyone assumes Mrs. Parks isn't about to tell it for the umpteen-millionth time.

Well, she did tell it. And talk about being around to hear history firsthand. Now I know that probably that if King and company hadn't had Mrs. Parks, they would have found someone else to help start the civil rights movements, because the time was ripe. But in fact it was Mrs. Parks and her determination to be treated fairly that did begin the whole thing. And to hear her tell it was one of those rare, incredible times when reporting gets so exciting that you can hardly stand it. I had a tape recorder, and I promise always to have a tape recorder at historical events from now on.

Her narrative was compelling because it

was so detailed and uniquely spoken: After all these years, she told her story as if she were telling it for the first time. She remembered who was sitting next to her and in front of her, and who got off before the arrest started.

So when it came to writing the story, I wanted the reader to hear the story just as I had heard it: a simple matter of doing a transcript of her taped narrative, and putting large blocks of it into the story.

I sometimes wrestle over this issue of letting the news subjects do my writing for me. But for the most eloquent ones, there's never any question: They tell it better than I could; that's why I've gone to see them.

To make sure the reader got the point, I started the story with the first direct quote block — something I really hate to do, thinking that reporters get paid, if for anything, for writing lead paragraphs.

The next step was simple: to explain what was going on, put enough background in — structural things.

Finally, the event which produced Mrs. Parks' retelling, the school play, and the interview I had with the teacher who produced the play had some dramatic elements — which required, of all things, actual reporting, so I added that.

I wish it were more complicated, but most clichés are true, including the one about how good stories tell themselves.

Struggle over 'stolen' land

Nicaraguan Indians fight their Sandinista 'liberators'

By Randall Richard
The Providence Journal and *The Evening Bulletin*, July 25, 1984

SAN JOSE, Costa Rica — The silhouette of the Sandinista patrol boat flickered in bone-white lightning off Captain Largo's port bow.

In an instant, the sky went black. The boat was gone. The sea was empty.

Only the ghost of the boat remained — a negative image frozen white on black by the shock of light on Largo's retina.

Largo closed his eyes to hold the image. Mounted on the bow was a gun — an M-30 capable of blowing his boat out of the water with just one burst.

Instinctively, he kicked the rudder to his left and braced for the sound of gunfire.

There was none — just a single, deafening clap of thunder.

LARGO'S 55-horsepower Evinrude was at full throttle but managed only an anemic cough as his boat swirled in the blackness and levitated atop unseen swells.

Bundled in clear plastic tarpaulin below decks were 76 Soviet-made AK-47 rifles. Lashed to the gunwales at the stern were two 55-gallon drums of gasoline.

The guns and the gasoline were destined for CIA-backed rebels in Tasbaponi — a Miskito Indian village 60 miles to the north on Nicaragua's Atlantic Coast.

A DIRECT HIT on one of the drums would mean a fiery death for the 20-year-old gunrunner and his three-man crew. Surrender would mean 50 years in a Sandinista prison.

Largo's options were few. Weighted down as he was, he had little chance of outrunning the Sandinistas in his ancient 25-foot turtling boat. He had no chance of outgunning them.

For a moment, he considered tossing the fuel overboard. But the rebels in Tasbaponi needed the fuel even more than they needed his guns.

Despite the odds, Largo decided to gamble.

He would have to outguess the Sandinista gunners and change course instantly after each burst of lightning to elude their fire.

Even without the patrol boat to contend with, the slightest miscalculation in such a boiling sea would end in disaster.

His only hope was that the flashes of lightning would be few and far between — and that the Sandinistas, in trying to stay afloat themselves, would be too busy to hunt him down.

AT THE NEW YORK BAR in downtown San Jose, Largo's front tooth gleamed gold as he drew a mug of beer to his thin black lips.

His second-in-command — a Miskito teenager — listened intently while grabbing at the plaster that encased his own bullet-riddled right leg. The teenager swung the leg slowly from under the table in a wide arc and lowered it gently onto a barstool as Largo spoke.

Despite the pain, the youngster grinned stupidly as his captain's tale unfolded. He was transfixed. It was as if he hadn't been there himself, as if he was waiting to find out whether they had both survived.

Largo spoke in the lyrical cadence of a Caribbean out-islander:

"If I had me a FAL, mon — an M-30, an M-50, even an MPG-2 — I hit the pilothouse and everything is done — all them guys are dead, mon — all mashed up ...

"Every six minutes, mon — every 10 minutes, the lightning come in the east. ... I tell my second: 'Hermano,' I say, 'hold south — 15 minutes.' If Largo guess right, mon, maybe next time the lightning come and the Sandinista be far off. Maybe not. Maybe Largo guess wrong. Maybe Largo dies."

Largo stopped, looked at Hermano and laughed, his gold tooth gleaming with pride over his decision to head south.

"Then I go to the key — to my dodging spot — to sleep. At 5:30 in the afternoon, Largo and Hermano go to Tasbaponi. The guys them were there waiting. Twelve come to meet us — hungry, mon, tired. Some have no boots, no bullets. I give them everything — coffee, AKs, bullets, gasoline. Then I shake them hands and say, 'Well, Largo, he has to go again.' The Miskito boys them brave, mon, he want to fight the Sandinista. Some day, mon, them boys be free."

FIVE YEARS AGO last Thursday — while young Sandinista rebels were marching triumphantly into downtown Managua — Largo was working with his father, diving for lobster in the still, emerald waters off Corn Island.

He was 15 years old at the time and like nearly everyone on Corn Island, he knew little and cared less about the fighting that had been raging for months across the mountains to the west.

Largo and his people live in a world apart — in culture, language, religion and tradition — from the Spanish-speaking Mestizos of the Pacific.

As far as Largo's people were concerned, the Sandinista war against the dictator Anastasio Somoza was something for the "Spaniards" to worry about. It had nothing to do with them.

The waves of terror and bloodshed that had washed over Somoza's Nicaragua had never reached the tranquil shores of Corn Island, or, for that matter, the entire Atlantic zone of Nicaragua.

Somoza's Nicaragua and his ravenous appetite for land and power — except for a few isolated pockets where he plundered gold and lumber — ended at the frontier town of Rama in the center of the country. It is at Rama that the dusty road from Managua abruptly ends and it is there that the journey east to Largo's home by riverboat is a journey into centuries past.

TO THE NORTH of Rama are the gold-mining towns of Rosita and Bonanza and the lush riverbeds of the Waspuk and mighty Rio Coco. To the south and east are rainforests, savanna, swamplands, lagoons and one of the largest coastal plains of Central America. This is Nicaragua's primitive and desolate La Miskitia.

Only one in 10 Nicaraguans lives there — mostly Miskito, Suma and Rama Indians or English-speaking blacks from Jamaica — but it comprises more than half Nicaragua's territory.

But for the gold to the north and the once-vast pine forests to the east, Somoza had paid little attention to the region. The few roads that were built were for hauling lumber to the rivers. There are even fewer schools and virtually no medical facilities. No one, until the Sandinistas came to power on July 19, 1979, had even bothered to link the territory to Managua by telegraph.

Today, La Miskitia is the site of a bloody Indian uprising against the 5-year-old Sandinista government in Managua.

Largo became part of this uprising more than a year ago, and like many of his Indian cousins in the towns and villages that dot the Atlantic Coast, he is fighting for only one thing — for the land and property that he says the Sandinistas stole from him.

IT WAS NOT until the Sandinistas came to the Atlantic Coast one month after their victory over Somoza — ostensibly to "liberate" Largo's people from centuries of oppression — that the troubles began.

However well-intentioned the victorious young Sandinistas might have been, they committed one blunder after another in their dealings with the Miskitos. They set up schools — but initially insisted that the Indians become literate in Spanish, not Miskito. They established farming cooperatives — but in the process took from them their ancient tribal lands.

Later, when remnants of Somoza's old Guardia Nacional started crisscrossing the Coco river — Nicaragua's border with Honduras — to launch hit-and-run attacks against isolated Sandinista outposts, the Sandinistas moved thousands of Indians off the river to "resettlement camps" in the center of the country. In the process, they destroyed a way of life that had gone pretty much unchanged since the days of Columbus.

By 1981, small bands of Indians were

attacking Sandinista outposts with rocks, spears and arrows. Today, they attack with the AK-47 rifles that Largo brings them.

LARGO'S BOSS is Brooklyn Rivera, one of the few Miskito Indians who had gone off to Managua to study and who had stayed to fight with the Sandinistas against Somoza.

Rivera abandoned the Sandinista cause in 1981 and now heads Misurasata — a coalition of Miskito, Suma and Rama Indians that is waging a complex and little-understood war along the Atlantic Coast.

"After the triumph of the revolution," says Rivera, "I quit my position of teaching math at the university in Managua. I felt I had to do something for my people and so I went home. They were in misery — suffering from discrimination. . . .

"I decided to organize my people so they could participate within the revolution. I had great faith in the revolution, I wanted them to benefit from it — so I helped create Misurasata.

"But when I spoke too strongly for my people, I began to have problems. The Sandinista commander gave me one week to define my position — to accept a position with the government — to renounce my people. If not, he told me, they would not be responsible for my life. . . .

"It is true, I told him — it is true that I am a Nicaraguan, a Sandinista. But I am a Miskito first."

A SECOND COALITION of Indians, Misura, is led by Steadman Fagoth Mueller — a Miskito of German ancestry — and is fighting the Sandinistas in the north, along the Honduran border.

Rivera and Fagoth are enemies, however, and each has allied his group with separate and competing groups of Spanish-speaking anti-Sandinista rebels.

Rivera's alliance is with another disenchanted Sandinista — Eden Pastora — the legendary Commander Zero of the Sandinista revolution who resigned as Nicaragua's deputy defense minister two years ago.

Fagoth's group is allied with the Nicaraguan Democratic Front (FDN) — the so-called contras who are led, in part, by former members of Somoza's national guard — the same people Rivera and Pastora helped defeat in 1979.

Even those within Nicaragua who support the Sandinistas — who say that Pastora and Rivera have sold out to the CIA in their lust for personal power — agree that there are important distinctions between their forces and those of the FDN-Fagoth alliance.

Pastora's troops, they say, concentrate on military targets, while the FDN engages in a terror campaign against civilians. Rivera's troops, they say, are "misguided" volunteers, while Fagoth kidnaps Indian youngsters to fight for him and kills those who refuse.

DESPITE THEIR ALLIANCE, even Pastora and Rivera have vastly different reasons for fighting the Sandinistas. Pastora's concerns about press censorship, democratic elections and Nicaragua's ties to Cuba and the Soviet Union are of little interest to Rivera and his Miskito Indians.

Like the young Sandinista rebels who poured into Managua five years ago — united against a common enemy but divided in what they expected from the revolution — they, too, have different visions of Nicaragua's future, their own dreams and soaring aspirations.

Rivera's goal is to force a change in Sandinista policy toward the Indians. Pastora's goal is to change the government itself. But Rivera's people say that since the CIA is far more interested in changing the central government in Managua than it is in Indian rights, the money it is pouring into its not-so-"covert" war in Nicaragua goes primarily to the FDN and, until recently, to Pastora.

As political orphans, the Indians have therefore had to turn to their Spanish-speaking allies for money and supplies — Fagoth to the FDN and Rivera to Pastora.

CIA funding for Pastora, however, reportedly began drying up about three months ago because Pastora remained adamant about refusing to join forces with the FDN in a coordinated campaign against the Sandinistas.

PASTORA SAYS he cannot join forces with the FDN for "ideological reasons."

Though he and Rivera are also fighting to topple the Sandinistas and are together in Washington today looking for new money to do it, Pastora says his group and Rivera's Misurasata are far different from the FDN and Fagoth's Misura.

Pastora describes some FDN leaders as

"bloodthirsty beasts" but says his army and Rivera's Miskitos make up a "truly peoples' army."

In an interview two weeks ago, Pastora said he suspects that those most bitter about his refusal to fight with the FDN may have been responsible for a bombing at his jungle headquarters last month — a bombing in which he and 15 journalists were injured and 10 people, including an American newswoman, were killed.

PASTORA SAYS he decided to quit his post in the Sandinista government after he saw a draft of a speech that was scheduled to be delivered by the Sandinista leadership on the second anniversary of the revolution.

"When I saw what that speech was saying about the future of my country, I decided I had to leave. I began to see clearly the direction that the revolution was taking. I saw more and more the nationalization of industries within the country, and I did not want to become involved in that particular process."

But even more than Sandinista speeches, it is Sandinista deeds and the fear of what might happen next that frightens Pastora and the two main dissident groups on the Pacific coast of Nicaragua today — the private-enterprise sector and the hierarchy of the Roman Catholic Church.

BUSINESSMEN and landholders are upset because the government regulates wages and prices, prohibits profits from being sent abroad and controls the flow of money through government-owned banks.

They say the government also arbitrarily exercises its authority to confiscate farmlands that are "underutilized" and businesses that are being "decapitalized" by owners who are either unable or unwilling to reinvest in their operations.

Also, a number of measures that were taken to help the poor quickly alienated the middle-class. Soon after coming to power, taxes were hiked sharply to pay for new social programs while rents were ordered cut by 50 percent for families paying $50 a month or less. While these measures won the Sandinistas many friends among the poor, it was a severe blow to property owners and landlords.

The hierarchy of the Catholic Church is troubled primarily by what it sees as Marxist indoctrination of schoolchildren, censorship, the arrest and imprisonment of suspected counter-revolutionaries without due process and a new draft law that has no provision for conscientious objectors.

Despite these concerns, there are many Nicaraguans — including those unhappy with the Sandinistas — who will admit they feel freer now than they did under Somoza, and that unlike Salvadorans and Guatemalans they need not fear soldiers bursting into their homes and massacring everyone inside.

THE CONCERNS that Rivera and his Indians have are far simpler. What they want is the freedom and independence they enjoyed by default under the Somoza regime.

In an interview at his headquarters in Costa Rica, Rivera conceded that the Sandinistas may be trying to divide him and Pastora by making several recent conciliatory gestures toward the Miskitos — gestures that include the release of 300 Miskito prisoners and a grant of amnesty for all Miskito rebels who are willing to lay down their arms.

Though he sees these gestures as a "positive step," Rivera bitterly denounces them as inadequate:

"We have been analyzing the amnesty decree.... But amnesty means pardon, and we are not so clear how the Sandinistas can pardon the Indians when it is they who repress the people, when it is they who arbitrarily imprison and persecute the Indian.

"They destroyed all the Indian villages. They massacred the Indian. How can they announce a pardon of these same Indians? This is a contradiction."

"We are obliged to think that they are trying to please some of their friends, and perhaps to drive a wedge between the Indians and Pastora.... The main problem that the Sandinistas have is with the Indian. They think that if they resolve the Indian crisis, all the other opposition groups will have less power and opportunity to struggle against them....

"This amnesty decree is a recognition of our Indian struggle. In the past, they have never accepted that they were fighting with the Indians. They always said that in the Atlantic region they were fighting only the Somocistas — the contras."

RIVERA SAYS his war with the Sandinistas will end if they agree to withdraw most military forces from the Miskito Coast, recognize Misurasata as the representative of the Indian people in Nicaragua, and "give freedom to the Indians to cultivate their own lands and fish in the river and sea without government control."

The Indians, he says, are not "separatists" as the Sandinistas insist, but are fighting for their own "regional government — something similar to a state within the United States.... As Indians and Nicaraguans, we will participate in all the national issues but we will have our own particular situation of control in the region...."

Rivera says he thinks there's a chance that the Sandinistas will agree to those conditions:

"I think they are already convinced and, in principle, agree — but according to their own interests. So, what we need to do is to agree on the details on how this can work.... We see the door open now to get some kind of peaceful solution. But it doesn't mean that we will stop our struggle. We will continue until one day they will sit down with us."

The main difference between his group and Fagoth's, he says, is that Fagoth "has closed the door to any possibility of negotiation or peaceful solution.... Why? Because his bosses (the FDN and CIA) say no — you don't have to say anything about the Indians because there is no Indian struggle....

"Here, we can say freely — even though we are in an alliance ... (with Pastora) that if we see any door opening to liberate the Indians, we will go home — we will walk. We don't have other political or ideological interests."

IT WAS INSANE, Largo now admits, far too dangerous for a gun-runner to linger in Nicaraguan waters. But he could not resist telling Hermano to set course for Corn Island after delivering the AK-47s to the Miskito warriors. He needed a glimpse of home.

"Largo and Hermano were tired, mon, cold. We sleep at my dodging spot but not so good. We sleep in the sand. The sand, mon, it is wet. If I sleep on the south part, I can't rest because there is too much sand fly. So Largo and Hermano go up to where the breeze is. Cold, mon, but we have to stand it. Better cold than the flies....

"At 5:30, Largo and Hermano wake up. I tell my second — 'Hermano,' I say, 'hold the wheel southeast for one half hour....

"We have only condensed milk, a few biscuits.... We are just sucking the sweet milk like this.... Well, I call my second, I say, 'Hermano,' I say, 'look at us, we are just sucking the sweet milk. We have fresh water but we have nothing to mix it in.' Hermano looks on me. I says, 'Hermano, we must have a glass.' It wasn't half an hour, mon, and there it was — a buoy glass floating in the water. Right away we start mixing the sweet milk.

"I says, 'Hermano,' I say, 'see how good the Lord is — all the time the Lord is with us' — and that's why Largo and his helper never have so much disappointment — because we always believe in the Lord. We know he is guiding us in this revolution."

AS IF ON CUE, Stevie Wonder's "You Are the Sunshine of My Life" started blaring from the greasy Wurlitzer in the San Jose bar. Largo absently swatted at the flies that circled the three mugs of beer.

"And then Largo and Hermano see Corn Island — just arriving — bigger and bigger, bigger and bigger. That's my home, mon. Then Largo looked. I see the boat hauling a trap — right on the side — one of my friends too — but Largo can't stop.

"Mon, just my feelings hit me — like when the time will come for Largo to go back home.... My helper tells me, he says, 'Largo,' he says, 'I know your feelings,' he says. I says, 'You know it boy....' He says, 'Largo,' he says, 'one of these days we will reach back home if we live.'

"So, I am looking on Hermano. I am looking on Corn Island. Largo sees the beach ... the part they call Long Beach. Largo sees the beach, mon, the water blue — the sand white. Just in a short time, mon, Largo feels like something cold run through his body — you know, like I want to shed tears. I pass so close to my family — to my people — but Largo can't go on the land.... You know, mon, the key — the rock. When I look on the rock, mon, I almost feel to cry. I say if Largo was on that rock, mon, for just one day, just one hour — Largo would feel much better. ..."

How I wrote the story

In 1982 I set out for the Miskito Coast to report on the flight of 13,000 Indians from their tribal lands along the Rio Coco River in northern Nicaragua. Naively, I expected to make my way through the jungle, cross the savanna, get the story and get out within three days. Five weeks later I finally managed to hitch a ride on an ambulance flight back to the 20th Century. It was one of those assignments every reporter dreams about. It had all the drama and otherworldliness you could ask for. It couldn't miss.

The story was fairly well received, and even won a couple of writing awards that year, but it was clearly a story that did not approach its potential. The story could have written itself (I'll explain what I mean by that later) — and would have turned out much better — if only I had let it. Unfortunately, I didn't, and for the next three years I suffered the guilt that comes with having confronted a story that I knew was much bigger and far better than my talent to tell.

Last year, on the fifth anniversary of the Sandinista revolution, I was lucky enough to get a second crack at the Miskito story. The setting and the context were not nearly as dramatic as they had been in 1982, but I welcomed the chance to deal again with what I believe is an extremely important, though still largely ignored, aspect of the Nicaraguan conflict.

Space is what I had thought I needed in order to do the Miskito story justice the first time round (five open pages of it in three days), and that kind of space is what I didn't have last year. It had to be done in one piece: the last day of a four-part series that set out to chronicle the Sandinista revolution from 1979 to 1984.

The title of the series was "Faces from a Revolution." The game plan was to tell the story of the revolution through the lives of 11 people: a revolutionary war hero who now heads Nicaragua's internal-security forces; another war hero who has since taken up arms against his former Sandinista comrades; the director of Nicaragua's only opposition newspaper; his brother, the publisher of the official Sandinista daily; a pro-Sandinista nun; a pro-Sandinista priest; a middle-class businessman; the Sandinista military commander of Bluefields; the Miskito Indian leader who is waging war against him; a Sandinista peasant soldier; and, finally, Captain Largo, the "contra" gunrunner. Day one of the series was an attempt to put the revolution in historical context and to place (politically, socially and physically) each of the main characters in the series on the day of the Sandinista "triumph": July 19, 1979. The next three days were designed to explain how each of the main characters got to where they are today (July 19, 1984).

Given the overall format of the series, there was little room to maneuver. The Miskito story, though far more complex than it was in 1982, had to be told in one chunk of copy — without the benefit of a sidebar. It had to stand on its own and yet serve as a natural conclusion to the series as a whole. It also had to explain why some men were fighting to overthrow what is still largely a popular government in Nicaragua. Largo — like the flight of the Miskitos from the Rio Coco in 1982 — was a reporter's dream. But this time I was determined not to make the same mistake, and Largo seemed the ideal vehicle to try to let the story tell itself.

As with most people from the Miskito Coast, where storytelling is a nightly campfire ritual, Largo's eye for detail was extraordinary and his language poetic. It was simply a matter of turning on the tape recorder, getting him to relax, demanding enough backup material to try to keep him honest, and letting him talk for five hours.

Letting the story tell itself — or, in this case, letting Largo tell it — did not mean simply pulling quotes from the tape. As poetic as Largo was, the story would have lost most of its effectiveness that way. Letting him tell the story in this case meant trying to crawl inside his head — it meant trying to see what he saw when he saw it on the deck of his turtling boat. To do that, I had to listen to key sections of the tape over and over, and, in doing so, I discovered what it was about his story that had impressed me most when I first heard it. It was the cadence of his storytelling — a cadence that lent an almost mystical quality to his story — as much as the drama of the story itself.

The trick, I figured, was to try to duplicate that cadence, build the suspense as he had done, and at the same time condense his rambling monologue into a manageable narrative. "In an instant, the sky went black.

The boat was gone. The sea was empty," though not his words, was Largo's cadence. He had been talking about flashes of lightning and did so in sentences that seemed to mimic the lightning itself.

As journalists we're trained to know a good story when we hear it even if it's shrouded in disjointed monologue. We do it almost subconsciously, and tend to dismiss it as a simple process of separating the wheat from the chaff. I suspect, however, that the process is far more complicated — that there is something more than the facts of a story, no matter how dramatic those facts might be, that make a story intriguing. In Largo's case, it was the rhythm of his storytelling — a rhythm he could adjust at will to turn less-than-extraordinary events (like finding a glass buoy) into the supernatural. As with most Miskitos, Largo's only exposure to literature had been the Bible, and the rhythm of his storytelling showed it.

After listening to Largo for 10 minutes I was jumping for joy. I knew I had my story. I had already traveled extensively throughout the Miskito Coast and had long since researched the facts of the story. But until Largo, the story had lacked a soul.

The next step was to try to do in my writing what we all do automatically while listening to a news source — sift through what he had revealed about himself and find a way to discard the extraneous without losing what it was about him and his story that gave both their special charm.

In a sense, it's like translating a novel from one language into another without losing the nuances of the original. Here, Largo's language was the English of a Caribbean out-islander. While it's a language far more powerful than the English of narrative journalism, it's also a language all but impossible to translate into print.

It depends on skills that Largo had obviously learned around the Miskito campfire. It requires well-placed smiles, frowns, raised eyebrows, a gold tooth and a variety of body gestures. It means playing to his listeners and instinctively using whatever props are available to him.

I noticed, for example, that when the music on the jukebox in the bar changed, so did Largo's rhythm in his storytelling. To capture that in print, it meant reworking the lead again and again — each time relistening to his account until I had come as close as I could to reproducing for the reader the same feeling I had when I first heard his story. That meant playing the same song for the reader that I had been listening to as Largo spoke, and interrupting his story with some of the same gestures he and Hermano had used as his tale unfolded.

Listening to just about anyone we interview involves using your eyes as much as your ears; you can't do that while scribbling notes on a pad. But especially when interviewing a Miskito storyteller like Largo, I'd be helpless without a tape recorder. I needed to look into Largo's eyes as he talked, to try to figure out when the lies, exaggerations or half-truths were creeping into his story, and to see what moved him as he spoke. I often find that the storyteller's mannerisms betray emotions that his words might not be disclosing. When those telltale mannerisms surfaced with Largo, I tried to get him to go back over that moment in his description of an event — again and again — until he let down his defenses and finally began to verbalize what he was feeling at that time.

The only other challenge was in deciding where to break Largo's story to provide some historical perspective, establish some of the main distinctions between Nicaragua's Pacific and Atlantic coasts, and try to explain the key differences between the various anti-Sandinista factions. Largo's courage, humor and torment said more about the Miskito problem in Nicaragua than I had managed in five times the space three years earlier. It was nice to get a second chance.

The Appalachian Trail:

Lessons in humility

By Berkley Hudson
Sunday Journal Magazine, October 21, 1984

Two tree frogs splashed into a stream and crickets were singing when we found Orville and Marjorie Fezler at dusk in the West Virginia woods.

We had heard the Fezlers were special and that, if we were lucky, we would meet them at Keys Gap Shelter that night. Along the Appalachian Trail, that's the way it is. A grapevine links a family of people hiking through America. The family always is changing and so is the AT, as it's known from Maine to Georgia. For nine days last month, photographer Jim Daniels and I were part of that family.

Orville and Marjorie Fezler were making camp when we walked up to the lean-to with its tin roof and wooden floor that gave room enough for four or five sleeping bags. Alone, they were resting from the day's seven-mile hike from Harpers Ferry. Marjorie just had returned from the outhouse. She ran to tell Orville the news of sparkling-clean facilities. "How many women," she asked, "do you know who get excited about a new privy?"

He is 58 and she is 57, not unusual ages for hikers on an unusual trail: the longest continuous, marked footpath in the world.

Right away they wanted to talk about what they were learning from 165 days and nights in the mountains and forests. Orville had been an engineer for the Apollo space program that put men on the moon. As a registered nurse, Marjorie had supervised a cancer ward where patients waited for death.

They retired last year, moving from Philadelphia to the Ozarks of Arkansas. "Too many people," she said, "don't have a chance to do the things they would like to do." After deciding to hike the AT, they set out last spring. It was much more than they imagined, at times bordering on survival in freezing rain and snow.

Now seasoned hikers, they were dressed in handsome, green corduroy shorts with deep pockets, their legs as tanned as leather and their physiques as supple and sinewy as saplings.

They spoke of how the Appalachian Trail was reminding them of lessons long ago forgotten while they raised their three children and shuttled around America to follow Orville's career with Boeing. With the mosquito netting strung securely over their sleeping bags, Marjorie spoke reverently when she said the Trail has taught her truths, obvious perhaps, but so real when actually realized: the importance of patience, humility and understanding.

Orville and Marjorie's memories called forth special faces and places. The New York City couple who shared their supper on the Trail. The monks who fed them at Graymoor Monastery. The woman who gave them her car keys so they could drive to a post office near the Trail to pick up a food package they had mailed to themselves. The park ranger who offered them supper at his house and then a ride. The trapper who had little but gave all. "It's just honest, sincere people," Orville said, "in the little towns that you normally wouldn't even be coming in contact with."

"Traveling the interstates," Marjorie said, "you don't even know they're there."

People gave even when the Fezlers weren't looking for help. Slices of pie, cups of coffee and relaxed conversation with strangers followed trips to laundromats of small towns they never before knew existed. The greatest surprise was that those with the least gave the most.

THROUGH THE WOODS of Keys Gap came the screech of car tires. It was a Friday night. Not far away was Route 9, a two-lane road where people, loaded with six-packs from High's Store, were driving fast.

Half the population of America is within a day's drive of the Appalachian Trail, a thin sliver of America that in some places provides barely enough room to squeeze through with a backpack and, in other spots, stretches as wide as the gravel or asphalt roads it traverses. Power lines in Maine, radio and television transmission towers in Georgia, mobile homes and general stores in North Carolina, suburbs in Maryland and rural towns in Virginia surround this fragile wilderness in 14 states, including all of New England except Rhode Island. New York City, Washington, D.C., and Atlanta are within 85 miles of the AT; Providence, 120 miles.

Sometimes civilization comes too close. Three years ago, two hikers were murdered in Virginia. This year, a woman whose hiking companion needed medical help was raped by a man who followed her onto the Trail after he took her friend to the hospital. Eventually, after she escaped and got help for herself, she returned to continue hiking.

Still, if there is wilderness left in the East, the Appalachian Trail passes through it. The Fezlers feared not humans, but animals, especially bears in the Smokies, where lean-tos with chain-link fences protect bears and humans from one another. Yet, Orville said, "We've had nothing but goodness all along the Trail. No bad experiences with animals or people."

Like Earl Shaffer, who in 1948 became the first person to hike the entire AT, the Fezlers started in Georgia last spring with plans to hike to Maine. They would start where people speak with one accent, and finish where another is heard. But at 10 miles a day, their pace was slower than expected and, realizing they wouldn't make it to Maine until October and worried that snow might inhibit their ascent of Mount Katahdin, they changed their plans in Virginia.

There, a priest offered them a ride to Boston and they linked up with the AT's northern end, hiking south through the New England section in summer. Now they were working their way back to Virginia, where they left off.

THE SOUTHERN END starts with Springer Mountain, north of Atlanta. It's Deliverance country, land of copperheads and rattlesnakes, shotguns and woodsheds, moss, mules and boiled peanuts. James Dickey's novel was set and filmed in northern Georgia country like Springer.

With the start of autumn, the temperature reached 90 and Atlanta radio was playing "Summer in the City." In the mountains, it wasn't much cooler. Working out of the back of his pickup truck alongside a two-lane blacktop, Herbert Gooch fanned himself with a red cap. He was selling apples and sourwood mountain honey at Turner's Corner, just a ways down from the Trail and not far from Gooch Gap, named for his forebears who lived on the Trail before there was an official AT. Never hiked on the Trail, he said — "You kidding?"

All around Gooch's curbside location, leafy green kudzu (the vine that was originally imported from the Orient to curb erosion in the South and, so the story goes, has choked cows to death) was strangling the red clay farmland and rusting chicken coops in the Georgia foothills, not far from Amicalola Falls State Park.

The state park at Amicalola Falls provides access to the Trail's start, with the top of Springer more than eight rugged miles away. The freezing cold water of the falls braids itself into silvery streaks 729 feet down the mountainside.

By car, we took a shortcut on a steep gravel road that winds through the rhododendron, azaleas and oaks. At Nimblewill Gap, the isolated road crosses a trail that leads to the start of the AT, more than two miles up and away.

Into the bees, bushes, briars and black-eyed Susans, we hiked toward Springer, the spot that six and seven months ago attracted some 400 hikers who wanted to walk with spring, all the way to Maine. Perhaps fewer than 50 of them made it or will make it. Going south to north is the favorite way because it allows hikers to avoid Maine's lingering winter and its black flies of early summer. By the time hikers arrive in Maine in August or September, moose, moss and a mile-high finish of boulders greet them with the Trail's end on Katahdin.

FIRST COMES SPRINGER. As we waded through waist-high bushes obscuring the rocky trail, morning sunlight filtered through the sassafras, the shagbark hickory and the tulip poplars and onto the Queen Anne's lace. A woodpecker was at work. The incline and the heat were causing my jogger's heart to beat faster and faster. My mind created its own diversions. Dreams came. What it would be like to hike more than 2,000 miles from Georgia to Maine? I smelled the woodsmoke of a Shenandoah campfire. I felt the coziness of a mummy sleeping bag at the end of a long day's hike in the Carolinas and tasted a mouthful of mountain water gulped wholesale from a dive in a waterfall pool someplace in Maine where pollution surely hasn't arrived.

The reveries ended fast. The thick, powerful body of a snake lay before our feet. "That a copperhead?"

The head was triangular and must be full of poison that kills. In the split-second before I could answer Jim, the snake itself answered. Its rattles shook and didn't stop shaking.

As it coiled, we stepped back further. It looked like a diamondback. Maybe there were others in the bushes. Still, we leaped through the dense undergrowth, finding our way back to the Trail beyond the snake. For the rest of the day, we heeded the guidebook's warning to beware of snakes.

AT THE TOP of Springer, we met Birdman and Joe. We had passed them earlier, the only people we saw on the Trail that day. They were two very good ol' boys, in their 20s, fresh out of the service, one from the Navy, the other from the Marines, and both from Georgia. They were out for a week's hike on the AT to think about what to do next in life.

Birdman had a chew of tobacco in his cheek and talked a lot. Joe didn't say much. A swallow-tail butterfly danced in the air. They looked out from the narrow view that Springer provides, with rolling green hills, short and tree-covered, unlike the treeless summits of New England where vistas abound.

At the soles of our boots was the bronze plaque that marks the AT's start. It reads:

"A footpath for those who seek fellowship with the wilderness." The day was hazy and in the distance was more than haze. It had a brown tinge, smog marking a new border of the wilderness.

Before leaving the summit, Birdman opened the mailbox on the side of an oak. In it was a notebook, a hikers' register, like the notebooks at campsites all along the Trail, part of the grapevine.

Birdman wrote something silly, unlike the metaphysical thoughts of thru-hikers. "Birdman and Joe stopped by. Tried to get a party going but there were some girls with no clothes that wanted to take our picture. Watch out for snakes. If we're not back by Saturday, send help."

IN HARPERS FERRY, W. Va., Clara Cassidy lives on a bluff not far from where the Trail crosses a valley rich with Colonial and Civil War history. The Shenandoah and Potomac rivers meet at this spiritual midpoint of the AT (the actual halfway mark is 75 miles north, in Pennsylvania). Harpers Ferry is home of the Appalachian Trail Conference, the organization that oversees the Trail.

When she was 48, Clara Cassidy started hiking the Trail in this part of the country. That was 34 years ago, when she was a manager in a Washington, D.C., department store and escaped to the mountains on weekends. Now, living in a house "built to my measure" four years ago, she provides a way station for weary hikers. They set up tents in her backyard by the garden or they enjoy the comforts of a house as cozy as a cocoon.

There she fashions handmade quilts and rugs from old coats and skirts, puts up homegrown tomatoes for juice (48 quarts so far this season), writes a newspaper column on people approaching their "topmost years" and fights for equality for older women. When she speaks, so do her eyes, which are almost as blue as the ridges she has hiked.

The vision of a Massachusetts naturalist, Benton MacKaye, launched the Trail and the Appalachian Trail Conference in the 1920s. MacKaye's idea sparked immediate interest in 1921 when it first appeared in the Journal of the American Institute of Architects. For the next 16 years, volunteers worked in the wilderness to link existing trails and create a unified route from Maine to Georgia. Today it passes through eight national forests and six national parks.

Amid fears that the AT was threatened by encroachment, Congress in 1968 and again in 1978 enacted legislation to protect the Trail, granting $90 million for the purchase of rights-of-way where the AT was endangered. So far, more than 80 percent of the Trail has been permanently protected and work continues on buying the remaining land.

Supervision of the Trail is done by an unusual combination of volunteer hiking organizations of the Appalachian Trail Conference, and federal and state agencies, particularly the National Parks Service and the U.S. Forest Service.

Much of the federal money, approved and pushed by the Carter Administration, has been spent during the Reagan Administration. Former Secretary of Interior James Watt never had a favorable image as a protector of the environment, but, says Larry Van Meter, executive director of the Appalachian Trail Conference, the AT was one of the few areas in which Watt gave strong support.

THE AFTERNOON we visited, Clara Cassidy told the story of a man who died of a heart attack on the AT while hiking two years ago in the Carolinas. She heard about it from a young hiker who came to stay with her. "After he talked with me a bit and saw what kind of person I was, he excused himself and said: 'I got something in my pack I think you'd like to see.' He brought what was called the Roving Register."

It was a notebook carried along the Trail to tell the story of the man who died. "Everybody who carried it, wrote in it. All the young people were saying what a grand way to go, that he died doing what he wanted. That's a terribly important thing. You think people who die in a nursing home are doing what they want to do? Not on your tintype.

"I wrote that up as a column to let people know they ought to go ahead and do what they want to do. So what if it's dangerous? You're taking chances, adjusting, trying to meet challenges. That's being young, I don't care how old you are."

Doctors, lawyers, out-of-work deep-sea divers and people like the Fezlers make their way to Clara's — but only if Jean Cashin of the Appalachian Trail Conference decides a hiker is deserving enough to be sent to Clara's, just around the corner and down the block from headquarters.

"I TRY TO GET a profile of the hikers," Clara said. "There isn't one. It's just the people willing to take chances, who are curious. A lot of them are loners and a lot of them getting their heads together.

"This year I had two sisters. One who had nursed a husband through a long illness. He died in February. She was walking off her grief. You read how awful the first months of widowhood are. Hers will be mixed up with mountains and streams. Her mind is not on her husband, but on where she'll put her foot next."

Clara keeps her own register. This year Winston the Wonderful came, hiking all the way from Key West and then onto the Trail north from Georgia. "He didn't carry a billboard. But he came on pretty strong." He is the veterinarian from Tuskegee College in Alabama everybody on the Trail was talking about, this man who billed himself as "The Great British-American-Jamaican."

"There are a few anonymous types. Silent or abstracted. So introverted they don't know how to make a connection.

"You've heard about the two Frenchmen that came? School teachers from Grenoble, France. Martin and Dominique. Dominique wrote a haiku in French." Next to his signature, Clara wrote the translation: I would like to come back. I envy the waves, their ability always to come back, come back.

WITH THE TEMPERATURE 40 degrees cooler than a week earlier in Georgia, the first day of autumn in Maine's Baxter State Park felt like winter.

In Baxter, you can still hear the call of the loon. Camp in the park and you're likely to see moose rambling the woods, along the gravel roads and trails, and the ranger at Daicey Pond in the shadow of Mount Katahdin will tell you: "Canoes a dollar an hour. Five for the day. Keep your own time."

This is the Appalachian Trail's northern limit, remote and relaxed. The boundary is marked by Katahdin's Baxter Peak, a monolith that dominates the 200,000 acres of the Baxter park and offers one of the AT's toughest hikes, just over five miles. Above timberline, part of the Trail is nothing more than boulders with iron hand-holds embedded in rock to keep hikers from sliding off sheer drops. Inclines are severe but not as extreme as the 1,500- to 2,000-foot drops along the mountain's Knife Edge Trail.

Katahdin lives up to its name, meaning "greatest mountain." Legend says that the mountain was created as a sacred meeting place for the council of gods. One deity, Pamola, was denied admission to the council and, forever holding a grudge, stirs storm clouds around the mountain in hopes of thwarting all who climb it.

There is a reward, however, for risking Pamola's wrath. On sunny days the summit provides a view that, owing to Maine's many lakes, appears as if it were formed by a giant mirror being shattered on the rocky peak, its pieces flying out across the countryside of spruce and fir.

On rainy days, even though the chance of slipping increases, the beauty does, too. When nature's varnish of rain slickens the pink and gray granite of Katahdin, it assumes beautiful hues underfoot.

PETER SHAK and Steve Alexander came last month from Chicago in search of this beauty. We found them at 7:30 in the morning, readying to climb the last 5.2 miles of the Appalachian Trail. For the previous week, they had hiked 110 miles on the Trail, from Monson, Maine. They would end their week's vacation from their engineering jobs at Motorola by climbing Katahdin on the first day of autumn.

Peter and Steve, both in their 30s, stuffed gorp (M & Ms, peanuts, raisins) and water and a rice-and-raisins mixture into their day packs as they signed the register on the ranger station's porch. The day before, in a Dartmouth College notebook hanging from a bulletin board, a young man who hiked from Georgia had written: "As you go you up, you will be filled with enthusiasm and awe. Once down, your perspective on the whole trip will have changed."

Also the day before, a trip up Katahdin inspired Laurie Messier from Annapolis, Md., to write for all who would read about the last miles of her more than 2,000 mile journey from Springer: "I feel it as a crowning of a great trip and an inspiration to continue doing what makes me happy. I'll see you in years to come, on the trails and wild places of America and Earth."

PETER AND STEVE made their way to the Katahdin Stream Trail. The morning sun brightened the red berries of mountain ash, the purple shades of wood asters and, most of all, the leaves, turning red and gold. The sound of Katahdin Stream Falls filtered through the trees. We made our way along a rough, moss-covered carpet of boulders and roots of spruce, maple and fir.

The wind stirred the paper-thin birch bark. To climb Katahdin, you need a good pair of hands, a good pair of legs and a good pair of boots. On this day, you needed plenty of warm clothes. Peter was wearing shorts but had on hat and coat and layers under that. It got colder and icier the closer we climbed to timberline.

At that point, our party of four split up, leaving Peter and Steve to go alone to the summit; Jim and I had been up two days earlier.

Beyond the tricky boulders, where the terrain levels out to become a tableland, they passed through rocky tundra that Henry David Thoreau first came upon when he climbed Katahdin in 1846. Just as then, arctic plants make up the vegetation. This flora is said to have been there since the last continental ice sheet. Reindeer lichens, bog laurel, mountain heath and willow create ever-so-subtle shades of green and red.

The wind was blowing clouds and freezing fog around the summit. To say it was howling is not to exaggerate. The temperature felt like 0. People appeared like apparitions in the clouds that obscured the summit. One hiker, then another, coming from another trail, would appear. When Peter and Steve reached the summit, they could see no more than 25 to 50 feet. Wind was shaping the rime ice, fog that freezes, on the rocks.

They stayed at the summit only long enough to take pictures of each other by the wooden sign that tells hikers they are at the northern end of the Appalachian Trail. An arrow points south. Springer Mountain,

Georgia, it says, is 2,050 miles that-a-way through the clouds.

Peter and Steve hurried down the mountain. In the warmth of boulders near timberline, they watched the clouds clear and the wind settle. Then they saw the view they were deprived of at the summit.

There were mountains and more mountains, looking like the backs of so many slumbering dinosaurs, and the sun was reflecting from the lakes and ponds in the distance for miles and it seemed like the two men could see forever.

ORVILLE AND Marjorie Fezler say they will not be the same when they go home again.

"The Trail taught us nothing lasts forever," she said. "Times change. Because times change, people's needs change."

"You see one bug eating another bug," he said. "Or see a plant is dying so another plant can live. You get pretty close to that. She may be 30, 40 paces or so behind me and we may not say a word for, golly, an hour or so. You look at things. You wonder. You see a tree growing. A little weed growing out of a crack of a rock. You think: How did it start?

"Everybody's hanging onto life. Life is so precious that everybody is fighting for that place in the sun. When you're out in the woods, you see that same competitiveness in nature. And that's all kind of hard to figure out sometimes."

Somewhere in the trees, a blue jay was making a racket. The Fezlers asked about Dorothy and Jeff Hansen of Neels Gap, Ga., where the AT goes right through the breezeway of the Hansons' hostel and store of stone and timbers.

Did they have their baby yet?

Yep. A girl, seven-and-a-half pounds and everybody's fine down south at the Neels Gap end of the Trail.

How I wrote the story

As the headline suggests, the Appalachian Trail teaches lessons to those who want to learn. My goal was to write about these lessons.

In the reporting and the writing, the Trail didn't teach me new lessons, but it certainly reminded me of lessons previously learned: the value of openness, flexibility and perseverance, as a reporter, writer, hiker and human being.

In a sense there was no "story," with a beginning, middle and end. It wasn't a dramatic cops-and-robbers narrative. This was of a more subtle nature. There was power — though different from a tale opening with a villain killing his victim with a .357-magnum.

The power would come from a stunning piece of geography — 2,100 miles of it running through 14 states. The drama would come from the humans who explore the Trail and explore their inner selves; and then there would be those who, by contrast, simply live along the Trail and don't give a hoot about matters such as inner exploration.

At the idea stage, I had no doubt that the story would work photographically; I wasn't as sure about the words. To make it work, I felt I had to be alert in the reporting for what my editor, Joel Rawson, has taught me about finding those things that trigger the reader's memory. In this case, I thought the sense experience of the outdoors would be powerful — touch, taste, smell, hearing and seeing.

In addition, I wanted to take myself as well as the reader to a place that was out of the way and extraordinary. And another element I felt I needed for the story to work was finding people — whether hikers on the Trail or people who live along it — whom I could care about and whom the reader, in turn, would care about.

With Will Durant as my inspiration, I found the Trail appropriate for journalistic pursuit. "Civilization," Durant wrote, "is a stream with banks. The stream is filled with blood from people killing, stealing, shouting and doing things historians usually record. ... On the banks, unnoticed, people build homes, make love, raise children, sing songs, write poetry, and even whittle statues. The story of civilization is the story of what happened on the banks."

The idea

The idea originated a full year before we were given the assignment. Photographer Jim Daniels suggested it when he and I were on a story, flying over Maine in August, 1983, and looking out the plane window at the majestic landscape.

Within a month, we did some initial research and proposed it. It was accepted and then rejected.

We waited a year and proposed it again. After some negotiations about where we would go and how long we would be gone, the idea was accepted and Sunday editor Mark Silverman gave the go-ahead for a magazine story with lots of color pictures. Photo and graphics editors George Rooney, Chip Maury, Dave Gray and Ray Lomax discussed with us approaches to consider.

It was decided we would go for two weeks in September, from Georgia to Maine. The story line would follow the geographic route of our journey, going from south to north, hot weather to cold, late-summer greenery of Georgia to early-autumn foliage in Maine.

Planning

We had a logistical problem from the start. If we dealt with the entire length of the Trail, how could we do it in two weeks? A *National Geographic* team had spent six months hiking the Trail. A recent New York *Times* feature on the Trail just in Connecticut — but 1 of the Trail's 14 states — made it appear that the reporter had spent no fewer than two days reporting and writing.

With the help of the news library and its computer system linked to data banks of other newspapers and magazines, I began to do research on the Trail. I also talked with friends who had hiked it from Georgia to Maine. And Jim researched the Maine end, where he had hiked Mount Katahdin a number of times.

We decided to get to the isolated areas by flying and using rental cars, to minimize the time we spent getting there. We made some campground reservations, in Maine and in Georgia, but we also allowed for spontaneity by not having any idea where we would stay some nights.

I also got information from the Appalachian Trail Conference, which oversees the Trail from its headquarters, in Harpers Ferry, W.Va. This helped us get an idea of terrain, distances and the likelihood of finding hikers. We even got names of long-distance hikers, their general locations and about how many miles a day they were traveling, in hopes of finding them.

Notwithstanding Will Durant's inspiration, by the time Jim and I left I was worried by the lack of a "hard-news edge." I feared I was lapsing into the ultimate of Jello journalism, a nature story that didn't even have a news element. No toxic waste. No fight between environmentalists and developers. Even James Watt, the Interior Department leader who was feared by environmentalists, vocally supported the Trail.

But the second day out, in the Georgia mountains, I quit worrying and started to relax. Oddly enough, that occurred soon after Jim and I had leapt around a rattlesnake, coiled and rattling in our path. I realized that our own experiences could provide plenty of drama — plenty to write about.

With writing coach Don Murray's encouragement, and with support from editors who nourish good writing, I am learning to trust my impressions and, when appropriate, to weave them into a story. I have revamped my notion of what reportorial objectivity means. It doesn't mean that, in the writing, I deny my instincts, reactions and impressions; nor does it mean that I puff up myself, my experiences or my point of view at the expense of journalistic fairness or accuracy. My obligation is to the story, and to using whatever techniques best serve the story — which means, of course, serving the reader.

Finding a voice

When I returned, I had the initial problem of finding a voice. It was the main problem I had in the writing — figuring out the relevance of our experiences to the story — but for the first two days of the writing I didn't know that was the problem.

I wrote what *The New Yorker*'s Calvin Trillin calls a "Vomit-out": an uncensored off-the-top-of-the head draft that encourages discovery of what a story is about. I've found this is a good approach when facing tons of notebooks, tapes, maps, guidebooks — tons of experiences.

Without looking at my notes or listening to my tapes, I "vomited out" 185 lines. The draft centered on our experiences in Georgia, our starting point, since I thought it would be easiest to write as we had traveled: south to north.

Because I didn't feel completely comfortable with what I had written, I showed it to magazine editor Bobbie Siegel. She said the writing sounding stiff in parts. It seemed, she said, as if I were afraid to say what I really wanted to say.

This was a crucial moment in the writing process; Bobbie's critique and the spirit of it helped me discover the source of the problem. Looking for what made the story stiff, I used the technique of switching the medium I was working in. I moved from writing and reading the story on the video terminal to studying a printout and marking it up with colored pens.

And I found the reasons the story was stiff: passive constructions; nonspecific language; and third person instead of first.

Story organization

Once I found the voice, I was able to address the story's organization. I wrote:

Theme: Nature teaches us about ourselves.
Through the Trail, they make discoveries about themselves and the people they meet.
Link to history: Gettysburg. Harpers Ferry. Indian wars. Boom towns.
You start with one accent and finish with another.

Using an outline, I broke the Trail up into three sections: 1) southern — Georgia and North Carolina; 2) central — Virginia, West Virginia and Maryland, 3) northern — Maine - New England. I wrote a short list of one-word dominant impressions from each section.

I began to discover that my overall dominant impression was that along the Trail there was a kind of family, complete with a family grapevine.

The pattern became very clear when we met the Fezlers, in the West Virginia woods. In Georgia, we had met Dorothy and Jeff Hansen, who, after hiking the whole Trail, had started a hostel, which put them constantly in touch with people at the Trail's headquarters, in West Virginia. Then a few days later, at headquarters, we met Jean Cashin, who tries to keep track of hikers who are on the Trail for any length of time. She led us to Clara Cassidy, just around the corner, who offers a way station. Both Clara and Jean led us to the Fezlers, in the woods, who knew that Dorothy Hansen was pregnant but didn't know whether she had had her baby yet. When Jim and I told the Fezlers that the Hansens had had a baby girl, I realized the beauty of this extended family out there in the woods.

I came up with the idea of splitting the scene with the Fezlers, and making the two halves the beginning and the end of the story. I would use the news of the baby's birth as an upbeat symbol for the growth and rebirth that the Fezlers, a retired couple, had undergone.

It seemed natural to go from the Fezlers in the lead back to the southern end of the Trail, in Georgia; wend the story north to Maine; and then end with the Fezlers' thoughts on their transformation.

On a piece of paper I wrote this as an outline:

Fez
Georgia
W. Va.
Maine
Fez

Once I had a clear theme and knew which characters would illustrate it, I began the task of going through my notebooks and transcribing my tapes with an eye and ear to what I wanted to extract.

I made printouts of my notes and underlined key quotes in red ink. Then I began building all this around my original vomit-out draft.

While writing this, it was important for me to conjure up in concrete terms what exactly we had experienced, and how that related to what the people we were writing about experienced on the Trail. A key element that shaped the writing was the richness of the experience that Jim and I had, working together as photographer and reporter. We spent 24 hours a day together in heat, cold, rain, fog and terrain that at times was physically demanding. We shared sunrise and sunset, peanut-butter-and-jelly sandwiches, and scallops sautéed on a camp stove. Nature didn't run on our schedule; we ran on hers.

As I wrote, I kept this in mind. I brought back little sandwich bags full of rocks and flowers and buckeyes; I laid them out on my newsroom desk while I wrote, and they helped me recall the hues and textures of what I had seen. I spread the contour maps around me. This helped bring vigor to the writing.

Because I had so much strong material, it was easier than usual to throw material out. Entire interviews and entire mountains went into the trash. The outlines and quote lists helped ensure I wasn't discarding anything valuable.

To get a sense of how the story sounded, I read it aloud in the newsroom's glass office. And for accuracy's sake and tonal quality, I read parts of it over the phone to some of the people I was writing about.

When I was finished, after several rewrites, I felt very satisfied. The response on publication showed that the writing and the photographs stirred readers, too. I immediately received phone calls at home from strangers who had read it, and letters and more phone calls came in the following weeks. When writer and reader are both satisfied, I suppose that is the true test of the worth of the effort spent on writing.

Building new lives

'Fragile' people find new security

Part three of a six-part series

By G. Wayne Miller
The Providence Journal and *The Evening Bulletin*, November 27, 1984

BARRINGTON — Lloyd Pattie's home is an elegant, gabled, neo-Victorian structure hidden behind hemlocks and pines and maples that line one of this coastal town's busiest streets. On a fine autumn afternoon, sunlight ripples through the trees, and the southeast wind smells faintly of salt and sea.

Pattie, 61, lives here with seven other adults. They share general chores, keep their own rooms, do their own laundry, but it's him they turn to when they have a problem. Got a question about cooking? See Lloyd. Trouble with the budget? Lloyd's your man. Feeling down? Guaranteed, Lloyd'll pick you up.

"I guide them along," Pattie says modestly, but with his distinctive smile — a wonderfully warm smile that fills his face and quickly endears him to strangers and friends alike.

He is a burly man — a bear, really — intelligent, articulate and likeable. His face is craggy, rich with character; his dark eyes alternately dance, probe, study, narrow to slits. His eyebrows are thick, his hair jet-black and perfectly neat.

Like everyone in Barrington House, a group home for the mentally ill run by Riverwood Rehabilitation Services, a non-profit social service agency, Pattie spent years at the Institute of Mental Health. He was locked in seclusion rooms, injected with drugs, moved from building to building. He had few visitors. Attendants scared him.

"No, I did not like IMH," he says softly. "They put me in the wrong wards. They had me in incontinent wards. I was not incontinent."

In October, 1983, Barrington House opened. Pattie was one of its first residents. There were a few initial difficulties, but his adjustment to life on the outside was generally smooth. The staff liked him. He got along well with them and with the other residents.

"The home here is immaculate compared to IMH," he says. "Beautiful. I feel secure. Oh, yes, I like the Barrington group home."

IN MANY RESPECTS, the script of Lloyd Pattie's life is lifted from a chapter of old-fashioned, God-and-country Americana: the story of an immigrant who landed young on these shores, became a citizen, served his nation in war, came back to marry and raise a family.

In other respects, it is the story of a man whose ambitions and dreams were shattered by what doctors diagnosed as schizophrenia — perhaps the most puzzling and debilitating of all mental illnesses.

The second of five children of French-Canadian parents, Pattie was born Jan. 13, 1923, in a small town in Nova Scotia. While still an infant, his family moved to Stoneham, Mass., where his father found employment as a general hand for a fuel company.

Early on, father taught son the value of work. Pattie's first job, when he was barely a teenager, was giving pony rides to children. On good days he earned $4. He saved some of his money, and spent the rest on trips to Boston, which he reached by streetcar.

He was in high school when he landed his second job, as a part-time clerk for Economy Grocery Stores — a small chain that later became Stop & Shop.

In 1941, Pattie graduated from Stoneham High School. War broke out. In 1942, after sailing through physical and IQ tests, he enlisted in the Army Air Corps. He spent much of the war stationed in Alaska, where he worked for the operations division of an air wing.

Peace came, and Pattie returned to Stoneham and his grocery store job. On Labor Day, 1948, he marrried a Rhode Island woman. They settled in Providence. Before long, he found work with a Providence rubber company.

He began as a laborer, but his mechanical aptitude propelled him swiftly up the ranks. His specialty was lining steel tanks with rubber, a process that made the tanks resistant to corrosive chemicals stored inside. In 1955, he was offered a job as a supervisor for a New Hampshire firm. Pattie and his family — which now included a daughter and two sons — moved to Nashua, where his last child, another son, was born.

In 1962, Pattie was offered a job back in Rhode Island. The family returned. They bought a house in Smithfield. The children were growing, and Pattie was deeply involved with them. They went on visits to the zoo, out for ice creams, walks in the woods, summertime dips in a nearby pond.

BUT GRADUALLY the tranquility of his life had been changing in subtle, disturbing ways. In his 20s and early 30s, he sometimes found himself irritable, out of sorts, angry — moods he could ignore, or explain away. Later the moods became darker, lasted longer, didn't seem to have easy explanations.

He began to think that people were conspiring against him, forging checks in his name, spreading lies to damage his good reputation. He got into arguments. He complained of feeling confused. Once, he was convinced that enemies had hung cameras and microphones in a tree to spy on him. Eventually, he developed an elaborate theory that the U.S. government, using million-dollar electronic machines, was controlling his life.

"From what I understand," he says, "at the beginning, people that we thought were my friends were my bitter enemies. They were talking nice to my wife's face, but behind her they were stabbing her in the back. Stabbing me in the back. I was hearing an awful lot of obscene language."

The family doctor prescribed tranquilizers. They did nothing. In June, 1963, he was admitted to a short-term ward at Chapin Hospital, then a public hospital run by the city of Providence. He was given electric-shock treatment and medication, and discharged after three weeks. Ten days later, he was readmitted. On Aug. 15, 1963, he was transferred to the IMH.

Doctors made their diagnosis: schizophrenia, paranoid type, comparatively late in onset. Cause: like all schizophrenia, unknown. Prognosis: utterly unpredictable.

AT BARRINGTON HOUSE, Pattie's favorite spot is a wooden dining-room chair. On a fine fall day, chances are you will find him relaxing there, sipping decaffeinated coffee and perusing the evening paper while he listens to WLKW, an easy-music station, on the radio he bought at the IMH.

Spend some time with him at that table and you will meet his housemates — a man and six women, 39 to 70 years old. All spent years at the IMH. All are chronically mentally ill, and probably will remain so for life.

To be sure, they have their eccentricities — one woman always loses the matches for her cigarettes, another occasionally talks to herself, the man sometimes yells for no apparent reason — but they are polite and friendly, quick to say hello and offer coffee and a snack to visitors.

Their illnesses, compounded by years of institutional neglect, have cost them many of the most basic skills of day-to-day living. They are, to use a social worker's description, "fragile" people, and they need help in solving emotional crises, budgeting, taking the bus, cooking, buying clothes — skills untroubled people take for granted.

"I lived in poverty and misery when I used to get discharged before from Rhode Island Medical Center," says Judy Costa, who was in and out of the IMH several times before the state finally gave her a home in Barrington House.

"You really have a chance to survive in the outside world with this kind of setup. You don't have to worry you won't have enough money to pay for it. You look like a decent, respectable person. People don't go around thinking of you as a criminal or a beggar."

THE FIVE-BEDROOM, two-story residence that became Barrington House was bought from a doctor on July 1, 1982. Using public bond money, the state paid $123,000, then spent an additional $89,708 for furnishings and extensive renovations. The home opened in October, 1983.

The state Department of Mental Health, Retardation and Hospitals gave Arn Lisnoff, Riverwood's head, a $110,000 annual contract to run the house. The contract, which is periodically renegotiated, reflects deductions for "rent" that residents pay from psychiatric-disability checks they receive monthly from Social Security.

Lisnoff — an innovative, compassionate young man whose vision and programs are greatly admired by MHRH and within the private sector — hired a staff of seven to provide 24-hour care. Like Lisnoff, the Riverwood staff is highly respected as capable and caring.

Besides Barrington House, Riverwood runs two other group homes, as well as a day program in Bristol, which Pattie and his housemates attend four days a week. The Riverwood Co-op, as the program is known, is an opportunity for residents to meet, talk over problems and learn conversational and housekeeping skills. Residents also play board games and discuss current events.

Pattie joins in discussions, and he is considered the finest checkers player at the co-op. Only rarely, however, does he participate in classes designed to hone members' social or housekeeping skills — unlike the others, he never lost those. And so he spends his days reading papers or magazines, or preparing lunch, or cleaning up, or helping the staff with menu planning and bookkeeping.

Barrington House residents make regular visits to the state-financed East Bay Mental Health Center (one of eight centers in the state) for counseling and medication that helps control the symptoms of their illnesses. Medical care is provided in private hospitals, and paid by Medicaid or Medicare.

An important component of life at Barrington House is recreation and socializing: weekend sightseeing trips and picnics, dinners at local restaurants, baseball games, cookouts, visits to the circus, movies, holiday parties — whatever residents agree they want to do, and can afford. Several members also attend Sunday Mass.

PATTIE'S FIRST STAY at the IMH ended when he was released in September, 1965. For the next 10 years, he lived on the outside. Twice during that decade, when he had difficulties with his family and his job, he was admitted to hospitals for short-term care.

Pattie's schizophrenia flared again in 1975.

Records indicate that he had become "combative," "nervous," "paranoid." He heard voices, was suspicious of people around him, had trouble sleeping and maintaining job performance. Twice that year, he was admitted briefly to the IMH.

On April 26, 1977, he was admitted again. He would not be released until October, 1983.

During this time, his wife divorced him and his family slowly drifted out of touch with him. They have yet to visit or write him in his group home.

UNLIKE MANY schizophrenics — those whose illnesses have lowered a curtain on the world around them — Pattie never lost his taste for current affairs.

His curiosity is active, his wit sharp. He reads the newspaper religiously, right down to the ads, and he catches TV and radio news. He can quote car prices, tell you the best cuts of meat on sale this week, discourse on Lee Iacocca, the '84 election, the space shuttle.

But spend time with him and you discover that he can be — to use the psychiatrists' term — "delusional." No one understands what triggers the process, but it happens occasionally.

When it does, Pattie hears voices no one else hears. He believes in forces of darkness and light. Believes that certain people can read his mind, a process he calls picking his head.

He believes in schemes — in particular, a master scheme he calls "The System." Government-financed and government-run, The System, he says, controls his life with electronic machines operated by the national networks.

No matter what the psychiatrists tell him, Pattie refuses to believe that The System does not exist. For over a decade, he has stubbornly argued that it is real.

HE FIRST DISCOVERED The System, he says, in the 1970s. His life was in turmoil.

"I was in my father's house in Massachusetts," he says. "I started sitting on the couch and thinking: Why is all this happening to me?

"Then I turned the radio on and I was listening to a program. I knew it was government because Jimmy Carter and Rosalynn Carter, Jerry Ford and Betty Ford were in my head like a picture.

"The system can put voices in a person's ear and bring information to a person. You can talk to them. They watch and they get information from you.

"The system machines are at NBC and ABC... CBS. It's hooked up to the radio and TV. It's the most powerful machine in the whole United States. The world. They say it's worth one million and some hundred thousand odd dollars.

"The System, come right down to it, is 24 years old, but no one knew much about it until 11 years ago. That's when it was made public. I don't mind carrying The System. Through The System, I'm living a dual life."

He pauses, remembering what the doctors have told him.

"They say, 'Well, you hear things.' Well, there's a lot of people hearing things if I'm hearing things because an awful lot of people have The System in their ears."

THESE DAYS, Pattie rarely talks about The System unless he's asked. Although he believes in it unwaveringly, he's smart enough to realize that most people — particularly strangers — aren't apt to want to hear about it.

And so, for most of the time, he keeps The System to himself as he settles contentedly into his other role — that of "father" to the residents of Barrington House. That role, combined with the security and low-stress environment of his group home, have made all the difference to Lloyd Pattie.

"I enjoy myself here," he says. "I feel protected in a way I didn't at the IMH. I would love to see my family, be reunited with them, be assured that everything is OK. But I know it's not time yet."

How I wrote the story

It sounds clichéd, and perhaps it is, but the trick to this story — the entire series, in fact — was portraying mentally disabled people as "people." Which means describing a severe disability in honest, accurate terms while still showing the reader that a schizophrenic has ambitions, talents, fears, happy and sad moments, a past and a future, just like the rest of us.

With Lloyd, the job was tough. The reason is obvious: His delusions are so deep, so bizarre to an outsider (at least initially), that they threatened to overwhelm anything else I wrote. Of course, I could easily have dwelled on those delusions and still written a credible story raising all sorts of issues and dilemmas, and fascinating the reader with the complexities of chronic mental illness.

But more than anything, I wanted to capture some of Lloyd's humanity.

So I decided early in the writing process that I would use a relaxed, almost conversational voice. No embellishments, no flair, no technocratic language, no aiming for the stylistic stars — just straightforward writing, the kind they forgot to teach us in college.

Naturally, I had spent several days with Lloyd, building his trust, learning his history, and so it seemed appropriate to begin his story with a description of the thing dearest to him, which is his new home. This also seemed a good way to immediately telegraph a message to the reader that Lloyd must be a good guy, right? Why else would he be welcoming us to come inside and visit with him for awhile?

Having set something of a homespun tone, I found it comparatively easy to slide into a history of Lloyd's schizophrenia, with all of the necessary details about electric shock and medications and paranoia and fright. Again, the key was steering clear of embellishment.

Most of the details about Lloyd's current delusion I kept until the end, however, and that was deliberate: By the time the reader gets to them, he already has met another side of Lloyd, the Lloyd-as-a-person side, and it's easier by then to accept his delusion.

I also managed, I think, to impart some of the information about Rhode Island's elaborate group-home system without beating the reader over the head with facts and figures. We as reporters have a tendency to abuse statistics, the idea being, I suppose, that lots of numbers add lots of credibility to a story. I disagree, unless it's for the business pages — and even there I have my doubts. A few numbers such as I used convey a sense of scale and importance much more economically and with less boredom than a deluge of statistics.

Not that everything was a breeze. A major problem was length. My original draft was about a third again as long as the one that made it into the paper, and the project editor insisted that was an absolute no-no. Because I liked what I had written, cutting it took about as long as writing it had taken. The cutting was accomplished in two ways: trimming quotes and condensing other sections that admittedly were overwritten. Fortunately, I was able to do most of the editing myself — which, no matter how painful, is usually the best way to fly, I have found. Except for one or two wonderful quotes that had to be sacrificed, I think the final, abbreviated product was better than the original.

One of the keys to this story, by the way, was establishing a strong relationship with the other group-home residents and with Lloyd, to the point that he allowed me to use his real name and be photographed straight on — features that are all too rare, unfortunately, in newspaper stories about the mentally disabled. Lloyd became my friend during the reporting phase, and I think the reader sensed that, and profited from it. I'd also like to think the piece did something to erase a bit of the stigma that surrounds the chronically mentally ill.

Lloyd, by the way, was very fond of the story, and, at last word, was doing fine.

A simple story of loss that speaks to all people

By Mark Patinkin
The Providence Sunday Journal, December 30, 1984

TIMBUKTU, Mali — We are all of us homeless this night. They are nomads who have lost their land; I am a traveler, far from everything I am part of. Together, we are spending Christmas Eve in the desert.

We are the oddest of couplings. They wear Moslem robes; I a flannel shirt. I grew up in Chicago and live now in New England; they've known only the Sahara. I have with me enough cash to cross the ocean in a morning. If they want to visit the nearest village, 10 miles distant, they must walk.

They have nothing. And tonight, I, too, have nothing.

I am in their camp. I am their guest. I am here because I want to know their world, what they had and what they lost. For this one night, we share our lives.

THE BEST WAY to get here is by Land Rover. My guide is a Western doctor.

He gives introductions, then leaves for his own Christmas. It is now only I and them.

The name of this tribe is Touareg. They live in newcomers' tents on the banks of the Niger. They came in from the deep desert only a month ago, driven by hunger, refugees all.

I am taken to the the tent of the chief. He gives me his hand, he tells me his name. "Hamzata," he says.

I tell him mine. We smile at each other's foreignness, and it brings us closer.

Only one thing about him speaks of wealth — his turban. It is blue and of fine silk. It must be the only thing of value in this camp. He has as much pride in it as I in the three things that have gotten me through this trip — my L.L. Bean shirt, my Swiss army knife and Ray Ban sunglasses. Little items, perhaps, but treasured things that have been with me for years — things necessary in this desert, and, right now, my only comfort.

The chief is well educated, fluent in French, but still we share less than half a language. My French is only marginal. This night, there would be many gaps to bridge.

I watch them unfold the visitor's mat, and light a fire for tea, rituals now familiar to me. But unfamiliar, too. I am thinking only of home.

I miss some things. I miss the winter ocean. I miss music, and movies, and the energy of the American spirit.

I wonder if it is snowing back home. Tree lights must be everywhere now. Here, I see only sand. Nearby, a tent of newcomers are settling to sleep without food. It is hard to feel the season in famine country.

I explain that it is Christmas Eve. I explain that in America, this is the best-loved of nights. They say they know about Christmas. It is not theirs, but they know it.

The chief motions to some of the others. He has them set up a special bed for me, in his tent. I tell him it's not necessary — it's bad enough I've imposed unannounced at 5 p.m. The ground would be fine. But he insists. I am his guest. It is important to him.

Soon, it begins to get cold. A fire is lit. I tell the chief I'm here to understand how his people came to be hungry.

It is simple, he says. They lived off cattle. The drought came. The grass disappeared. The cattle died.

"There must be more of a story than that," I say.

Yes, he says, there is. There is a story of

loss here that speaks to all peoples who have lost something dear. But he did not want to take my time with it.

More tea is poured. More men come around. We gather close to the fire.

WHY THE DESERT, I ask. Americans would consider it a banishment.

That makes him smile. It is the opposite, he says. Desert, for them, is freedom itself. All men, he says, have an ache for land. With the nomad, it is only keener. It is why they choose not a piece of land, but a world of it. This way, they can even own night.

He began to tell me of the good times, the fat times. They were wealthy then. They'd have been wealthy even in America. Hamzata's family — just he and his brothers — owned 1,000 cows. Had he been born in Texas, he'd have been a rancher.

As his ancestors had for centuries, he, too, followed the rhythm of the desert. From October to May, they would find a stand of grass, and this would be the time of settlement. And it was a good time. But they could not shake the love of road, the need for road. Even the cattle knew the rhythm of this movement, and were themselves restless by June.

Now they would follow the time of wandering, a week here, a month there, the stars guiding them, the camps numbering 100 souls, though they did not call them camps, they were families.

And they brought with them a culture, hiring learned men to join them during the season of teaching. Always, from the sale of cows, there was money to buy comforts in town, where their wealth was regarded with awe. Good times. Fat times.

THE CHIEF did most of the talking. The others gave him the respect of their silence. I had to struggle with the French, but slowly the same words were coming again and again.

"*Avant.*" Before.

Before, when things were good, they had fresh steak every night, and fresh camel milk, too, which is the best of all milk. There was guitar music, and even hunts, the dogs tracking gazelles, the chiefs following on their horses.

"It sounds like the perfect life," I say.

Yes, says the chief. It was ... *avant.*

Before. Before the sun became a constant thing, the nurturer of life changing to the enemy of it, the grass curling under it, the animals beginning to die, dying year after year, until, last May, the last of them was gone. And a world gone with them.

"And now?" I ask.

Now they are trying to find a new way of living. They are trying to learn cultivation of crop and a rootedness of their own. Now, there is no steak, only rice from UNICEF, and not always that. If the women sell their crafts in town, there is dinner. If not, there is none.

And around me, I can feel how it is ending. I can feel the ache of loss, the confusion of men and women who no longer have the things that make them what they are.

"*Les peuples ont faim,*" says the chief. It is another phrase I would hear throughout the night: The people are hungry.

SOON, THE COLD becomes too much. We go into the tent. And he takes out an album of photographs. A nomad with a Polaroid.

He brings a lantern over and begins showing me what times looked like when times were good. His camels ... his cows ... his soul. It is important to him that I see this. He understands I am a journalist. This is for history, he says. So people will know there was once such a life.

I had expected we would sleep without food. But as we leaf through the album, I smell cooking.

He says it is because I am a stranger who cared enough to come. Tonight, there would be dinner, a true feast. They were preparing the meat from one of the last of their desert sheep, meat they'd until now been saving for more difficult times. The women bring it to the tent. The chief begins cutting the portions with a dull sword. I see he is having trouble, and offer him my Swiss army knife. He marvels at it and cuts the rest with ease.

Sixteen of us are in the tent. There is enough for each of us to have five bites. There is a seriousness to eating here, a respect for it that only people like this can know. The chief eats only half his portion. He insists I have the rest. He says he isn't hungry.

When it is done, we go back to seek the fire's warmth.

There is no talk for a while. Then I ask how hard this has been for them.

The chief says it is the hardest thing in experience, leaving the one life you know. Even the secrets understood only in their hearts are secrets that tie them to the desert. How do you give that away, he asks. How do you start over — not after a lifetime, but after an ancestry?

We stand and talk for more than an hour. I tighten my flannel shirt. I notice he is shivering.

"Is there no clothing?"

"If there is no food . . ." and he lets the sentence go at that.

More phrases become familiar with repetition. *Rien à manger* — nothing to eat. Or simply, rien.

Whenever I bend to take a note, two of the men bring lanterns to help me. Slowly, I begin to feel an unexpected kinship. We are all far from home.

There are only two beds in the tent, the rest of the floor is sand. The chief takes one, I am given the other. At 10 p.m., we say good night. The lanterns are put out.

"*La Noël joyeux,*" I say into the dark. "*Tu comprends?*"

"*Ah, oui,*" he says. "*Je comprends.*"

CHRISTMAS EVE in the Sahara. I lie there for an hour, but cannot sleep. The cold comes into the tent, and into my bed. I walk outside for the embers of the fire. I am alone.

When this sky is clean, there is no sky like the Sahara sky. Under a full moon, you can read a newspaper. It helps me understand the draw of this place. When nature imposes a harshness, it seems to give back a beauty as great.

And now I find myself thinking about the things I've seen this month and what they mean.

What I've found here in this Touareg camp is what I've found everywhere: A man had a life he loved, the weather changed, and now he can't even feed his children.

I was where I'd begun in Ethiopia, in a tent city, hot by day and cold by night, where people of the land had gathered by force of weather, people now dependent on nations alone.

But here, as there, in the midst of this pain, I find a familiar twist of hope. There is a knowledge of spirit among famine victims here, a knowledge that says if you lose everything, you can still have civility, and there is wealth in that. I have never known the hospitality I've been given this night.

And I will always remember the hungry of Ethiopia, days from death, walking past a disabled food truck, ignoring its load of wheat, because touching it would have been theft.

I try again to sleep. I drift in and out. Finally, morning comes.

I RECOGNIZE this morning. I have seen it before. It was the morning of the Korem feeding camp, at least on one level. Here, now, as happened there, the children come to me. I can walk nowhere without the children. And always, they grow quiet and content when I give them my hand.

Why is it that they, and the adults, too, are drawn to Americans so? I did not expect that. There is a warmth for our country I had not known existed. And it has nothing to do with politics or allegiances, only with what the people here see — that when there is pain, this nation reaches out.

And I realize more than ever before, that what we are, and what we stand for, rests with that compassion.

BEFORE I LEAVE, the chief wants me to see what I've come to see. We walk to the newcomers' tents. I notice he is squinting hard into the sun. Soon, we pause at one tent, and there we find a true child of famine, one of the more troubled of this flock. The chief embraces him.

The child, to him, is a stranger. But to see the hurt in his face, it could be father and son. The little arms are so small. He holds him close long after I am finished with my photographs.

"*Rien à manger,*" he says. "*Rien à manger.*"

There is a kinship here Americans don't know. The greatest of this people feels truly diminished by the difficulties of the least of them.

I ask the chief about this. My French cannot keep up with him, but I do not need it. I know, from a month in famine country, what he is saying. That we are one family here. Joined together by weather. And joined also by the little we have. The things we do not have are things that join us, for he who, like me, has nothing, is my family.

We hear the grind of an engine. A half mile distant, we see the doctor's Land Rover.

We walk back to the main camp. The chief tells me to wait, then disappears into his tent. Soon, he emerges. He is carrying his blue silk turban. He places it in my hands.

For you, he says.

I take off my L.L. Bean shirt and hand it to him. Then I give him my Ray Ban sunglasses and Swiss army knife.

"For you," I say.

Christmas morning in the Sahara.

I climb into the Land Rover.

"Until next time," says the chief.

I say it, too. We begin to drive away.

And as we do, I turn to look back at these people who have been changed but not broken by hunger.

And as I leave this place, I am thinking one thought: One world.

How I wrote the story

I'd never written from the Third World before. I soon discovered something longtime correspondents take for granted — that the journalist abroad spends more energy getting stories back home than getting the stories.

In Africa, you can't rely on telephones. The main tool is the telex.

Don't get me started on telexes. Most look like 1962 supermarket cash registers, send material without paragraphs, and even, in some countries, have keyboard letters in the wrong place. I often ended up sending all my M's as W's, all my A's as Q's.

This story was the last of a series of 18 first-person articles I wrote during a month-long trip through famine country. In the research I did before leaving, I read that there was hunger in Timbuktu. I guess I hadn't even realized Timbuktu was in Africa. I figured any reporter who uses that dateline could die happy.

There was a more serious reason for choosing it. Foreign stories are probably one of the first things readers pass on their way to the sports pages. I thought this twist could help draw them. The same reasoning, I think, is why my paper decided to send a columnist on this assignment to begin with: to try a first-person-journey approach.

We also decided to try filing daily. We managed to do it, but only because of one lucky development: The Ethiopian government took more than a month to give me a visa. At first, that was frustration itself; I'd hoped to get there in days. The month, however, gave me time to draw story ideas from relief agencies, to send telegrams making appointments, to plot out an almost hour-by-hour itinerary. It turned out I needed it. You can't get much done in the Third World unless you arrive with a notebook full of local phone numbers and contacts with Land Rovers gassed up to take you around.

The writing of this piece was particularly important to me, chiefly because it was the last of the series. We often neglect endings of stories, but in some ways I think they're more important than leads; it's the final point readers take away. In a larger sense, the last of a series has the same impact, and I hoped this one would catch the themes I'd been writing about for a month — hope and humanity in famine country.

I don't think I could have done it had I not come up with this idea. I think most reporters agree that the great editor's cliche "there's no such thing as a dull assignment, just dull reporters" is nonsense. The best of journalism, it seems, always comes from the best of ideas. The old Christmas Eve angle may not have been the most original, but it struck me as a good conclusion for this series.

I broke a rule in coming up with the idea. One of the first things I was told by one of the first editors I worked for was never to go into a story with preconceived notions: Find out what it's about when you get there.

I came up with this idea, and even the

essence of the lead, two weeks before I left for Africa, while I was playing tennis. It held up, and it taught me how sometimes it helps to know exactly what you're looking for, even in so foreign a situation as this.

Again, planning made this story possible. If I had parachuted in, figuring I could work anything once on the ground, it would never have come together. Weeks before getting there, I'd telexed the UNICEF headquarters in Mali's capital, Bamako, about my hopes of finding a nomad camp near Timbuktu. The director there was kind enough to radio up to his Timbuktu coordinator, Marion Van Densen, to help me out.

She was at the airstrip to meet me, and eventually handed me off to some Italian doctors who knew of a tribe of nomads who'd come in from the desert. The doctors drove me there at dusk on Dec. 24, introduced me, and left me with my French-English dictionary.

At first, I thought the language barrier could hurt the story. I was able to understand only a third of what was said, if that. Then I realized I could use the language problem. That was part of it — the bond we managed even with minimal communication.

I approached the writing in the same way I'd approached the other stories, as a first-person chronological account of the evening.

I also find that any story is moved by dialogue, and first person can be helped by including the reporter's side of the conversation.

There were one or two devices I stole from others. I've always admired Murray Kempton, the *Newsday* columnist, for the way he gives his writing a special resonance by salting it with what I'd call statements about the way things are. I remember a piece he did on former Philadelphia Mayor Frank Rizzo's attempt to regain office. Kempton described Rizzo's newly humble campaign style, then added, "There has come to Rizzo, as happens with all bullies, the time when he wants no longer to be feared, but only loved."

I tried to do that throughout this piece, ending descriptive paragraphs with such phrases as "When nature imposes a harshness, it seems to give back a beauty as great."

I also think that stories should be circular, coming back to their beginnings. I almost missed that with this piece. On the first draft, I hadn't mentioned any of the gifts involved — the turban, the knife, the shades — until the last few paragraphs. On proofreading, I saw it might be more effective to foreshadow them. I went back and put in the paragraph about the chief's turban being his most valuable possession, as well as my own shades, knife and shirt being my own.

Finally, I think that echoing certain phrases can help to give a piece a thread. I remember reading a piece on Vietnam that began, "Every war has its saying. Ours was 'You'll get over it.'" The writer used that phrase — "You'll get over it" — a few more times, and it seemed to double the power and focus of the story.

I tried that to a lesser extent with a few phrases in this piece, such as the one in the chief's remembrance of his past life: "Good times, fat times." And again with "*Avant. Before...*" And a final time with the French phrase "*Rien à manger.*"

In a larger sense, I tried to do the same thing with the final two words of the story. In the middle of one of the earlier pieces I'd filed from Africa, I used the phrase "One world." It struck me as a good way to end the whole series. To make it echo, I used it one more time in the middle of another piece. And then ended this one the same way. It was another preconceived notion that helped me write this — I knew even before I got to Timbuktu that I would end the story with that phrase.

One soldier's story:
A cocky adventure that turned out wrong

By Joel Rawson
The Providence Sunday Journal, April 28, 1985

Bennington, Vt. Memorial Day, 1980

I do not care much for flags and parades anymore. I do not stand for the anthem in theaters or salute the flag at ball parks. I cannot articulate why except to say that it stems not from anger but sadness.

Still we are here, Stephan, my 9-year-old son, and I, a veteran of Vietnam. We sit on the lawn in front of a bank. The grass is still brown from the winter with clumps of green where the spring is trying to break through. Around us are strangers, all waiting for the parade to turn the corner and come up our street.

Once, I liked parades enough to volunteer for a drill team and had, through practice, developed the crisp but casual salute necessary if one is a pilot. Of all the military ceremonies, the one I found most moving had been retreat. The entire post would come to a halt, columns would stop marching, cars would stop and the drivers step out, all the soldiers would come to attention and salute as the flag was lowered at sunset and bugle music floated in the evening air.

Stephan fidgets. He is big for his age, his jeans a little short at the ankles, his face that of a child. He has clear blue eyes that can can search your soul.

However, his questions are ordinary.
Were you in the war?
Yes.
Did you kill anybody?
No.
Did you win?
No.
Did you fight the Germans?
I wonder if fathers can ever talk to their sons about anything, let alone war, without lecturing them.

Can you be honest?
I hated it. The loneliness ... the smell of burning kerosene ... being so tired I fell asleep trying to land a plane ... quivering against the ground as the rockets came in with a sound like tearing cloth ... losing.

I loved it. Flying low up the beach, the prop tips so low they kicked up sand ... the sound and pyrotechnics of night fighting on the perimeter .. the wonderful swaggering feeling of being young and carrying a gun.

I look at him and all I can see is the terrible fragility of life, and feel the moment the heart flutters to a stop and life passes out of the eyes.

And I lecture. War is the worst thing human beings can do to each other.

I wonder today if I can stand and salute, and what that will be teaching him. And it is then the parade turns the corner. In the lead is the honor guard from the VFW. They are dressed in khaki but they are old now. The cadence isn't too sharp and one of them carries his rifle a little off angle. World War II guys. The Mount Anthony Union color guard carries the flag out front, red, white and blue in the morning sunlight. Their flag, I think. Theirs, not mine.

Around us people are beginning to stand.

Orono, Maine. 1966

YOU DO NOT understand how cocky we were.

I am visiting a friend, Bob Fitzpatrick who teaches French at the University of Maine. He is married to Sylvie, a Frenchwoman. A second woman is visiting; she is returning to France from Saigon and has stopped in to see Sylvie.

We are sitting in the small living room and Bach is on the hi-fi. Sylvie's friend describes a drive from the city of Saigon to Vung Tau, a resort town with a wonderful beach on the South China Sea. She had been with a small party riding in a private car through the countryside when they came to a roadblock. Armed Viet Cong tax collectors. The point she is making is that it was daylight on a main highway and the highway did not belong to the government or the Americans. They convinced the Viet Cong that they were French and were allowed to pass.

If they had been American?

She shrugs.

I have read Bernard Fall's books *Street Without Joy* and *Hell in a Very Small Place* in which he described the French war in Vietnam. The French had been relatively poor. Coming back from defeat in Word War II, they depended on the U.S. for guns, planes and ammunition and they did not have the wealth of America. Fall told how their soldiers were ambushed on the highways and were trapped in muddy forts far from their supplies. The Communists chopped them to pieces.

Now I lean forward and explain that it cannot happen to us. We will not travel the roads. We have helicopters. Thousands of them. You have, of course, heard of the 1st Cavalry, the world's first airmobile division. It lifts entire battalions over mountain ranges and rivers. It cannot be ambushed or cut off.

I am a newly-commissioned second lieutenant headed for flight training. I have been taught, and I believe, that warfare is the application of force to inflict a nation's will on another.

I have been taught, and I believe, that the nation with the greatest amount of money, the greatest number of men and the greatest industrial output will win.

It was so in the American Civil War, in World War I, in World War II.

It is a matter of mathematics. Combine that with superior technology and we cannot lose.

I have not yet read Che Guevara's diaries or about Mao's Long March or even Tolstoy's *War and Peace*.

The helicopter, I tell them, the Hueys. We will not repeat the mistakes of the French.

Sylvie's friend looks at me with an expression of total bewilderment, and then her face closes and the eyes flash hard for the briefest of seconds before she turns brightly to Sylvie and speaks in French.

I have been taught, and I believe. And I have been dismissed as an idiot.

Ozark, Ala. 1967

THE FLAT WHAPPING sound of the Hueys' rotor blades waken us on a Sunday morning. Janeen and I go outside dressed in bathrobes to watch a chain of helicopters circling and landing on a small hill on the farm across the road.

Later on at the post I ask what is going on. Oh, pinnacle landings.

Why on Sunday?

We're behind schedule. Training seven days a week. Vietnam needs pilots.

The Huey helicopter was Vietnam's truck, it hauled infantry into battle, groceries to the kitchens, mail to the troops, generals to briefings, dead to morgues.

Its muttering fills the background to the movies The Deerhunter and Apocalypse Now. Even today, when I hear them fly over my home, the noise will stop me in midstride.

The Huey's peculiar sound will become the theme song of the war.

DaNang. August, 1968

STATON DRINKS A breakfast Pepsi Cola as we look at the Viet Cong corpses. They lie amid the red flower blossoms the explosion of their satchel charge blew from the trees. Flies walk into their mouths and dust lies on their open eyes. They are stacked like hunting trophies for all the Vietnamese to see.

A Special Forces sergeant takes photographs.

They had attacked the night before and the explosion had gone off with a bang in a drunken sweaty dream and I'd fallen out of bed in my shorts groping for my revolver in the dark. I ran for the roof and fell on the tar and gravel too shot full of adrenalin to be scared.

Two stories down, the street corner was lit by a gasoline fire from a burning personnel carrier. There was a bank on the corner with a walled courtyard and across the street from the bank was a compound where a Vietnamese infantry battalion lived. A panicked machinegunner in the compound fired into the air, his bullets ripping into the tree limbs in front of my face.

The streets were bordered by sewage ditches and I saw somebody crouched running down one and pointed my pistol at him, but I didn't pull the trigger and somebody else killed him.

A bank guard stepped around the wall and fired into the ditch, cool as a man potting cans with a BB gun. When the magazine was empty, he stepped back, reloaded his carbine and did it again.

I got up and ran down from the roof. As I turned the corner at the bottom of the stairs I was looking into the muzzle of a .45 pistol held by Major Greene. "Jesus Christ," he said. "I almost shot you. Get back on the roof." The Viet Cong had backed into a culvert and the infantry came out and threw hand grenades in until they were all dead. Except for one girl which they captured.

In the morning, I had showered and put on fresh pressed fatigues. As Staton and I wait for the truck to take us to the airfield we examine the carnage.

The four Vietnamese soldiers manning the personnel carrier had been asleep inside the machine. The Viet Cong had snuck up the ditch. Behind them was the wall surrounding the bank; in front, the Vietnamese compound. They had been trapped in the ditch with no way of retreating. Either by plan or through ignorance they had embarked on a mission which was suicide.

The woman who threw the satchel charge onto the personnel carrier did not get back to the ditch before the explosion caught her and cut her legs off. She had dragged herself across the street and fought from the ditch until killed.

Whoever those Viet Cong were, they had come to fight us until they died. It is their deaths, coming two months after my arrival in Vietnam, that forces me to realize there is nothing at stake in the war that means enough to me to die for. From then out I know that I am simply putting in time, trying to survive 365 days.

I am a volunteer, signed up for the adventure of it, signed up because of a romantic notion we were the new centurions on the frontiers of the American Empire. Fed on Victory at Sea, Hemingway novels and John F. Kennedy's speeches. I turned down a chance to work at a staff job, choosing instead to fly.

I am a volunteer officer in an Army filled with kids drafted out of high school. The sons of the poor. The sons of the ghetto and the farm, the sons of workers and the middle class. They had less reason than I to be there. We are all trying to survive 365 days.

At Fort Knox, Kentucky, I'd been assigned to train recruits. One evening I'd seen a marching column of men. They had been dressed in baggy field jackets and helmet liners. The column climbed a hill, the men bent forward against the slope, and I remember thinking how much they looked like a column of slaves from pictures of the building of pyramids. And I remember feeling pity for them because they were so much younger than me. I was 23.

At the gate to the bank we find the girl captured the night before. Her body lies in the driveway. We are told she is a local girl, 16 years old.

A newspaper placed over her face lifts in the breeze. She has been shot in the head and the bone structure is so shattered her face looks like it is painted on a deflated, dark ball.

Flying

WE ARE OVER the hill country along the Thu Bon River south of DaNang on a reconnaissance mission. The heat haze rises into the air shrouding the horizon but we can see straight down to the brilliant green jungled hills and the grassy valleys.

We circle a set of coordinates waiting for things to develop. The radio is crackling. The FACs and fighter bombers chatter on the UHF. On FM some Vietnamese are shrieking at each other. Occasionally we can listen in on the North Vietnamese. We all use the same radios, the same frequencies.

The propeller noise beats on the aluminum fuselage and the sun beats in through the plexiglass and the skin on my face is tight and prickly.

An authoritative voice comes onto the radio: "This is DaNang DASC. DaNang DASC. All aircraft. Heavy artillery warning." That is the euphemism for an Arclight. A B-52 strike. The voice reads a map location.

We check our position. It is time to go someplace else. The time between the warning and bombing is only a few minutes. We tuck the nose down and run.

The bombs fall in a valley. At first they appear as winking lights in gray smoke. Then the air is tinged brown with earth, and as the cloud rises thousands of feet, it changes to green, the color of cholorophyl, of pulverised vegetation.

At the briefings they tell us how many artillery missions are fired on targets we "acquired." How many airstrikes, how many infantry insertions. The information is designed to keep our morale up because ours is a war by remote control. We fly and gather data, the data is processed and then analyzed, probabilities are weighed, targets assigned, and on occasion the B-52s fly.

As I stare back over the wing at a mile-long valley being shattered, I wonder if the target was one of mine and I wonder if there really is anybody down there.

Saigon. Thanksgiving 1968

WE WAIT for three days for an airplane to be fixed so we can take it back to DaNang. At night we drink in various bars. During the day we stay in the hotel room located near a hospital. All day the sound of the Medevac Hueys comes whapping through the windows. Wounded coming in from the field. From the Iron Triangle. From the Delta. These are not casualties of a big battle. They are the wounded from little firefights and booby traps, of night rocket attacks and heat exhaustion. This is General Westmoreland's war of attrition.

He had hoped to trap the enemy where our fire power could kill him, where our wealth would count. We devised the body count to keep track of how we were doing. In the end it appears the only accurate count was of our own dead and wounded.

All day the sound of the Hueys come into the hotel room. I am long past going outside to watch.

Flying

I AM RIDING co-pilot with Richardson. We are calling it a day on a late afternoon flight. As we fly north up the coast from Chu Lai to DaNang the sun is low over the mountains to the west. The orange light of evening touches the belly of cloud and reflects like golden fire from the paddies. The coast runs under the nose, a curl of surf stretching to the horizon.

To keep the tension down, pilots are allowed to quit any day during their last week. My buddy, with whom I will be going home, quit five days ago. This is my last flight, on my last day. I have stuck it to the end. It is a point of pride.

I put a foot up on the dash and watch the country going past, trying to burn it in so I will remember it always.

There are so many shades of green to get right. The actual purple of the sky. That gold with dark strips of dike dividing.

Providence, R.I. April, 1975

WHEN THE collapse finally comes, I am working on the newspaper and each night the pictures arrive from the wire services.

At first they are distant images, but with the fall of DaNang the pictures are close to home. They show the beach with thousands of refugees in lines wading out to waiting ships, an Asian Dunkirk. They show Boeing 727s jammed with desperate Vietnamese, some clinging to the wings and landing gear only to lose their grip and plunge to their deaths on the very runways from which I had flown.

In the end there is a single image. Saigon is gone. The last helicopter perches on our embassy roof. A thin line reaches up toward it. In my mind I can feel it lifting, feel the turbine winding up, the blades taking bigger bites of air as she begins to tremble and lift. I can smell the burning kerosene on the wind and hear the whapping sound.

Bennington, Vt. Memorial Day, 1980

FROM WHERE Stephan and I sit on the grass, we can see the stone spire of the monument to the Battle of Bennington.

In the summer of 1777, a British force ventured south from Canada, down Lake Champlain with the hope of capturing New York State and cutting New England off from the Southern Colonies.

A raiding expedition of 800 men under Lt. Col. Friedrich Baum was split from the main force and sent into Vermont. They were Germans from Brunswick and Hesse, British soldiers and American Tories.

The Colonists raised a force of 1,500 men from New Hampshire, Massachusetts and Vermont, a Colonial militia of farmers, shopkeepers and artisans against professional mercenaries from Europe. The British expedition dug in on an 863-foot high hill west of Bennington overlooking a valley of a small river.

You can go there now on an August day. The earthworks the Hessians dug still show, gentle mounds under the grass, and there is a plaque telling about the battle.

On August 17, the Americans snuck around behind and attacked across a low saddle of fields. They fought with muskets and cannon until the Hessians' ammunition blew up and then the fighting was with bayonets and rifle butts, sabres and pikes. More than 200 men died on that hill in an area the size of a football field.

Today there are black-eyed susans and goldenrod in the fields and sumac, white birch and maples in the woods. You can look at the green of the corn and hay fields across the valley and see the moving cloud shadow on the hills.

The Americans took their prisoners and dead back to Bennington. You can find some of them buried in the yard of the Old First Congregational Church where a marble monument carries their names — Head, Post, Pettingill, Eastman, Conant, Cunningham, Harris, Hicks, Hooper, McAffee, Moore, Perkins, Proctor ... Names from a great American victory in the War of Independence.

We have become a nation of names on monuments, but they are no longer all to victories.

I wonder, for a second, if they ever drink to Bennington in the beer halls of Hesse.

Then as the color guard comes up the street, I take Stephan by the elbow and we stand and salute the flag.

How I wrote the story

The story grew from Don Murray's first visit to the *Journal-Bulletin*, in 1981. He ran a seminar for editors, in which he made us write a piece. Trying to find an idea, I turned to the Memorial Day parade in Bennington. That morning had troubled me, and I remembered it and the dilemma. I was struck also by the historical significance of the Battle of Bennington, and the parallel stories of the Hessian mercenaries defeated in America and the Americans defeated in Vietnam.

Although the story was not finished then, I thought it could be turned into a free-lance piece. *Yankee* was in mind. During my August vacation that summer, I took a day and went to Bennington, where I visited the *Banner* and read its parade account. I also went to the museum in Bennington containing battle artifacts. A visit to the battlefield gave me some detail for the fighting, but the most valuable part for me was to walk part of the route the Americans took and note the kinds of plants growing today and just look around. On the way back from the battlefield, I stopped at the church and wrote down the names in the graveyard.

I never did get around to the free-lance story. The notes went into a desk drawer and fell from mind.

As the 10th anniversary of the fall of Saigon approached, Mark Silverman, Chips Quinn and I got together in the glass booth in the back of the newsroom to talk ideas. I got onto a rant about the picture of the Huey helicopter lifting refugees off the Saigon embassy roof, and how that picture more than any other symbolized the war to me.

Mark said, OK, so why don't you write a piece?

So, OK, I did.

These are the decisions that shaped it.

The style is a deliberate effort to write in tight scenes, each of which has a point unto itself (colored threads in the cloth) or contributes to the understanding of the whole (the stout white canvas). The device is the dateline. I'm trying to find a shorthand that will carry the story ahead without tying the reader up with background. This is evidence of the considerable influence Joan Didion's writing has had on me. She has also convinced me of the power of the short piece. (Buy her latest, "Democracy," a short novel about politics, war, the hydrogen bomb, marriage and murder, and you'll see what I mean.)

The second decision was where to begin — which became where to end.

Bennington is the key scene. I tried putting it all at the beginning. I tried putting it all at the end. I tried beginning with the difference between myself and Steve's very conservative grandparents, whom we were visiting.

Then I took my own advice and Ernest Hemingway's. Each time I talk about writing at newspapers, I conclude with a passage from "A Moveable Feast" in which Hemingway describes how he starts. Cut away all the scrollwork, he says, and begin with a simple declarative sentence. I thought about what the story was and decided it was about that salute and why the salute was so difficult. That gave me the courage to write the first line and stick with it.

A key element of storytelling is to pose a dilemma early on and then solve it — my own advice. The dilemma is, Will he salute? The answer comes at the end. I split Bennington in half. That scene now neatly served as two vehicles. The lead sets up the characters and the problem; the end allows the comparison of the battle to Vietnam. We are moving toward the salute. After that there was nothing further to say. And that gave me the last line.

This outline resulted:

Bennington, Memorial Day, 1980
Helicopters
Orono, 1966. We were so sure

DaNang, summer 1968. What's worth dying for war and politics, war is not diplomacy by another name, they fight to kill, the barroom The Aytollah and limits of power Nixon on the beach and the changing nature of war

Saigon, Thanksgiving, 1968. War by machine and data analysis, garbage in - garbage out, Westmoreland's body count

1975, the newsroom and the wirephoto images of the beach and DaNang, defeat changes the way you think, no longer so sure

Bennington, Memorial Day, 1980

All of the points did not survive the writing, but the above outline served as the rough guide and a reminder of the points I wanted to touch.

The themes of the piece are flags and memorials and helicopters and Vietnam and defeat. The story is about teaching kids a father and a son. It is the core of the story, and all the rest is wrapping.

A point that bothers me: How do I know Staton was drinking a Pepsi? I wrote an account of the bombing in 1970; I kept it and used it as notes for this piece. The Pepsi can is in there, but I can no longer see it in my mind's eye. Which leads us to how far to trust memory: I don't know. In places like the scene in Orono, I can remember some details, but not others. Time of year is lacking. I remember a gray day, but not whether it rained or snowed. I remember the Bach. I can't remember the woman's name. I would not dare put quotes on dialogue. The last flight with Richardson happened; its details exist in my mind as images so sharp and vivid they could be happening now. Yet I have no document, no photograph, and I ask myself, "Is it true, or has it changed through 16 years to become more imagination than reality?" I don't know. I trusted the memory.

I got a first draft written and showed it to Chip Scanlan. He did what good editors do: praised the piece and then fixed it. He suggested a rewrite of the Bennington history, as it was too stiff — like a textbook, he said. He ordered up a rearranging of material so that the image of the dead girl's head — "a dark deflated ball" — was emphasized. He spotted both the weaknesses and strengths, and got me to work on both.

Summer dreams, vacation fantasies and the annual purge

By S. Robert Chiappinelli
The Providence Journal and *The Evening Bulletin*, July 29, 1985

Do you ever notice your reaction on the first week back from vacation?

I don't mean the dragged-out feeling, the horrid realization that 10 a.m. is not 4 p.m. as your body and mind insist.

I'm referring to something more than that, a nagging irritation.

I mentioned that last week to a friend also freshly returned. He felt the same way. He went home that first day in a lather about things that normally roll off his back.

It seems to happen without fail to me.

I have to undergo a purging that first work week, a playing out of emotions that recur vacation after vacation. Every time I come back, I feel diminished somehow. Perhaps it's a gnawing feeling that life has only so many vacations and I've spent another.

More likely it's wrestling with a different dragon. Vacations, I think, create an impression of life offering more — a free-to-be-me feeling.

Returning to work, on the other hand, confirms that the relaxed life we nibble on briefly will never be our main course. The treadmill resumes here.

THE WEEK OF return involves reconciling myself to being here for the long haul. It also involves realizing deep down that it is not so bad at all, that I really don't want the life of the rich and the famous, that each ounce of glitter costs a pound of permanence.

Vacations also deceive me into thinking I own time. It's takes a while to realize I'm the same renter I always was.

After each respite, I think I can actually organize my life, budget my time. I return home resolved to dispatch the compost pile of mail cooking on the dining room table, the bundle of investments, magazine subscriptions, insurance and bills I can't decide on or don't have the money for at the moment. Just 10 minutes at the pile, an unexpected phone call and a kid's scraped knee or two, confirms that the pile is forever.

Then I return to work, to the accumulated junk mail, to the same unfinished pile of things on my desk and to what seems like a week of rerouting phone calls for others — even my phone is no longer my own, I moan — and the week of vacation seems from another time.

THIS YEAR WE spent 10 days roaring back and forth to South Bend, Ind., and staying at Notre Dame, my alma mater, under an alumni program. You can ride tandem bikes, swim, play handball, racquetball, tennis and basketball, jog, golf, watch VCR movies, roam the campus, relive the memories and generally behave like a jock trying to relax. I did most of the above.

Life's grittier side scraped us this time, though. Someone smashed our car window, and we spent two days getting the $155 replacement. Then on the return trip we consumed nearly two hours futilely searching for a room in Wilkes-Barre and Scranton, Pa. Spurned at every turn, we drove on through the night and arrived exhausted at 5:15 a.m.

That should have been enough to make me welcome returning to work.

NO SOONER was I in the newsroom door than I was sent to cover a small flood at a senior citizens' home. No easing back in. And no boffo lead-off story. I got to lunch late because of deadline rewrite and then was dragged out of lunch to cover a bank robbery.

Later I was asked to do a throw-away story and to work a Saturday — I already had plans and didn't have to — but both contributed to my post-vacation blues. I began to feel as appreciated as your average dowel.

Then the check for my vacation week arrived. We receive vacation pay in advance, but I am always struck by the regular check that the company also issues for bookkeeping purposes.

The check is pink, like the usual one, but covered with dozens of Xs and has "Void" written on it 19 times. I always feel void when I receive it.

NOW AS I close out my first week back, I am still rebounding toward the times when I love this job's chance to chronicle life's ups and downs.

As I type, a 32-year-old next to me wonders if he is middle-aged. Middle age is always one year older than you are, I reply in my 44-year-old wisdom.

I begin looking forward to next week, thinking about a series and a project the staff has planned. I think about an article I read during the week about George Scott, the former Red Sox first baseman, knocking around Fenway Park, hoping someone will offer him a job in baseball.

And I realize that if dreams and vacation fantasies did come true and I had grown up to play for the Red Sox, I could be like Scott, all done, left only with an aging body and memories. And I realize how lucky I am.

Hey boss, got a little flood I can cover?

How I wrote the story

The first ingredient of a post-vacation-blues story is a vacation — which I am prepared to take again in pursuit of another column.

One thing I have discovered in writing a column is that the more uncomfortable I feel while writing a story, the more people respond to it.

You might call it the squirm effect.

I squirmed last year when I wrote about turning 44, and I squirmed again when I wrote about my post-vacation blues. Both columns got a lot of response, even though I wondered all through them why anybody would care. But apparently misery does love company.

Along that line, another column lesson is: When things get bad, write about them. It took a while for that to register, but once it did, it proved a wonderful outlet. Feeling low that you are about to be executed for murder? No sweat: Just write about it. You'll feel positively upbeat for your last meal.

That was kind of the way it was the first day back at work.

I slogged through that small flood in a senior citizens' home, and then arrived late to a brown-bag quality-circle meeting of reporters, and then was yanked out in midbite to go cover a bank robbery.

Things continued to pile up over the next few days. I never got a moment to explore the rubble on my desk and to figure out where I was before I left. Instead, more scraps joined the pile.

I mentioned my downer to a few other newshounds and found they often experience the same feelings. So I decided to write about them.

I started with a question: "Do you ever notice your reaction on the first week back from vacation?" — because that seemed conversational and also would allow the millions I thought would be uninterested to answer "No" or "I don't care," and move on. Better to lose them immediately than bore them.

From there it was a matter of examining my feelings and getting them down — the squirming process. I thought briefly about checking with psychiatrists, psychologists and the like to establish a pattern, but decided that would be too much like work, and might not lead anywhere.

So I went back to the feelings of diminishment and the whisking away of the brief freedom I enjoyed.

All this was percolating when I read Peter Gammons's *Globe* story on George Scott, the former Red Sox first baseman. (Scott played and managed in Mexico for several years, and said he became "affluent" in Spanish.)

The usual purging was taking place as I wrote, and by the time I got to Scott I was feeling better. So I wound up with the request for another little flood to cover. I knew the editors would accommodate me.

And here are a few more observations about my reporting and writing process:

The first is that a surprising number of readers really care about what I and other writers experience.

As reporters we usually operate as disinterested observers. That distance can be really valuable. I think of it as the "Mr. Reporter" role. It's not really Bob Chiappinelli out there; it's just some guy doing his job.

The Mr. Reporter role saw me through several stories I might not have done had I stopped and thunk.

Once a city editor — the same one who sent me out to cover a guy walking nude down a pedestrian mall, resulting in a lovely picture of my interviewee looking comfortable and me looking like a whipped dog — dispatched me to check out a guy walking a lion on a leash outside the *Journal*.

Old Mr. Reporter grabbed his pad and pencil and went to work. The guy was promoting the circus, I learned, and people were giving him a wide berth. Everyone, that is, except me.

Mr. Reporter didn't realize what he was into — or what was into him — until later, when I viewed a picture showing me diligently jotting notes while the lion clawed playfully at my pants leg.

Another time, as I walked into work, an old man stopped me in the middle of downtown and asked where to catch a bus. He told me that he used to be a singer, and suddenly, in the middle of morning rush hour, he began singing to me — loudly.

For a minute I thought of chasing a squirrel up a tree. Then Mr. Reporter kicked in. That wasn't Bob Chiappinelli out there embarrassed; it was Mr. Reporter. He just takes notes, observes and doesn't really get involved. The incident became a column.

It's easier on the psyche operating on that level.

But there is another level, the level of human emotions, which we infrequently write about. Yet all people share that level — the doubts, the mortality, the hang-ups, the little joys we're shy about flaunting.

It took me years to realize that, and to get myself to try to share some of those doubts and joys. But in retrospect, most of the stories I got good feedback on operated on that level: dealing with a sudden melancholy that hit my son when he was 4, recounting my discomfort at being a stranger at a party, struggling with turning 44, the age at which my father died.

I'm not tremendously at ease spilling my guts. Few of us are. But I always admire people who wrench something from deep inside and share it.

What it comes down to, I think, is that it is OK for reporters — the Fourth Estate, the champions of the First Amendment — to let on that we are human beings, not just smart tape recorders who can craft a lead and build a pyramid upside down.

People like to see us smolder at mowing the lawn, get taken by glib salesmen and flinch as parents in the face of relentless kid-caring chores.

As for actually writing such stuff, well...

First, a sense of humor helps. We all have flaws that we can deal with only by laughing at ourselves. I butcher home-repairs jobs. I always lose 10 yards on every carry — I go to dig a hole and break the shovel. There's columns in them there frustrations, folks.

Being honest is important, too. You don't have to have happy endings or draw tremendous morals. You're just some poor stiff living life, and a lot of poor stiffs out there are happy just having that shared with them.

Finally, realize what a tremendous outlet writing is.

It's therapeutic. It's work, but it organizes and focuses your thoughts, pinpoints your problems, and somehow makes you feel a little better about them. You're rewarded for your embarrassment and reluctance by a cleansed feeling, and frequently by subsequent support from others.

When I wrote about turning 44, I said how vulnerable and diminished I had felt for the past few months. Several strangers then called, and some wrote lengthy warm, caring notes in response. That was one of the nicest experiences I've ever had.

One thing Chip Scanlan has mentioned to me is the question of writing to a limit (something I'm hardly doing now).

That can be rough. Often I will finish a story by 2 o'clock and spend two hours paring it.

I follow the Joel Rawson technique for that, first going through and finding grafs where one or two words tag over onto a new line. A little weeding in a few of those gardens sometimes is all you need.

Other times, though, I have to chop larger weeds. That usually becomes an individual choice, depending on what I think I can spare from the story, which quotes are similar, etc.

Writing a column every week — let alone four times weekly, as our Mark Patinkin does — can be draining. And a problem with the weekly column is that I'm always shifting gears; I'm a general-assignment reporter four days a week and a columnist the fifth. I don't feel I have free rein to criticize someone I might be writing a news story about the next week. But that's all right; I'm not much of a crusader anyhow.

One way I cope with the weekly demand is to realize that no matter what, that space will be filled. We are eminently disposable. The paper always comes out; it never has all-white pages. Then, too, every columnist, I bet, has written a column about having nothing to write.

Desperation often drives me out on the streets, and that is a good place to be. We reporters do a lot by telephone and don't really see the interaction of people, so we benefit from going into that rich grove.

Well, I'm just about done.

But, you know, it's been a while since I turned 44. Coming back from vacation was a bummer. And writing this has taken quite a bit of time.

So if you're so inclined, just write or call me, and gush about how great I am.

And to show how fair-minded I am, I'm willing to accept calls from those who think I should be laid to rest in a tiny inverted pyramid.

Just ask for Mr. Reporter.

The natural

By Bill Parrillo
Sunday Journal Magazine, April 6, 1986

No one knows where it started. Or how. Or why. Or when.

Maybe it began with the brown bat. Yes, maybe the brown bat. Wade Boggs loved that bat — dark brown on the barrel, light brown at the handle. There were a lot of hits in that round piece of wood. Singles into the gaps, doubles down the left-field line. Even an occasional home run.

The bat would split and he would nail it back together. Another crack, another nail. Maybe it would need two nails. And some tape. A piece of wood would chip away and Wade Boggs would glue it back. For three years, that bat, held together with glue and tape and nails, just kept ringing out hits.

One day, however, Boggs took a mighty swing and the bat disintegrated into a zillion pieces that no amount of glue could put back together. Young Wade was beside himself.

There go all those line drives to left center and right center. There go all those smashes up the middle. Wade Boggs figured he'd never get another base hit the rest of his life.

His lucky bat was gone. His career was over.

Distraught, he went to every sporting-goods store around his home, in Tampa. And St. Petersburg. And Clearwater. No brown bats. Not like the one he had.

"We even searched through warehouses filled with bats," remembers Winfield Boggs, Wade's father. "Couldn't find another bat like that nowhere. Finally, I got this Pete Rose bat. You know, one of those signature models? I told him, 'Now, Wade, why don't you try this one? Seems to do all right by him.'" Boggs reluctantly agreed. He allowed as how what was good enough for Pete Rose might be good enough for him. And the line drives kept coming.

Wade Boggs was 10 years old.

OR MAYBE it all started during the spring training of his rookie year, 1982. He went over to his mother's house for supper one night and had her lemon chicken. The next day, he went 5 for 6: line drives everywhere. He thought back to the lemon chicken. That night, he had chicken again. The next day, three more hits.

Now, four years and two American League batting titles later, Wade Anthony Boggs, star third baseman of the Boston Red Sox, eats chicken 365 days a year.

And the line drives keep coming.

Superstitious? Of course. Eccentric? No doubt.

But Wade Boggs can afford to be both. Barring injury, this week he will begin his fifth big-league season, ready to add to his already staggering accomplishments. A year ago, for example, he batted .418 at Fenway Park with an on-base percentage of .500. That's right. He reached base one out of every two times at bat. In four seasons, he has compiled a career batting average of .351. Line drives, indeed.

His start defies any kind of modern perspective. When you talk about Wade Boggs and his numbers, you don't talk in terms of Rod Carew or Dave Winfield or Stan Musial, even. You have to go back a bit. Back to Wagner and Speaker and Cobb. Back through the corridors of time to another place and another era.

After only four baseball seasons, Wade Boggs is now chasing the legends of the game. Then again, he always has been something of a natural.

IT WAS THREE spring trainings ago that a man walked up to Ted Williams one day at the Red Sox camp in Winter Haven, Fla., and showed him a snapshot of a young child swinging a bat in his backyard.

Williams took a look, blinked and looked again.

"Now let me tell ya somethin'," boomed Teddy Ballgame in his best John Wayne voice. "Now that is a perfect swing."

It was Wade Boggs's swing. He was 18 months old.

"He just loved to swing that bat," remembers Winfield Boggs. "It was one of those plastic kind. I gave it to him for Christmas. I'd get home from work and he'd be waiting, bat in hand, ready for me to pitch him the whiffle ball. After a couple of years, we changed to a tennis ball — I'd pitch and he'd hit it. And he'd only stop when he either got tired or it was time for supper. But, to be honest, it was always supper that stopped him. Wade never got tired. He never got tired of hitting."

WINFIELD BOGGS, 60, is a career military officer living in Tampa. He and his wife, Sue, have three children: an older son, Wayne, who is an air-traffic controller at O'Hare Airport, in Chicago; a daughter, Ann, a nurse practitioner; and Wade, who was born in 1958, when the senior Boggs was stationed in Omaha, Neb.

There were moves to Puerto Rico and Brunswick, Ga., before the Boggs family settled in Tampa, when Wade was 10. All along, his best coach was his dad, who was a top-flight pitcher in fast-pitch softball. He knew the game.

"To be honest, I didn't show him much," says Winfield Boggs, who speaks with a pleasant Southern drawl. "Everything he did seemed to come natural. I never taught him how to swing. I never taught him how to throw a ball. The first swing was a natural swing. The first throw was a natural throw. He just loved the game. We used to get baseball games on the Armed Forces Network, and Wade would just sit in front of the set and watch.

"I mean, he was 3 years old," the elder Boggs continues. "Most kids that age get fidgety after five minutes and do something else. Not Wade. He'd watch the whole game. And he was a great mimic — he'd pick things up from watching the players. Like sliding: He'd put this piece of cardboard down in the backyard and he'd slide on that cardboard ... tuck one leg under the other, slide and just bounce right up. He knew how to hook-slide when he was 3 years old."

THOSE WHO KNOW Wade Boggs — those who really know him — talk about the fire that burns inside him. His desire to play the game. His passion to hit a baseball. His obsession to be the best.

"You watch him for only one day, you're not going to be impressed," says Joe Morgan, Boggs's manager at Pawtucket. "But you watch him for a month, and you find out there's something inside that boy. Something that drives him. I don't know what it is. Only thing I know is, very few have it."

David Fyfe, Boggs's coach at H.B. Plant High School, in Tampa, remembers the practices. He especially remembers the Saturday-morning practices.

"We'd start at 9 o'clock, but I'd always arrive a half-hour early to get things ready," recalls Fyfe. "I'd get there and look out in the parking lot, and there would be Wade, sitting in his little red Mustang, waiting for me. There he was, the only car in this big, empty parking lot. In three years, I never beat him to practice.

"I've always said this," Fyfe continues. "Just like Patton was born to fight wars and Yeager was born to test-fly airplanes, Wade Boggs was put here to hit baseballs." Boggs is 27 years old now, is married to Deborah and has a daughter, Meagann, 7. On Deborah falls the burden of preparing any one of 13 different chicken dishes.

Let's see now, there's lemon chicken, and barbecued chicken, and baked chicken, and Italian chicken, and on and on. At various times, certain dishes become hotter than others.

For example, Boggs might eat lemon chicken one day and then bang out two base hits. The next day it might be baked chicken, and he'll get three hits. The day after, it's Italian chicken, followed by no hits in two at-bats, with one walk; the Italian chicken is sent to the bullpen. The baked gets a few extra starts.

Crazy, you say? Perhaps. But it's just a part of the well-ordered world of Wade Boggs.

FOR A NORMAL night game at Fenway Park, Boggs starts to get himself ready shortly after noontime. That's when he begins pulling on his mask of intensity; that's when he begins shutting out the rest of the world. "Building my cocoon," he calls it.

He arrives at the park every day at the same time, 3 p.m. He spends the next hour just relaxing around the clubhouse. He might read a few pieces of mail; maybe kibbitz a little with Vince Orlando, the Sox's longtime clubhouse man. He'll watch others play cards, but he won't play ("waste of concentration," he says).

One hour after having arrived, he'll go out and field some grounders. At precisely 5:17, he will take batting practice. Then he'll return to the clubhouse, change his shirt and walk down the cool of the underground runway that leads from the clubhouse to the dugout. At the dugout, he'll pull up a metal folding chair, lean back and start playing "catch" with the wall, flipping a baseball off the wall and catching the rebound in his glove.

All the while, the cocoon gets thicker.

AT EXACTLY 7:17, Boggs will do a few pregame wind sprints in the outfield, and then he'll play a little catch in front of the Red Sox dugout. He plays catch with one teammate for a whole season.

"I pick him out on opening day," says Boggs. "I just decide then. No other reason."

Playing catch with Wade Boggs seems a dubious honor. Three years ago, Boggs's partner was Jeff Newman, a catcher. Two years ago, it was Gary Allenson, another catcher. Last year, it was Dave Sax, yet another catcher. Since then, both Newman and Allenson have been released and, at this writing, Sax is on the fence. Memo to other Sox players: If Wade Boggs asks you to play catch, run the other way.

Whatever, for Boggs it's all part of the big picture. The more that he can make routine, the fewer the sur-prises.

"I just don't like to change things," he explains. "If something I do is successful, why change? A routine makes everything feel on an even keel. It's less hectic; you're more relaxed ... less apt to rush things. I only do this with things I can control. Like I arrive at the park the same time every day. But if I get caught in a traffic jam and arrive late, no problem; I can't control that."

NOW WATCH Wade Boggs stepping into the batter's box. The focus has narrowed to baseball's classic battle — Pitcher vs. Hitter — and Boggs is the picture of control. The infielders and the outfielders are just so many blurs; the crowd is just a babble. Wade Boggs's eyes are riveted on the pitcher, baseball in hand.

"I just talk to myself ... always positive things," says Boggs. "I remind myself to relax. The big thing is getting a good pitch to hit and then hitting it hard. It really doesn't matter where the ball is, inside or outside. And it doesn't matter what the pitch is ... fast ball, curve, change-up. I don't guess; I feel ... I have a feeling for what's coming."

In the battle of wits, he works the count, always looking for his pitch. It's the essence of the game.

"I work the count like a blackjack player works his hand," says Boggs. "That's the challenge. Play against the dealer. You're working your hand against his. If there's a pitch I can't handle, I try fouling it off. I can foul off five ... six ... seven pitches in a row. I'm pretty good at that. I'm just trying to work the count in my favor."

BUT, INCREDIBLY, that's where Wade Boggs has changed the rules of the game. For example, normally when the count is no balls, two strikes, it's the pitcher who is in control. That's the time he can get cute — throw one in the dirt or tease the batter with a change-up just out of the strike zone.

But if the count goes 0-2 to Boggs, he's just warming up. Indeed, a year ago he batted an incredible .392 after the count had reached no balls, two strikes against him. More often than not, he would work the count back to 2-2 or 3-2, and then jump on his pitch.

"It's the best game there is," Boggs says of his daily duels. "Every at- bat is a different at-bat."

He says he tries to treat every at-bat as if it's match point at Wimbledon; as if it's the ultimate at-bat. As if it's the last at-bat he'll ever have.

"Wade Boggs," says Walt Hriniak, the

Sox's hitting coach, "may be the best two-strike hitter in the history of the game."

"The thing that's amazing is that he hits every ball as if it were pitched right down the middle," adds teammate Dave Stapleton. "You know that's not possible, of course. You know a lot of pitches are either low or off the plate. But he hits every ball solid."

FOR ALL THAT, baseball people have always tried to change Wade Boggs's style. At a strapping 6 foot 2 and 200 pounds, he's the classic line-drive hitter, yet people think the liners should be landing in the seats, instead of the gaps in the outfield. It has always been that way.

At Plant High School, Boggs had 9 homers in 18 games in his junior year. The next year, the pitches started coming in differently — a little outside, a little more outside and outside even more than that. Since the scouts wanted him to keep slugging, Wade Boggs was now swinging at a lot of bad pitches.

"He was in a terrible slump," says Winfield Boggs. "He didn't know what to do. So we went to the public library and we got Ted Williams's book on hitting, and we sat down and we read it from cover to cover. That's where Ted tells you to be patient and go with the pitch."

In the second half of the season, Boggs was the talk of Tampa baseball, with 28 hits in 32 at-bats.

When he was drafted by the Red Sox, in 1976 in the seventh round, it was the same thing: Be quicker ... pull the ball ... go for the seats.

"He was really worried again," remembers Winfield Boggs. "He called me up and he said, 'What should I do, Daddy?' I told him, 'Normally, you do what your employer asks you to do. But baseball is a little different. If they want to change you and they're wrong, they're not gonna care. They'll just start working with someone else.'

"I told him, 'Go see Mr. Williams,'" the elder Boggs continues. "'Ask him what you should do. And then do what he says.'"

A DAY LATER, young Wade Boggs paid a visit to the master. He asked the master's advice.

"You go with what you feel comfortable with," Williams told him. "Don't change anything you can't handle. And don't let anybody change your swing." Boggs says he felt better after that.

The irony is that Boggs's hitting guru is now Hriniak, whose hitting theories are largely in conflict with Williams's. But Boggs has been able to walk a very thin line, seemingly taking the best from both. Williams remains a hero.

Besides, Boggs is obsessed with hitting just as Teddy Ballgame was. Legend has it that Williams once could recite the first 100 big-league homers that he had hit: He could remember the name of the pitcher, the kind of pitch it was and where the ball landed.

With Wade Boggs, you name a pitcher and he comes close to telling you how many hits the pitcher has gotten. Quite often, he's right on the button.

Ron Guidry?

"Seven for 28," says Boggs. "First hit was a double off the wall. A slider on the outside. The other six were singles."

Charlie Leibrandt?

"Seven for 14," he says. "One homer."

Matt Young?

"0 for 14," he replies with a wince.

He is, first and foremost, a hitter — and hitters walk and talk with a confidence that borders on arrogance. It was that way with Cobb and Speaker; it's that way with Pete Rose and Wade Boggs.

If Boggs has any apprehensions about the upcoming season, they revolve around his recent arbitration case, which he lost, and so he will be paid $1.35 million for the year, rather than the $1.85 million he was asking. Things got ugly, and now Boggs worries about his reception the first time he steps to the plate at Fenway.

"I know I'm being painted the villain; I'm the bad guy," he says. "But money was never the issue. All I wanted was assurance I'm going to stay in Boston. I want to follow Williams and Yastrzemski. I want to spend my whole career here."

HIS RELATIONSHIP with his sister, Ann, is another side of Wade Boggs. When, last fall, Ann was stricken with multiple sclerosis, it left the Boggs family stunned.

"That," says Boggs, "is something that

always happened to someone else. Now it was hitting home."

He searched everywhere for help. When someone told him about a doctor in Houston who was having success with a certain treatment, Boggs had Ann flown there.

"She's improving now, all things considered," says Boggs. "She's able to walk now, with the help of a walker. Hopefully, she'll improve even more."

He goes on, "It makes you reexamine things — not everything is baseball. Now I've got two goals for 1986: Win another batting title and help my sister as much as I can. And not in any special order."

IT'S A NEAT little baseball field they have at Plant High: new outfield fence ... new bleachers, that which wrap around the backstop ... lights ... a press box ... a new concession stand in the works. A very nice field.

Every year, as of the day after Christmas, Wade Boggs returns to his old school's field to begin workouts for the following season. He practices right alongside the Plant High kids, and it's quite a scene: Wade Boggs, American League batting champion, standing in line, waiting his turn at the batting cage.

This past winter, the people at Plant decided their baseball field needed a name. But before you can do something like that, you have to poll all sorts of groups — the students, the booster club, the PTA, the faculty and, of course, the baseball team.

"I met with the student body and I asked for nominations," says Beth Shields, Plant High's principal. "They stopped after Wade Boggs. Same with the faculty. And the boosters. The thing is, it's not like he's some big star who goes away and never comes back. He's here every day. Frankly, it was a natural."

Of course.

How I wrote the story

This was an interesting piece to do — for a lot of reasons.

For one thing, in developing the information I learned more about the subject, Wade Boggs, than I thought was possible. I mean, after having done a half-dozen (minimum) newspaper columns on Boggs, in all sorts of scenes and circumstances all the way back to his minor-league days in Pawtucket, I thought I had a pretty good idea what this guy was all about.

Not quite. Which was one of the reasons it was fun. But let's begin at the beginning.

When the idea for the story was first suggested, the light bulb flashed instantly with two thoughts.

First thought: I had heard a story once in spring training about Wade Boggs's father or cousin or someone showing Ted Williams a snapshot of Boggs swinging a bat when he was 18 months old, and how Williams had remarked that it was "a perfect swing."

Second thought: Get the snapshot. And wouldn't it look great if we could get Boggs to make the same swing 26 years later?

I called Boggs's agent, Alan Nero, a former Rhode Islander now living in Chicago, and asked about the story and the picture.

"Yeah, it's true," said Nero. "In fact, I got the snapshot in his file."

Perfect. He sent the snapshot, and Mary Murphy took care of the picture of the modern-day Boggs matching the swing at Winter Haven, Fla.

The next thing I did was make a list of people I wanted to talk to about Boggs. I decided to limit the number of "big league" people on the list — maybe a couple of teammates and maybe his hitting coach, Walt Hriniak. I also wanted other people — George Digby, the guy who scouted him in high school; Joe Morgan, his minor-league manager; David Fyfe, his high school coach; his high school principal; his buddy next door; his dad. At some point, however, you have to call a timeout — you could find yourself talking to the immediate world.

In any case, the best of the bunch was Wade's father, Winfield Boggs, a retired career Army officer. He was terrific. He was a baseball father but not in an obnoxious, oppressive way. He gave me the story about how they looked around for another brown bat when Wade's favorite one finally had disintegrated, and he told me about father and son invading the library on a Saturday afternoon to find Ted Williams's book, "The Science of Hitting." And how they read it from cover to cover in hopes of helping young Wade get out of a batting slump.

It was getting good.

The next thing was deciding where to talk to Boggs himself. I had two choices: the first few days of spring training, or Boggs in New York at some arbitration hearings. Spring training would make the thing almost a deadline piece, so I opted for New York.

I spent two days with Boggs in New York City: a couple of dinners surrounded by the arbitration hearings, a few cab rides, a session in his room and a long session in the lobby of the Grand Hyatt. I got a newspaper column out of the arbitration hearing, and I was able to separate that from the *Magazine* piece.

Another thing that I found interesting: The more the piece started coming together, the more Wade Boggs began taking on the traits of all the great athletes with whom I've come in contact. That may sound like an oversimplification, but it still never ceases to amaze me.

Almost without exception, people like Ted Williams, Pete Rose, Larry Bird, John Hannah, John Havlicek, Jack Nicklaus and Boggs have all had the same singular obsession with being the best. The same is true, obviously, in business, the arts, etc., but it's no less true on a baseball field.

But maybe the most intriguing thread that was developing was how easily everything apparently came to Boggs, especially early on in his career.

Winfield Boggs said he never had to teach him to swing a bat — the first swing was the right swing. George Digby, same thing. Ted Williams: "Don't let anybody change your swing."

Yeah, right. The Natural. But this wasn't going to be Roy Hobbs, and there wasn't going to be any woman in white standing up in the stands at the crucial moment.

Still, I became fascinated with the fact that Boggs was, indeed, a natural hitter. Just as I became fascinated with his obsession with detail and routine, and the fact that he still works out on his high school field with the high school kids.

Now, to put it together. I decided this would work best in segments — some of them scenes, some of them just segments.

The lead?

The snapshot and the Ted Williams story were obvious — but too obvious. Besides, that was good enough to go anywhere and not lose anything.

Boggs and chicken? No, Wade Boggs was a helluva lot more than eating chicken.

His obsession with hitting was a strong point. His obsession at age 12 made it even better. Besides, I loved the brown-bat story.

I mean, I had a favorite bat like that once. A Gil McDougald model. I used it for two years playing for the West End Tigers — made the all-star team, even. But then, as I got older, the pitchers began throwing harder, and then came the curve balls . . .

But that's another story. I liked the Wade Boggs story better.

Chapter 9

Bookbag: A reading list for writers and editors

In 1981, the *Bulletin of the American Society of Newspaper Editors* asked Donald Murray, John Bremner, who teaches journalism at the University of Kansas, and Roy Peter Clark, who organizes and directs writing seminars for the Poynter Institute for Media Studies in St. Petersburg, Fla., to answer the question "Which books should every newsroom have?" Their suggestions, numbering more than 60 textbooks, anthologies and style books, can be found in "Improving Newswriting," published by the ASNE.

"It would be easy," Murray said in his reply, "to list a hundred books that could be read with profit by working nonfiction writers, but such a list should come from the writers and editors in a particular city room."

Such a list — suggested by *Journal-Bulletin* writers and editors and bolstered by examples from the ASNE bibliography — follows.

Reading about writing: books on writing, coaching, editing, language and style

● "A Writer Teaches Writing." Donald M. Murray. (Houghton Mifflin. 1985. Revised edition.) A fascinating introduction to the process approach to writing.

● "Writing for Your Readers: Notes on the Writer's Craft from the Boston *Globe*." Donald M. Murray. (The Globe Pequot Press. 1983.) A collection of essays written while Murray was the *Globe*'s writing coach.

● "Write to Learn." Donald M. Murray. (Holt, Rinehart & Winston. 1984.) The writing process examined in absorbing, enlightening fashion. A college text worth a spot on every writer's bookshelf.

● "Read to Write." Donald M. Murray. (Holt, Rinehart & Winston. 1986.) Murray teaches the lessons of writing and rewriting through case studies of writers at work and his comments in a college reader that can help any professional.

● "On Writing Well: An Informal Guide to Writing Nonfiction." William K. Zinsser. (Harper & Row. 1980. 2nd edition.) "The single best book on writing available today" — Donald Murray.

● "The Elements of Style." William Strunk Jr., with revisions, an introduction and a chapter on writing by E.B. White. (Macmillan. 1979. 3rd edition.) The classic book on style.

● "Best Newspaper Writing, 1979, 1980, 1981, 1982, 1983, 1984, 1985, 1986, etc." Edited by Roy Peter Clark and Donald K. Fry. (Poynter Institute for Media Studies, 556 Central Ave., St. Petersburg, Fla. 33701.) Reprints of stories that won the American Society of Newspaper Editors annual writing awards; illuminating interviews with the writers; and helpful essays. A valuable collection.

● "News Reporting and Writing." Melvin Mencher. (William C. Brown. 1981.) A textbook helpful for the beginner or veteran.

● "Effective Writing and Editing." Edited by Elwood M. Wardlow. (American Press Institute, 11690 Sunrise Valley Drive, Reston, Va. 22091. 1985.) A useful and inspiring collection of tips, techniques and advice from the American Press Institute.

● "Editors on Editing: An Inside View of What Editors Really Do." Edited by Gerald Gross. (Harper & Row. 1985. Revised edition.) Focusing on the book-publishing world, this collection of essays also contains useful advice for newspaper editors *and* writers.

- "Max Perkins." A. Scott Berg. (Dutton. 1978.) Invaluable advice for writers and editors in this biography of the man who edited Hemingway, Fitzgerald, Thomas Wolfe, James Jones.

- "Poison Penmanship: The Gentle Art of Muckracking." Jessica Mitford. (Vintage Paperback. 1980.)

- "Writers at Work: The *Paris Review* Interviews." (Penguin Books. Six volumes, dating from 1957.) Interviews with Updike, Hemingway, Cheever, Didion, Frost and many others.

- "The Careful Writer." Theodore M. Bernstein. (Atheneum. 1965.) He was the guardian of style at the New York *Times*.

- "The News at Any Cost: How Journalists Compromise Their Ethics to Shape the News." Tom Goldstein. (Simon and Schuster. 1985.) A provocative exploration of ethics that stimulates fresh thinking about reporting and writing. Goldstein reported for the New York *Times* and *The Wall Street Journal*.

- "Make Every Word Count." Gary Provost. (Writer's Digest Books. 1980.)

- "The Literature of Journalism: An Annotated Bibliography." Warren C. Price. A sequel: "An Annotated Journalism Bibliography: 1959-1968." Warren C. Price and Calder M. Pickett. (University of Minnesota Press. 1968.)

- "First Person Singular: Writers on Their Craft." Compiled by Joyce Carol Oates. (Ontario Review Press. 1983.) An inspiring collection of essays and interviews.

- "The Triggering Town: Lectures and Essays on Poetry and Writing." Richard Hugo. (Norton. 1979.) Helpful advice from a poet.

- "Writing the Australian Crawl: Views on the Writer's Vocation." William Stafford. (University of Michigan. 1978.) Another poet with worthy counsel for any writer.

- "Hemingway's First War: The Making of 'A Farewell to Arms.'" Michael S. Reynolds. (Princeton University Press. 1976.) Unique insight into the role of revision.

- "A Moveable Feast." Ernest Hemingway. (Bantam. 1967.) Reflections on a writing life.

- "The Years with Ross." James Thurber. (Little, Brown. 1959.) A memoir-profile of Harold Ross, the *New Yorker*'s original editor. A funny book remarkable for Ross's sensible advice on writing (as well as some of his idiotic notions). Of most value to writers is Thurber's exemplary style.

Reading for inspiration: examples of good writing

- "A Treasury of Great Reporting." Edited by Louis L. Snyder and Richard B. Morris. (Simon and Schuster. 1962.) "Literature under pressure" from the 16th Century to modern times.

- "The Literary Journalists." Edited by Norman Sims. (Ballantine. 1984.) Magazine and newspaper stories by Tracy Kidder, Jane Kramer and others. Includes an essay on the writers and their work habits.

- "The John McPhee Reader." Edited by William L. Howarth. (Vintage Paperback. (1977.) Introduction describes the *New Yorker* writer's work habits.

- "Essays of E.B. White." (Harper & Row. 1977.)

- "The Orwell Reader: Fiction, Essays and Reportage." (Harvest Paperback. 1961).

- "In Cold Blood." Truman Capote. (Random House. 1966.)

- "Fame and Obscurity." Gay Talese. (Bantam Paperback. 1971.) A collection of profiles — on Sinatra, DiMaggio, New York

City — by a writer who uses "fictional techniques for factual situations."

- "The World of Jimmy Breslin." Jimmy Breslin. (Viking. 1967.)

- "The New Journalism Anthology." Edited by Tom Wolfe and E.W. Johnson. (Harper & Row. 1973.)

- "Mission Beyond Darkness." J. Bryan and Philip Reed. (Duell, Sloan & Pearce. 1945.) A reconstruction of a bombing raid in World War II, it is a masterful guide for anyone writing that form.

- "The Friends of Eddie Coyle." George V. Higgins. (Ballantine. 1981.) A master of dialogue.

- "Slouching Towards Bethlehem." Joan Didion. (Washington Square Press. 1981.)

- "Division Street," "Working" and "The Good War." Studs Terkel. (Pantheon.)

- A group of feature writers and editors from around the country came up with this list at a seminar at the Poynter Institute for Media Studies:
  - "Hiroshima." John Hersey.
  - "Crime and Punishment" and "The Brothers Karamazov." Fyodor Dostoevsky.
  - "Cannery Row." John Steinbeck.
  - "Invisible Man." Ralph Ellison.
  - "Fame and Obscurity." Gay Talese.
  - "The Maltese Falcon." Dashiell Hammett.
  - "Essays of E.B. White."
  - "Poems and Sketches." E.B. White.
  - "Confessions of a Knife." Richard Selzer.
  - "The Collected Stories of Flannery O'Connor."
  - "The Postman Always Rings Twice." James Cain.
  - "A River Runs Through It" and other stories. Norman Maclean.
  - "The White Album." Joan Didion.
  - "The Orwell Reader," especially the essays "Shooting an Elephant" and "Politics and the English Language."

Periodicals with the potential to inspire

- *The Writer.*
- *Writer's Digest.*
- *Columbia Journalism Review.*
- *Washington Journalism Review.*
- *ASNE Bulletin.*
- *Nieman Reports.*
- *Mother Jones.*
- *The New Yorker.*
- *The Atlantic.*

An interviewer's reading list

- "The Craft of Interviewing." John Brady. (Writer's Digest Books. 1976.)
- "How I Got That Story." (Overseas Press Club and Dutton. 1967). Top reporters give behind-the-scenes accounts of how they covered great news events.
- "The Reporter's Handbook." (St. Martin's Press and the Investigative Reporters and Editors. 1983). An investigator's guide to documents and techniques.
- "Murderers and Other Friendly People." Denis Brian. (McGraw-Hill 1973). The public and private world of interviewers.
- Truman Capote's interview with Marlon Brando. (*The New Yorker.*) Nov. 9, 1957.
- Alex Haley's interview with Malcolm X. (*Playboy.* May, 1963.)
- Lillian Ross's interview with Hemingway in "Reporting." (Dodd, Mead paperback. 1981.) A reprinting of her *New Yorker* pieces with an introduction by the author.
- "The New Muckrakers." Leonard Downie Jr. (New American Library. 1976.) Seymour Hersh, Bob Woodward and Carl Bernstein, and others tell how they do it.

" *Books on writing — and manuals on sex — can be helpful, but they are no substitute for the act itself.* "

— **Don Murray**

PN 4781 .H5 1986 c.1

FEB 4 '88
APR 18 '88
MAY 1 '88
JUL 14 '88
JUL 12 '89
SEP 21 '89
FEB 9 '90
FEB 05 '96